What We Choose to Remember—and What We Are Allowed to Forget

Memory, Power, and the Architecture of Remembrance

What We Choose to Remember—and What We Are Allowed to Forget

Memory, Power, and the Architecture of Remembrance

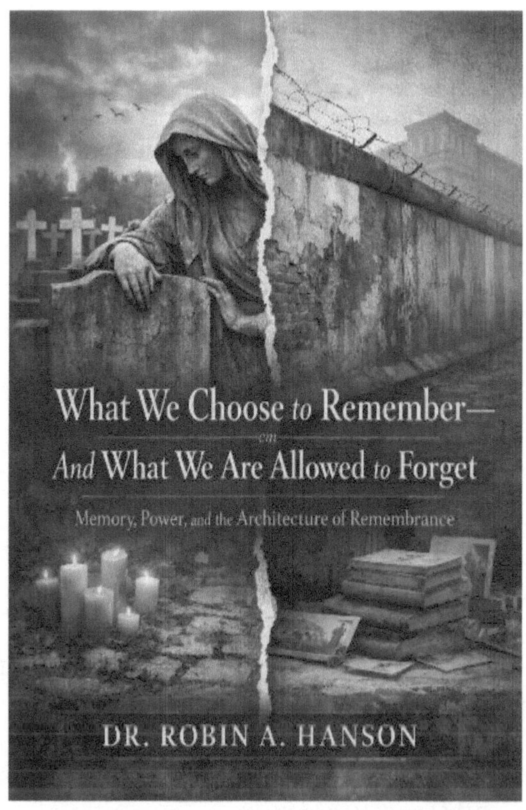

Robin A. Hanson, PhD

Galiah Institute
Galiah Publishing Company

Printed in the United States of America

For more information contact Galiah Publishing.

ISBN: 978-0-9823423-4-3

Other works by the author include:

- The Threshold Chronicles: The Melissa Aradan Series
- Sacred Women of the Andes: Keepers of Balance, Water and Cosmic Memory
- Eternal Echoes: Death and Remembrance in America
- An Amazon Legacy: Memories of Lives Lived as a Warrior Woman

Table of Contents

Prologue

Memory, Power, and the Architecture of Remembrance

This book is about memory, but not in the abstract. It is about how memory is organized, regulated, displaced, and made visible—or invisible—through cultural practice. It is about who is remembered, how they are remembered, and what must be forgotten in order for certain stories to remain intact. Most of all, it is about patterns: patterns of containment, erasure, normalization, and justification that repeat across time, geography, and population, often under the protection of reasonableness.

Memory is not neutral. It is not a passive accumulation of facts or an innocent inheritance handed down intact. Memory is shaped by institutions, rituals, language, and space. Cemeteries, monuments, exhibitions, archives, and even omissions function as technologies of remembrance. They do not merely reflect values; they enforce them. What is preserved, what is sanitized, and what is excluded tells us as much about power as any law or decree.

The chapters that follow move deliberately across domains that are often kept separate: burial practices and national mythmaking; women's bodies and scholarly legitimacy; sexuality and suppression; confinement, internment, and displacement; spectacle, performance, and monumentality; symbol, fertility, and ancient memory. These subjects are not assembled to provoke shock, nor to argue equivalence between disparate histories. They are brought together because they share a common logic. Each reveals a way in which culture manages memory in order to stabilize itself, particularly when confronted with bodies, identities, or histories that resist containment.

This is not a book of moral ranking. It does not seek to declare one injustice greater than another, or to collapse historical specificity into general accusation. Comparison is used here only to reveal trajectory—to show how early stages of exclusion, classification, and containment often appear reasonable, even necessary, when they are first introduced. The most dangerous systems rarely announce their final form. They begin with language that reassures, structures that appear temporary, and boundaries framed as protective rather than punitive. By the time harm becomes undeniable, it has already been normalized.

Several chapters rely on proximity rather than distance. They ask the reader to sit with familiar landscapes—cemeteries, fairs, monuments, museums—and recognize them not as inert backdrops but as active participants in memory-making. Others move into less comfortable territory, examining how bodies that did not conform—women, queer people, racialized populations, the incarcerated—were disciplined, erased, or reframed to preserve dominant narratives. The intent is not to indict the reader, but neither is it to absolve them. Recognition requires proximity. One cannot understand how memory functions without acknowledging one's own position within it.

Visual material appears sparingly and intentionally. Where photographs are used, they are framed as evidence, not spectacle. They are meant to slow the reader, not overwhelm them. Care has been taken to avoid sensationalism and to preserve historical integrity. The purpose of these images is not to equate experiences, but to illuminate how similar structures emerge when populations are rendered manageable and disposable under the logic of the state. What matters here is not sameness, but sequence.

This book also resists the idea that memory is only held in official records. Symbols, rituals, and embodied knowledge preserve histories long after formal acknowledgment has failed. The final chapters turn toward ancient and suppressed symbolic systems not as romantic recovery projects, but as reminders that memory often survives where power least expects it—encoded in myth, ritual, and bodily knowledge that persists beneath sanctioned narratives.

The chapters are arranged to create movement rather than argument. The book begins with the management of death and burial, because that is where cultures often reveal their deepest anxieties about belonging and exclusion. It moves through the regulation of living bodies, into systems of confinement and displacement, and then outward again into performance, monumentality, and spectacle. Only after these structures have been made visible does the book turn toward symbols and deep time, where memory is neither fixed nor easily controlled. The conclusion does not offer resolution. It offers responsibility.

This is not a book that promises comfort. It is also not a book that demands despair. It asks instead for attentiveness—for a willingness to notice patterns that are often dismissed as coincidental or inevitable.

The hope, if there is one, lies not in reassurance but in recognition. Once patterns are seen, they cannot be unseen. What is done with that knowledge remains an open question.

Chapter One

The National Cemetery and American History

Section I

The Making of American Memory

The National Cemetery occupies a distinctive position in the American landscape, one that cannot be understood solely through its function as a burial ground. While it originated as a practical response to the unprecedented scale of death produced by the American Civil War, it quickly evolved into something far more complex. The ordered rows of identical markers, the regulated rituals of commemoration, and the perpetual care provided by the federal government transformed these sites into spaces where personal grief intersects with national meaning. In this convergence, the National Cemetery became both sacred ground and political terrain, a place where the state, the citizen, and the dead are bound together in a relationship that continues to shape American ideas of identity, belonging, and legitimacy.

The approach taken in this book aligns with scholarship concerned less with fixed interpretation than with the conditions under which meaning becomes possible. It shares affinities with thinkers such as Victor Turner and Arnold van Gennep in treating ritual and liminality as structuring forces rather than symbolic residue; with Clifford Geertz in reading cultural spaces as texts that must be interpreted through thick description; and with Roland Barthes in attending to moments where meaning exceeds intention or slips beyond articulation. It also resonates with work in memory studies and material culture that understands remembrance not as a passive archive but as an active, negotiated process shaped by space, embodiment, and power. These perspectives do not supply a single theory to be applied, but a set of sensibilities—ways of noticing how authority, silence, and reverence are produced and sustained in ordinary practices. This book proceeds from that shared orientation, allowing sites of remembrance to reveal their own logics through close attention rather than theoretical imposition.

Cemeteries have long served as liminal spaces, positioned at the threshold between the living and the dead. They are locations where societies confront mortality, memory, and continuity, and where beliefs about the afterlife and the meaning of death are made visible through material form. In the United States, the National Cemetery intensifies this function by linking death explicitly to service, sacrifice, and citizenship. Unlike private or churchyard cemeteries, which primarily reflect familial or religious affiliations, National Cemeteries are organized and maintained by the state. This involvement imbues them with an authority that extends beyond personal remembrance, situating individual loss within a broader narrative of national purpose.

The visual impact of a National Cemetery reinforces this transformation. The uniformity of the headstones, identical in size, shape, and material regardless of rank or social standing, communicates an idealized vision of equality in death. This aesthetic order contrasts sharply with the chaos and violence that produced the graves themselves, offering visitors a sense of resolution and control. The landscape suggests permanence, stability, and continuity, qualities that are deeply reassuring in the face of mass death. At the same time, this uniformity masks the social hierarchies and exclusions that shaped both military service and burial practices, creating an appearance of unity that is more aspirational than actual.

From its earliest iterations, the National Cemetery functioned as a symbolic extension of the nation-state. The decision to centralize the burial of Union dead and to mark and record their graves represented a significant shift in the federal government's relationship to individual citizens. Prior to the Civil War, responsibility for burial typically rested with families or local communities. The creation of National Cemeteries signaled a new understanding of the state's obligation to those who died in its service, as well as a recognition of the political value inherent in commemorating that sacrifice. By assuming perpetual care of the graves, the government asserted its role as guardian not only of the living nation but also of its dead.

Robert Bellah's articulation of *American civil religion* provides a useful framework for understanding how national cemeteries and commemorative practices acquire moral authority without relying on explicit theological doctrine. Writing in the late 1960s, Bellah argued that the United States sustains a parallel religious structure—complete with sacred texts, rituals, symbols, and sites—that operates alongside, and sometimes independently from, institutional Christianity. This civil religion does not replace traditional faith, but it borrows its grammar: sacrifice, martyrdom, covenant, and redemption are transposed onto the nation itself. Within this framework, the deaths of soldiers are not merely historical losses but consecrating events, and the spaces that contain them become sanctified through collective ritual rather than divine decree. What is crucial for the present analysis is that civil religion functions by naturalizing national power through reverence. By framing state violence and mass death as sacred sacrifice, it converts political history into moral inevitability, shielding institutions from scrutiny while inviting emotional allegiance. Cemeteries, monuments, and commemorative ceremonies thus operate not simply as sites of remembrance, but as liturgical spaces in which the nation rehearses its own legitimacy.

This guardianship carried profound symbolic weight. The land itself became sanctified through bloodshed, and the presence of the war dead served to legitimize the authority of the federal government. In this sense, the National Cemetery operates as a form of civil religious space, where secular power adopts the language and structures traditionally associated with the sacred. The rituals performed within these cemeteries—military funerals, Memorial Day observances, presidential wreath-layings—mirror religious ceremonies in their formality, repetition, and emphasis on collective participation. Through these performances, the values of patriotism, duty, and sacrifice are reinforced, and the memory of the dead is woven into an enduring national narrative.

At this early stage, it is important to note that none of this requires cynicism. Sacredness and political utility are not mutually exclusive. The power of the National Cemetery lies precisely in its ability to operate as both at once, allowing reverence to coexist with authority without appearing contradictory.

The sacred character of the National Cemetery is further reinforced by its role as a site of pilgrimage. Visitors come not only to mourn specific individuals but also to engage with the broader story the cemetery tells about the nation itself. Walking among the graves, reading names and dates, and observing the symbols etched into stone, individuals encounter a tangible representation of American history. The cemetery thus functions as a text, one that communicates cultural meanings through spatial organization, material choices, and ritual practices. Unlike written histories, this text is experienced bodily and emotionally, shaping understanding through presence and participation rather than argument alone.

The appearance of unity, however, depends on what remains unexamined.

Yet the National Cemetery is not a neutral or passive space. Its design, regulations, and rituals are the products of deliberate choices made within specific historical and political contexts. Decisions about who is eligible for burial, how graves are marked, and which ceremonies are sanctioned reflect prevailing ideas about citizenship and belonging. The cemetery's sacredness does not place it outside the realm of politics; rather, it makes it an especially powerful political instrument. By framing national sacrifice in sacred terms, the state elevates its authority beyond ordinary critique, presenting its narrative of history and identity as both natural and inevitable.

This blending of sacred and political functions allows the National Cemetery to serve as a bridge between individual memory and collective identity. For families, the grave of a loved one offers a focal point for grief and remembrance, a physical location where loss can be acknowledged and endured. For the nation, those same graves form a collective monument to endurance, unity, and moral purpose. The tension between these perspectives is ever-present, as private sorrow exists alongside public symbolism. The power of the National Cemetery lies in its ability to hold both simultaneously, allowing personal and national meanings to coexist within the same landscape.

At the same time, this coexistence raises important questions about whose memories are preserved and whose are marginalized. The appearance of unity conveyed by the cemetery's orderly rows can obscure the contested realities beneath the surface. While the landscape proclaims shared sacrifice, it also reflects the social divisions and exclusions that shaped American society during the periods of its development. Understanding the National Cemetery as sacred and political space therefore requires attention not only to what it commemorates but also to what it conceals.

In recognizing the National Cemetery as both a site of reverence and a mechanism of state authority, it becomes clear that its significance extends far beyond its boundaries. These cemeteries participate actively in the construction of American historical consciousness, shaping how past conflicts are remembered and how national identity is defined. They offer reassurance in the face of loss while simultaneously reinforcing a particular vision of citizenship grounded in service and sacrifice. As such, the National Cemetery stands as one of the most potent symbols of the American nation, embodying the complex interplay of memory, power, and meaning that continues to define its history.

The cemetery's calm does not resolve these tensions; it contains them.

Section II - Death, Citizenship, and Civil Religion

The transformation of the National Cemetery from a practical burial solution into a symbolically charged national institution rests on a deeper cultural process in which death, citizenship, and collective belief become intertwined. In the United States, the association between military service and moral worth has long depended upon the idea that sacrifice for the nation confers a form of elevated status. The National Cemetery gives this belief physical form. Through its structure, rituals, and permanence, it translates individual death into a public affirmation of citizenship and binds personal loss to the survival and legitimacy of the state.

The American Civil War marked a turning point in this process. The scale of death was unprecedented, and the nation lacked established mechanisms to absorb such loss without fracturing under its weight. In response, the federal government began to assume responsibility not only for the bodies of the dead but also for the meaning of their deaths. By organizing, marking, and maintaining graves, the state imposed order on chaos and provided a narrative that framed loss as necessary, purposeful, and ultimately redemptive. Death in service to the nation became more than an end to life; it became a contribution to a collective moral project.

This reframing of death aligns closely with the concept of civil religion, a system of shared beliefs, symbols, and rituals that invests the nation itself with sacred significance. Civil religion does not replace traditional religious belief but operates alongside it, drawing on familiar forms of reverence to sanctify political ideals. In the context of the National Cemetery, civil religion manifests through ritualized commemoration, symbolic language, and the elevation of the war dead to near-mythic status. The soldier's willingness to die for the country is implicitly linked to religious notions of sacrifice, redemption, and eternal remembrance, lending spiritual weight to political allegiance.

The cemetery's role in this system is both subtle and profound. By granting burial in a National Cemetery, the state affirms that an individual's life and death matter beyond private relationships. The grave becomes a marker not only of mortality but of belonging. Inscribed with name, rank, and service, it situates the deceased within an official historical record, ensuring recognition by future generations. This promise of remembrance addresses one of humanity's most persistent anxieties: the fear of being forgotten. In offering literate immortality through stone and registry, the National Cemetery provides reassurance that service to the nation secures a lasting place in collective memory.

At the same time, this promise reinforces a particular definition of citizenship. Citizenship, as expressed through the National Cemetery, is not merely a legal status but a moral one, earned and validated through service and sacrifice. The landscape communicates this message through its disciplined order and standardized markers, which emphasize conformity to shared values over individual distinction. Rank, wealth, and social standing recede in importance, replaced by the common identity of citizen-soldier. This idealized equality suggests that the nation recognizes all who serve as equally worthy of honor, even as social realities complicate that claim.

Ritual plays a crucial role in sustaining this framework. Public ceremonies conducted within National Cemeteries are carefully structured performances that reaffirm the connection between death and national purpose. Military funerals, Memorial Day observances, and presidential appearances follow established patterns that emphasize solemnity, respect, and continuity. Through repetition, these rituals normalize the association between sacrifice and citizenship, embedding it deeply within cultural consciousness. Participants and observers alike are reminded that the nation endures because individuals were willing to give their lives on its behalf.

These rituals also function as moments of collective education. They teach audiences how to interpret the landscape and the graves within it, guiding emotional responses and reinforcing accepted meanings. The presence of national symbols—flags, uniforms, formal addresses—frames the experience, directing attention toward ideals of unity, duty, and honor. In this way, the National Cemetery becomes a classroom of sorts, where lessons about national identity are conveyed not through argument but through embodied experience and shared observation.

Yet the power of civil religion lies partly in its ability to mask complexity. By presenting national sacrifice as sacred and unquestionable, it discourages critical examination of the social and political conditions that produce war and death. The reverence accorded to the cemetery can render it immune to scrutiny, positioning it beyond ordinary debate. This elevation serves the interests of the state by stabilizing national narratives and minimizing dissent, even as it offers genuine comfort to those who mourn.

The National Cemetery thus occupies a dual role. It is a place of solace and meaning for individuals grappling with loss, and it is a mechanism through which the state articulates and perpetuates its vision of citizenship. These functions are not mutually exclusive; rather, they reinforce one another. Personal grief finds resolution within a larger story of national endurance, while the state's narrative gains emotional legitimacy through intimate acts of remembrance. The cemetery's power derives from this mutual reinforcement, which binds private emotion to public ideology.

Understanding the National Cemetery as an expression of civil religion clarifies its enduring influence on American culture. It reveals how deeply notions of death and belonging are embedded in national identity and how the management of the dead shapes the living. The cemetery does not merely reflect existing values; it actively participates in their creation and transmission. By sanctifying sacrifice and linking it to citizenship, the National Cemetery continues to define what it means to belong to the nation, even as the meanings of service, identity, and inclusion evolve over time.

Section III - Ritual, Memory, and the Performance of Nationhood

Ritual provides the mechanism through which the meanings embedded in the National Cemetery are activated and sustained over time. Without ritual, the cemetery would remain a static landscape, its symbols mute and its messages fragmented. Through repeated, structured performances, however, the cemetery becomes a living space of memory, one in which the past is continually re-presented to the present. These rituals do not merely commemorate the dead; they perform the nation itself, reaffirming shared values and reinforcing the bonds between individual citizens and the collective identity.

Public rituals associated with National Cemeteries emerged organically in the aftermath of the Civil War, shaped initially by personal grief and local custom rather than by centralized authority. Families and communities sought ways to honor those lost in battle, bringing flowers, flags, and quiet gestures of remembrance to gravesites. Over time, these acts coalesced into more formalized observances, such as Decoration Day, which later became Memorial Day. As participation broadened and the scale of these ceremonies grew, the federal government recognized their potential as instruments of national cohesion and gradually assumed a guiding role in their organization and symbolism.

The formalization of these rituals marked a significant shift in their function. What began as intimate expressions of loss evolved into public performances with clearly defined roles, scripts, and meanings. Military precision, hierarchical order, and the presence of political leaders signaled the transformation of commemoration into an expression of state authority. Through these ceremonies, the nation presented itself as unified, grateful, and enduring, even as the underlying realities of social division and contested memory persisted. Ritual thus served to stabilize national narratives by emphasizing continuity and shared purpose.

Memory, as enacted through ritual, is not a simple act of recall but a process of selection and emphasis. The ceremonies conducted in National Cemeteries highlight particular aspects of the past while minimizing others, shaping collective understanding of history. The focus on sacrifice, honor, and unity directs attention away from the causes and consequences of conflict, encouraging reverence rather than critique. In this way, ritual memory smooths the rough edges of history, offering a version of the past that is both emotionally resonant and politically useful.

The physical setting of the National Cemetery amplifies the impact of these ritual performances. The orderly arrangement of graves, the carefully maintained grounds, and the controlled access points create an environment conducive to solemn reflection and disciplined behavior. Visitors are guided, both implicitly and explicitly, toward appropriate modes of conduct, reinforcing the seriousness of the space. This choreography of movement and attention ensures that rituals unfold within a context that supports their intended meanings, blending material form with performative action.

The interplay between ritual and memory also operates on a deeply personal level. For individuals attending ceremonies or visiting graves outside formal observances, the rituals provide a framework for interpreting their own emotions. The shared language of honor and sacrifice offers a way to articulate grief and loss that aligns with broader cultural expectations. In participating, individuals connect their private experiences to a collective story, finding meaning through association with something larger than themselves. This connection can be both comforting and constraining, as it channels emotion along established paths.

At the societal level, ritual memory contributes to the construction of what might be called an imagined community, one bound not by direct interaction but by shared symbols and narratives. National Cemeteries function as focal points for this community, anchoring abstract ideas of nationhood in tangible form. The repetition of ceremonies across time and space reinforces the sense that these values are enduring and universally accepted. Even those who do not attend in person are exposed to these rituals through media coverage and educational narratives, extending their influence beyond the cemetery walls.

The performative nature of these rituals underscores their role as acts of communication. They convey messages about who belongs, what is valued, and how the nation understands itself. Silence, music, uniformed presence, and scripted speeches all contribute to this communication, shaping perception through sensory and emotional engagement. The power of ritual lies in its ability to communicate without argument, presenting its messages as self-evident truths rather than contested interpretations.

However, this very power invites critical reflection. The emphasis on unity and shared sacrifice can obscure the uneven distribution of honor and recognition within the cemetery itself. While rituals proclaim collective memory, the physical landscape may tell a more complicated story of inclusion and exclusion. The performance of nationhood, while compelling, rests on choices about whose sacrifices are foregrounded and whose are marginalized. Recognizing this tension does not diminish the emotional significance of ritual but rather situates it within a broader understanding of how memory is shaped and maintained.

Through ritual, the National Cemetery becomes an active participant in the ongoing construction of American identity. It stages the nation repeatedly, presenting a vision of continuity that links past, present, and future. In doing so, it offers a sense of stability in the face of loss and change, even as it subtly directs interpretation and allegiance. The rituals enacted within these sacred grounds ensure that the cemetery remains not merely a place of burial, but a dynamic arena where memory and meaning are continually negotiated.

Section IV - Cemeteries as Texts of American Identity

The National Cemetery can be read as a cultural text, one that communicates meaning through material form, spatial organization, and regulated practice rather than through written narrative alone. Like any text, it requires interpretation, and like many powerful cultural artifacts, much of what it conveys operates beneath conscious awareness. The arrangement of graves, the choice of materials, the inscriptions permitted, and the rituals enacted within its boundaries collectively express assumptions about identity, belonging, and value. In this sense, the National Cemetery does not simply record history; it participates in its construction.

Material culture offers a particularly revealing lens through which to examine these spaces. Headstones, pathways, fences, and monuments function as symbols that encode social meaning. The standardized markers of the National Cemetery, uniform in appearance and aligned with military precision, present an idealized vision of equality and order. This visual grammar suggests that service to the nation transcends individual difference, uniting the dead under a shared identity as citizen-soldiers. Yet this apparent equality is carefully curated, masking the historical realities of differential treatment and access that shaped who was buried where and under what conditions.

Spatial organization reinforces these messages. The deliberate separation of the cemetery from surrounding landscapes, often marked by walls or gates, establishes a clear boundary between sacred and profane space. Once inside, visitors encounter a carefully managed environment that guides movement and perception. Central axes, prominent monuments, and designated ceremonial areas direct attention toward sanctioned narratives of honor and sacrifice. Peripheral spaces, by contrast, often receive less emphasis, both visually and ritually, reflecting implicit hierarchies of significance.

These spatial cues operate subtly, shaping understanding without the need for explicit instruction.

Inscriptions on headstones further contribute to the cemetery's textual quality. The information allowed—name, rank, unit, date—reflects institutional priorities, privileging military identity over personal biography. Religious symbols, when present, signal affiliation while remaining constrained by regulation, ensuring that individual expression does not disrupt the overall coherence of the landscape. Through these limits, the cemetery balances personal remembrance with collective representation, allowing individuality to appear only within prescribed bounds. What is absent from the stones can be as telling as what is inscribed, pointing to the values and assumptions that govern commemoration.

Reading the National Cemetery as text also highlights the role of interpretation in shaping meaning. Visitors bring their own experiences, beliefs, and expectations to the landscape, engaging with its symbols in varied ways. For some, the cemetery affirms a sense of pride and belonging, reinforcing faith in national ideals. For others, it may evoke discomfort or ambivalence, especially when the promises of equality and inclusion implied by the landscape conflict with lived experience. This interpretive openness does not undermine the cemetery's power; rather, it demonstrates the complexity of its symbolic function.

The concept of studium and punctum provides a useful framework for understanding this interplay. The studium of the National Cemetery encompasses its broad cultural meanings: patriotism, sacrifice, unity, and continuity. These themes are communicated through the overall design and ritual use of the space, offering a shared field of understanding accessible to all visitors. The punctum, by contrast, emerges in individual encounters—a single name, a date that resonates, a personal connection that pierces the general narrative. Together, these modes of engagement allow the cemetery to operate simultaneously as a national monument and an intimate site of reflection.

As a cultural text, the National Cemetery also reflects the power relations embedded in the society that created it. Decisions about design, regulation, and ritual are shaped by dominant cultural perspectives, often privileging certain narratives while marginalizing others. Over time, these choices become naturalized, their origins obscured by repetition and reverence. The cemetery's authority derives in part from this naturalization, which presents its messages as timeless rather than historically contingent. Recognizing this process invites a more critical reading, one that attends to both what the landscape proclaims and what it silences.

This critical reading does not negate the cemetery's emotional or symbolic significance. Rather, it deepens understanding by situating the space within the broader currents of American history. The National Cemetery emerges as a site where ideals are asserted, negotiated, and sometimes contradicted. Its text is not fixed; it evolves as regulations change, new burials occur, and interpretations shift. Yet its core function remains consistent: to anchor national identity in the tangible reality of the dead.

By approaching the National Cemetery as a text, it becomes possible to see how American identity is inscribed onto the landscape through material choices and ritual practice. The cemetery teaches, persuades, and reassures, often without overt instruction. It invites reverence while shaping understanding, offering a vision of the nation grounded in sacrifice and continuity. In doing so, it reveals both the aspirations and the limitations of the stories Americans tell about themselves, written not only in books and speeches but in stone, soil, and ceremony.

Chapter Two

Segregation, Race and Reconciliation in the National Cemetery

Section I - Order, Control, and the Management of the Dead

The creation of the National Cemetery System was, at its core, an exercise in order imposed upon chaos. The American Civil War produced death on a scale previously unknown to the nation, overwhelming existing burial practices and exposing the absence of a coherent governmental policy for the management of the war dead. What emerged in response was not merely a logistical solution but a system that reflected prevailing social hierarchies and cultural assumptions. From its earliest implementation, the organization of the dead revealed how power, authority, and identity continued to operate even beyond death.

Initially, the federal government's concern centered on efficiency and identification rather than equity. Orders issued by the War Department focused on the proper recording of deaths, the marking of graves, and the consolidation of burial sites to facilitate future recovery and commemoration. Wooden headboards bearing names, units, and dates were intended to preserve individual identity while maintaining administrative control. These early measures established the foundation for what would become a standardized national system, one that privileged uniformity and record-keeping as tools of governance. In doing so, the state asserted its authority over the bodies of those who died in its service, transforming the dead into subjects of bureaucratic management.

This management, however, was never neutral. Decisions about where bodies were buried, how they were marked, and who was included within designated burial grounds reflected deeply ingrained distinctions between loyalty and rebellion, inclusion and exclusion. Union soldiers were prioritized for retrieval, identification, and reburial, their remains gathered into newly established national cemeteries that symbolized the legitimacy and endurance of the federal government. Confederate soldiers, by contrast, were often left where they fell, buried hastily on battlefields or in makeshift graves near hospitals and prison camps. When they were reinterred, it was frequently in segregated sections or separate cemeteries altogether, reinforcing their status as defeated enemies rather than honored citizens.

The management of the dead thus extended wartime hierarchies into the postwar landscape. Burial practices translated military outcomes into spatial form, marking distinctions between loyalty and defeat in ways that endured beyond the battlefield. Separation of Union and Confederate remains served not only practical ends but symbolic ones, inscribing national belonging into the ground itself.

Once established, these distinctions did not require explanation. They were reinforced through repetition, maintenance, and habit, becoming features of the landscape rather than decisions subject to debate.

Race further complicated this system of control. As African Americans entered military service in significant numbers, the question of their burial exposed the limits of the nation's professed ideals. Federal regulations did not initially specify how African American soldiers were to be interred, yet prevailing social norms filled the gap. Black Union soldiers were typically buried within national cemeteries but relegated to peripheral sections, physically separated from white troops. This spatial marginalization reflected a hierarchy in which race superseded shared service, signaling that citizenship remained conditional despite military sacrifice.

The inclusion of formerly enslaved civilians added another layer to this management strategy. African Americans who lived and worked under federal supervision, such as those residing in Freedmen's Village on the Arlington Estate, were buried within the national cemetery system alongside Black soldiers. This practice underscored the government's view of race as a defining category, collapsing distinctions between civilian and military status in favor of a racialized identity. The result was a burial landscape that simultaneously acknowledged African Americans' relationship to the state while reinforcing their subordinate position within it.

Control over burial practices extended beyond the placement of graves to the regulation of commemoration itself. The federal government established rules governing headstone inscriptions, monument erection, and ceremonial observance, ensuring that expressions of remembrance aligned with sanctioned narratives. These regulations curtailed individual and local agency, replacing diverse mourning practices with standardized forms that supported national objectives. In doing so, the state harnessed the emotional power of death to reinforce its authority and legitimize its version of history.

The management of the dead also involved strategic silences. By focusing on order, uniformity, and collective sacrifice, the National Cemetery system obscured the violence and inequality inherent in its creation. The visual calm of aligned headstones concealed the contested processes that determined who lay beneath them and under what conditions. This silence was not accidental; it was integral to the cemetery's function as a stabilizing symbol. By presenting death as orderly and resolved, the landscape discouraged inquiry into the social conflicts that persisted beyond the war's end.

Yet the very need for such control reveals the fragility of the narratives it sought to sustain. The separation of bodies, the regulation of symbols, and the management of ritual all point to an underlying anxiety about memory and meaning. The state's efforts to impose coherence on the dead reflect an awareness that burial practices shape how the living understand the past. In organizing the dead, the government organized memory, directing interpretation toward unity while containing the disruptive potential of unresolved conflict.

This initial framework of order and control set the stage for the more explicit forms of segregation that would follow. As the National Cemetery system expanded and matured, the principles established in these early practices hardened into enduring patterns. The management of the dead became a means of managing difference, embedding social hierarchies into the very ground of national remembrance. Understanding this process is essential to reading the National Cemetery not only as a place of honor, but as a landscape where power, identity, and exclusion are materially and permanently inscribed.

Section II - Confederate Segregation and Sectional Power

The segregation of Confederate dead within the National Cemetery system reveals the extent to which burial practices functioned as instruments of postwar power. While the Civil War had ended on the battlefield, its ideological and emotional conflicts persisted in the treatment of the dead. Decisions about where Confederate soldiers would be buried, how their graves would be marked, and whether they would receive perpetual care became proxies for unresolved questions about loyalty, legitimacy, and national identity. Through these decisions, the federal government and the public alike negotiated the terms of reunion and reconciliation in ways that were spatial, symbolic, and deeply contested.

In the immediate aftermath of the war, federal policy reflected a clear hierarchy of allegiance. Union soldiers, having died in service to the recognized government, were deemed worthy of retrieval, identification, and inclusion in National Cemeteries. Confederate soldiers, by contrast, occupied an ambiguous position. As combatants who had fought against the United States, they were excluded from the initial vision of national commemoration. Many were buried hastily near battlefields, hospitals, or prison camps, often without durable markers or formal records. This neglect was not simply the result of limited resources; it functioned as a continuation of wartime judgment, extending defeat into the realm of memory.

In the South, the absence of federal care for Confederate graves was experienced as both an insult and a trauma. Families and communities confronted the reality that their dead lay scattered, unmarked, and vulnerable to decay. In response, Southern women organized Memorial Associations to locate, exhume, and reinter Confederate remains, often at great personal and financial cost. These efforts represented more than acts of private devotion. They constituted a deliberate assertion of Southern identity and autonomy in the face of federal authority, reclaiming control over memory through grassroots action. Confederate cemeteries became regional shrines, spaces where the narrative of the "Lost Cause" could be preserved and transmitted.

In the North, the presence of Confederate graves presented a different challenge. Confederate prisoners who had died in Northern camps were often buried in segregated sections of local or military cemeteries, receiving minimal care and attention. Over time, deteriorating headboards and neglected grounds drew criticism from some Northern officials and citizens, who appealed to humanitarian and Christian principles in calling for improved treatment. These appeals framed care for Confederate graves not as endorsement of their cause but as an obligation owed to the dead. Even so, such arguments gained traction slowly, constrained by lingering resentment and the political influence of Union veterans' organizations.

The eventual inclusion of Confederate graves within the sphere of federal responsibility marked a significant shift in national policy. When the government agreed to assume care for Confederate graves in the North and to permit the burial of Confederate remains in designated sections of National Cemeteries, it signaled a willingness to redefine the boundaries of national belonging. This inclusion, however, was carefully circumscribed. Confederate graves were segregated from those of Union soldiers, often grouped in distinct sections with different markers. This spatial separation allowed the government to acknowledge shared sacrifice while maintaining a clear distinction between loyalty and rebellion.

Arlington National Cemetery provides a particularly revealing example of this negotiated inclusion. The decision to establish a Confederate section within Arlington carried powerful symbolic implications. Located on land once owned by Robert E. Lee's family and seized by the federal government during the war, Arlington embodied Union victory and authority. Allowing Confederate graves within its bounds represented an act of magnanimity, yet the segregated placement ensured that the narrative of Union triumph remained intact. The Confederate Section VI functioned as both a concession and a containment, incorporating the defeated dead without fully integrating them into the national story.

This form of segregation reflected broader patterns of sectional power. By controlling the terms of Confederate inclusion, the federal government asserted its role as arbiter of reconciliation. The state determined when and how former enemies could be commemorated, shaping the memory of the war to emphasize unity under federal supremacy. At the same time, segregation provided space for Southern sensibilities, acknowledging the depth of regional attachment to the Confederate dead while limiting the political implications of their commemoration. The result was a carefully balanced landscape that sought to soothe tensions without erasing the moral judgment of the conflict.

The politics of Confederate segregation also illuminate the performative nature of reconciliation. Public ceremonies honoring Confederate dead, when permitted, were often framed in ways that emphasized shared valor rather than contested causes. This shift allowed for emotional closure while sidestepping questions of slavery, secession, and responsibility. The spatial separation of graves reinforced this selective memory, enabling visitors to engage with the idea of sacrifice without confronting the ideological foundations of the

Confederacy. In this way, segregation functioned as a mechanism for managing not only bodies but narratives.

Despite these efforts, the presence of Confederate sections within National Cemeteries remained a source of unease. For some, they represented a necessary step toward national healing; for others, they symbolized an unwarranted honor bestowed upon those who had taken up arms against the nation. This ambivalence underscores the unresolved nature of sectional memory in the United States. The cemetery landscape, with its ordered divisions and controlled symbolism, offers an appearance of resolution that belies ongoing tension.

Confederate segregation within the National Cemetery thus reveals the limits of reconciliation achieved through commemoration alone. By incorporating the defeated dead in a separate and contained manner, the state managed to project an image of unity while preserving the hierarchy established by war. The ground tells a story of compromise shaped by power, one in which inclusion is conditional and memory is carefully curated. Understanding this story is essential to recognizing how the National Cemetery mediates the relationship between past conflict and present identity, using space and ritual to negotiate the fragile boundaries of national belonging.

Race would expose the limits of this system more starkly than sectional loyalty ever could.

Section III - African American Soldiers, Freedmen, and Racial Hierarchy

The burial of African American soldiers and civilians within the National Cemetery system exposes the most persistent contradiction embedded in the landscape of national remembrance. While the Civil War redefined citizenship in legal terms, particularly through emancipation and constitutional amendment, burial practices revealed how deeply racial hierarchy remained entrenched in American culture. The treatment of Black soldiers and freed people within National Cemeteries demonstrates that service to the nation, even unto death, did not dissolve the boundaries of race. Instead, those boundaries were reinscribed spatially, quietly, and with enduring consequences.

African Americans entered the war initially as laborers, contraband, and wards of the federal government before being formally enlisted as soldiers. When Black men began to serve in the United States Colored Troops, their participation challenged prevailing assumptions about race, loyalty, and citizenship. Yet this challenge was met with resistance that extended beyond the battlefield. Federal burial policy, while nominally inclusive, reflected the social realities of segregation that governed American life. Black soldiers were eligible for burial in National Cemeteries, but their graves were commonly placed in separate sections, often at the margins of the cemetery grounds. This peripheral placement signaled conditional acceptance, acknowledging service while maintaining racial distinction.

The spatial segregation of African American graves was not mandated by explicit statute but emerged through administrative practice and cultural expectation. Cemetery superintendents, operating within the norms of their time, reproduced patterns of separation that mirrored civilian life. The result was a burial landscape that conveyed hierarchy through distance and placement rather than through overt prohibition. Black soldiers lay within the sacred space of national commemoration, yet apart from the central axes and prominent monuments that defined the dominant narrative. Their presence was sanctioned but subordinated, visible yet marginal.

The inclusion of freed civilians within National Cemeteries further underscores the primacy of race over status. At sites such as Arlington, African Americans who had lived in federally supervised communities were buried alongside Black soldiers, regardless of their civilian status. This practice collapsed distinctions between military and non-military dead in ways that did not occur for white civilians, who were generally excluded from National Cemeteries. The decision reflected the government's perception of freed people as wards rather than full citizens, their identity defined more by race and dependency than by individual roles or contributions. Burial thus became another arena in which racial identity overrode claims to equal citizenship.

These practices carried significant symbolic weight. Burial in a National Cemetery conveyed recognition by the state and participation in the nation's collective memory. For African Americans, this recognition was partial and constrained. The segregated sections communicated a message that Black sacrifice, while acknowledged, did not warrant full integration into the national story. The uniformity of headstones within these sections mirrored that of the broader cemetery, yet their location conveyed a different meaning. Equality in form existed alongside inequality in space, producing a landscape that simultaneously affirmed and denied belonging.

Public rituals reinforced this hierarchy. Early Decoration Day and Memorial Day observances often neglected African American graves, leaving them undecorated even as white graves received attention. When Black communities organized their own commemorations, they did so largely outside the official framework, asserting their right to honor their dead in the absence of institutional support. These parallel rituals highlight the disjunction between the ideals proclaimed by national commemoration and the realities experienced by African Americans. The cemetery, rather than resolving this tension, made it visible through omission and separation.

The persistence of segregation within National Cemeteries also reveals the depth of racial ideology in postwar America. Unlike the segregation of Confederate dead, which was eventually reframed as a matter of reconciliation between former enemies, racial segregation lacked a comparable narrative of resolution. Black soldiers had fought and died for the Union, yet their burial reflected an assumption that race constituted an enduring and defining difference. This assumption required no formal justification; it operated as a taken-for-granted truth, embedded in administrative decisions and spatial arrangements.

Photographic and documentary evidence from the late nineteenth and early twentieth centuries underscores the emotional impact of this hierarchy. Images of African American mourners tending graves in isolated sections capture the quiet resilience of communities denied full recognition. These scenes contrast sharply with the grandeur of official ceremonies elsewhere in the cemetery, revealing the uneven distribution of honor and visibility. The cemetery thus functioned as both a site of inclusion and a record of exclusion, preserving evidence of racial inequality in stone and soil.

The burial of African American soldiers and freedmen within National Cemeteries challenges any reading of these spaces as unambiguously egalitarian. While the landscape proclaims unity and shared sacrifice, its internal divisions tell a more complicated story. The segregation of Black graves demonstrates how national memory can accommodate inclusion without equality, recognition without integration. By examining these practices, the National Cemetery emerges as a crucial source for understanding how race shaped the lived experience of citizenship, even in death.

This racialized landscape did more than reflect contemporary attitudes; it helped normalize them. By embedding segregation into a sacred national space, the cemetery lent moral legitimacy to social hierarchy, presenting it as natural and enduring. The consequences of this normalization extend beyond the boundaries of the cemetery, influencing how generations of Americans understood the relationship between service, race, and belonging. In this way, the treatment of African American soldiers and freedmen within the National Cemetery system stands as one of the most telling indictments of the limits of postwar reconciliation and the enduring power of racial division in American life.

By this point, the cemetery's surface coherence begins to fracture. What initially appeared as order reveals itself as sorting, and what seemed commemorative begins to read as regulatory.

Section IV - What the Landscape Reveals That Texts Conceal

The National Cemetery, when approached as a physical landscape rather than solely as a documentary record, reveals dimensions of American history that written texts often obscure or soften. Official reports, legislation, and commemorative speeches tend to emphasize intent, policy, and declared ideals. The ground itself, however, records practice. In the placement of graves, the organization of sections, and the patterns of care and neglect, the cemetery preserves evidence of social priorities that were rarely articulated openly. These material traces expose how power operated quietly, embedding hierarchy and exclusion into spaces ostensibly dedicated to unity and sacrifice.

Written records of the National Cemetery system frequently frame segregation and exclusion as administrative necessities or temporary accommodations shaped by circumstance. The landscape tells a different story. Segregation appears not as an anomaly but as a consistent organizing principle, one that structured the cemetery from its earliest development and persisted well into the twentieth century. Confederate sections set apart from Union dead, African American graves placed at the margins, and civilian freed people buried according to race rather than status all demonstrate how identity categories were spatially enforced. These divisions were not incidental; they were integral to how the cemetery functioned as a social and political instrument.

The power of the landscape lies in its resistance to revision. While texts can be edited, reinterpreted, or forgotten, the physical arrangement of graves endures. Paths worn by decades of visitors trace routes of attention and neglect, reinforcing which sections are seen and which remain peripheral. Monuments rise in some areas while others remain marked only by rows of identical stones. Even when policies changed and official rhetoric shifted toward reconciliation or inclusion, the earlier spatial decisions remained visible, their meanings accumulating rather than disappearing. The cemetery thus acts as a palimpsest, layering successive interpretations over a foundation that cannot be erased.

This persistence complicates narratives of progress. Claims that the nation moved steadily toward greater unity or equality after the Civil War falter when confronted with the enduring segregation inscribed in sacred space. The cemetery does not allow easy closure. It holds together moments of inclusion and exclusion, honor and marginalization, forcing them to coexist within the same ground. This coexistence challenges the comforting assumption that national ideals naturally translate into lived reality. Instead, it demonstrates how ideals are selectively applied, constrained by prevailing social hierarchies even at moments of profound moral reckoning.

The contrast between ritual performance and spatial reality is particularly revealing. Ceremonies conducted in National Cemeteries proclaim unity, shared sacrifice, and collective memory. These performances draw attention to central monuments and prominent sections, reinforcing a cohesive national narrative. Meanwhile, segregated sections often remain outside the focal points of ritual activity, their presence acknowledged only obliquely or not at all. The disjunction between what is celebrated and what is sidelined underscores how ritual can mask inequality even as it claims to transcend difference. The landscape quietly contradicts the performance, offering a counter-narrative for those willing to look.

Reading the cemetery as evidence also highlights the role of silence in shaping historical understanding. Many forms of discrimination leave little trace in official documentation precisely because they were considered normal or unremarkable at the time. The absence of explicit prohibition does not indicate the absence of exclusion. In the cemetery, silence takes physical form in empty spaces, peripheral placements, and the lack of commemorative markers. These silences speak to assumptions so deeply ingrained that they required no justification. The ground bears witness to these assumptions, preserving them long after the language that sustained them has faded.

The National Cemetery thus serves as an underutilized primary source, one that complements and complicates traditional archives. It demands a mode of reading attuned to materiality, spatial relationship, and embodied experience. Walking through the cemetery, one encounters not only names and dates but patterns that reveal how the nation sorted its dead. These patterns invite questions that texts alone may not prompt: why certain groups are clustered together, why some areas are emphasized and others overlooked, why equality in death is proclaimed but unevenly realized. Such questions arise organically from the encounter with the space itself.

Engaging with the cemetery in this way also alters the ethical stakes of historical interpretation. The landscape confronts visitors with the consequences of abstract policy, translating bureaucratic decisions into human terms. Segregated graves are no longer statistics or footnotes; they are visible reminders of lives shaped by exclusion even in death. This visibility resists the distancing effect of written analysis, grounding interpretation in tangible reality. The cemetery insists that memory is not only constructed through words but also through places that shape how history is felt as well as known.

In revealing what texts often conceal, the National Cemetery challenges scholars and citizens alike to reconsider how national identity has been built and maintained. It exposes the gap between professed ideals and practiced values, showing how unity was pursued through control rather than equality and reconciliation achieved through containment rather than integration. The sacredness of the space amplifies this challenge, lending moral weight to the evidence it preserves. The ground does not accuse or defend; it simply remains, holding the traces of decisions made and consequences endured.

By attending to the cemetery as landscape, the contradictions of American memory become unmistakable. The National Cemetery stands as both a testament to collective sacrifice and a record of enduring division. It affirms the nation's desire to honor its dead while revealing the limits of that honor. In doing so, it offers a fuller, more honest account of how citizenship, race, and power have intersected in the shaping of American history. This account, written in stone and soil, endures as long as the graves themselves, challenging each generation to read it with care and to reckon with what it reveals.

Chapter Three

And the Two Shall Never Meet: The Liminal Borderland of Cemeteries and Death

Section I - The Cemetery as Borderland

The American cemetery occupies a space that is neither fully of the living nor entirely of the dead. It exists as a borderland—material, cultural, and psychological—where the binary oppositions that structure human understanding of existence are brought into sustained contact. Life and death, presence and absence, sacred and profane, material and immaterial converge within its bounds. The cemetery is not simply a place of disposal, nor merely a site of remembrance; it is a constructed environment through which societies negotiate the most profound rupture in human experience: the separation of the living from the dead.

Human cultures have always required a physical locus for death. Birth requires no such structure, as the living body itself occupies space and demands recognition. Death, by contrast, removes the body from the social world while leaving memory, attachment, and identity unresolved. The cemetery emerges as a response to this rupture, providing a tangible framework through which absence can be rendered present and loss made intelligible. By situating the dead within a defined landscape, societies impose order on what would otherwise remain an unbounded and destabilizing experience.

As a material artifact, the cemetery reflects an external system of meaning constructed through cultural symbols, spatial organization, and ritual practice. Headstones, pathways, inscriptions, iconography, and plantings collectively form a language that communicates shared assumptions about identity, continuity, and the afterlife. Yet this external system does not operate independently. It is activated only through the interpretive engagement of the living, who bring to the cemetery their own memories, expectations, and embodied responses to death. Meaning emerges through the interaction of these internal and external systems, rather than residing solely in either.

The borderland quality of the cemetery is therefore not limited to geography. It is equally cognitive and emotional. Visitors experience the cemetery through sensory engagement—sight, touch, sound, and movement—while simultaneously processing loss, memory, and self-awareness. The act of standing before a grave requires an individual to negotiate personal mortality while confronting the trace of another's life. This encounter situates the cemetery as a liminal space, one that suspends ordinary social time and permits reflection on transitions that resist full articulation.

Within this liminal environment, material objects take on heightened significance. Ordinary items—stone, metal, wood, images—are imbued with symbolic weight through their placement and context. Among these objects, the photograph occupies a distinctive position. Unlike names or dates, photographs assert the visual presence of the deceased as they once were among the living. When introduced into the cemetery landscape, photographs disrupt the expected distance between life and death, inserting vitality, personality, and immediacy into a space otherwise marked by stillness and finality.

Understanding the cemetery as a borderland allows for an examination of how material culture functions as a mediator between worlds. It reveals how societies manage memory not as a passive repository of the past, but as an active, negotiated process shaped by environment, ritual, and perception. In this space, memory is stabilized through material form while remaining vulnerable to interpretation, decay, and transformation. The cemetery thus stands as both a site of continuity and a reminder of impermanence—a place where meaning is continually made, challenged, and renewed.

Section II - Photographs as Material Memory Technologies

Among the material objects incorporated into the cemetery landscape, the photograph occupies a singular and powerful role. Unlike inscriptions, symbols, or iconographic motifs, the photograph presents an indexical trace of the living body. It does not merely signify identity; it asserts presence. In doing so, the photograph functions as a technology of memory—an externalized mechanism through which the living stabilize, negotiate, and transmit remembrance across time.

Photographs differ from other funerary markers in that they originate outside the cemetery. They are created within the realm of the living, often long before death occurs, and for purposes unrelated to mourning. Portraits commemorate milestones, relationships, and moments of vitality. When later introduced into the cemetery, these images undergo a profound transformation. Removed from their original context and embedded within a funerary setting, they acquire new meaning through juxtaposition with death, absence, and ritualized remembrance.

This transformation is not passive. The photograph does not simply illustrate the deceased; it actively reshapes the experience of the cemetery encounter. Where names and dates abstract identity, the photograph particularizes it. The viewer is confronted not with a symbolic stand-in for the dead, but with a recognizable human face—one that once occupied the same social and physical world as the living observer. The photograph collapses temporal distance, creating a momentary convergence between past vitality and present absence.

As a material artifact, the photograph operates through both external and internal systems of meaning. Externally, it conveys culturally legible information: gender, age, social status, religious affiliation, ethnicity, and historical period. Clothing, posture, props, and photographic style situate the image within broader social narratives. Internally, the photograph activates subjective response. Memory, imagination, empathy, and identification emerge through the viewer's own experiences and emotional frameworks. Meaning arises through the synthesis of these systems rather than through either alone.

The photograph's power within the cemetery is heightened by its embodied nature. Unlike text, which requires literacy and interpretive translation, the photograph engages the senses directly. Vision initiates recognition before cognition intervenes. The immediacy of this encounter renders the photograph particularly effective as a mnemonic device, capable of eliciting affective response even in viewers with no personal connection to the deceased. In this way, photographs extend remembrance beyond familial boundaries, inviting communal participation in memory.

Importantly, the photograph also destabilizes the cemetery's expected visual grammar. Cemeteries traditionally communicate death through absence—through the stillness of stone and the finality of inscription. The introduction of photographic images interrupts this logic by reintroducing signs of life. Faces gaze outward. Eyes meet those of the visitor. The dead appear, paradoxically, animated within a space devoted to repose. This visual disruption compels the viewer to confront the unresolved tension between life and death that the cemetery is designed to manage.

As technologies of memory, cemetery photographs do not preserve meaning unchanged. They are subject to reinterpretation, decay, and shifting cultural frameworks. Weather erodes images, photographic styles age, and social conventions evolve. Yet this vulnerability does not diminish their function. Rather, it underscores the dynamic nature of memory itself. Remembrance is not fixed; it is continually renegotiated through material form, context, and perception.

By situating photographs within the cemetery borderland, societies externalize memory in a form that is both durable and contingent. The photograph becomes a site of encounter where personal recollection, cultural narrative, and material presence intersect. In this role, it serves not merely as decoration or identification, but as an active participant in the ongoing management of memory at the boundary between life and death.

Section III - Encounter, Interpretation, and the Work of Memory

The encounter between viewer and photograph within the cemetery is neither neutral nor incidental. It is an interpretive event shaped by bodily presence, cultural knowledge, and personal history. Unlike images encountered in domestic or archival settings, cemetery photographs are experienced in situ, within a landscape explicitly marked by death. Confirmation of mortality precedes interpretation. The viewer knows, before any conscious analysis begins, that the person represented is no longer living. This knowledge frames the encounter and conditions the meanings that follow.

Interpretation unfolds through the interaction of external cultural codes and internal cognitive and emotional responses. Clothing, hairstyle, photographic format, and compositional conventions situate the image within a recognizable social and historical framework. These elements provide the viewer with an initial orientation, allowing the photograph to be read within shared systems of meaning. Yet this external legibility does not exhaust the image's significance. The photograph simultaneously invites an inward turn, prompting memory, imagination, and empathetic projection that exceed culturally prescribed interpretation.

This dual process aligns with the distinction between collective comprehension and personal affect. The photograph communicates through recognizable signs, but it also elicits responses that are idiosyncratic and often ineffable. A viewer may be drawn to a particular image without fully articulating why, sensing a resonance that resists rational explanation. Such responses arise not from the photograph alone, but from the convergence of image, setting, and the viewer's own experiential archive. The cemetery amplifies this convergence by situating interpretation within a space already charged with emotional and existential significance.

The body plays a central role in this interpretive process. Movement through the cemetery, the act of stopping before a grave, the orientation of the viewer's gaze, and the physical proximity to the photograph all contribute to meaning-making. The encounter unfolds temporally rather than instantaneously. Initial recognition may give way to prolonged attention, followed by reflection, discomfort, or identification. In this way, memory is not simply recalled; it is actively produced through embodied engagement with material form.

Cemetery photographs also introduce an asymmetry of vision. The depicted subject appears to gaze outward, meeting the eyes of the living observer. This visual exchange disrupts the customary separation between the living and the dead by creating the illusion of mutual presence. The viewer becomes aware of being seen, even as they look. This reversal intensifies self-awareness and situates the observer within the scene of mortality. The photograph thus functions not only as a site of remembrance, but as a mirror through which the living confront their own temporal position.

Importantly, the meanings generated through these encounters are not fixed. They shift according to the viewer's relationship to the deceased, cultural familiarity, and emotional state. A photograph may evoke tenderness in one observer and unease in another. For family members, the image may reactivate intimate memories; for strangers, it may provoke curiosity, empathy, or avoidance. The same photograph can operate differently across time, as personal circumstances and cultural attitudes toward death evolve. Memory, in this context, is not preserved intact but continually reconfigured through repeated encounters.

The interpretive work performed at the cemetery therefore extends beyond the individual image. It encompasses the viewer's negotiation of loss, identity, and belonging within a broader cultural framework. By engaging photographs in this setting, individuals participate in a collective practice of remembrance that bridges private experience and public space. The cemetery becomes a site where memory is neither wholly personal nor entirely communal but produced through their intersection.

Through these encounters, photographs mediate the ongoing relationship between the living and the dead. They invite reflection without closure, recognition without resolution. In doing so, they reveal memory as an active process—one that requires participation, interpretation, and repetition. The cemetery photograph does not simply recall a life once lived; it compels the living to continually renegotiate the meaning of life, death, and continuity within the borderland they share.

Section IV: Selection, Authority, and the Politics of Representation

The photograph displayed within a cemetery is rarely a neutral or self-evident artifact. Its presence reflects a series of choices made by the living—choices shaped by grief, memory, cultural expectation, and power. The individual represented in the image is most often not the individual who selected it. Instead, the photograph functions as a posthumous representation constructed by survivors, revealing as much about those who remember as about the one remembered.

Selection is therefore an act of authority. Families choose images that align with culturally sanctioned narratives of identity: youth, respectability, marital unity, religious devotion, military service, or familial role. These choices stabilize memory by privileging particular moments over others, effectively condensing a life into a single visual statement. What is omitted—illness, aging, conflict, ambivalence—disappears from the public record, replaced by an image that conforms to collective ideals of how a life should be remembered.

This process of selection underscores the cemetery photograph's function as a representational negotiation rather than a documentary truth. The image does not claim to show the deceased as they were in totality; it presents the deceased as they are meant to be seen. In this sense, cemetery photographs operate as curated memories, shaped by social norms and emotional needs. The authority to choose becomes an authority to define identity beyond death.

Power is further embedded in the placement and orientation of photographs. Images positioned prominently on headstones, often above inscriptions or names, assert visual dominance within the funerary landscape. The gaze of the deceased—fixed, frontal, and enduring—meets the visitor repeatedly, reinforcing presence through repetition. This visual hierarchy grants the image a form of agency, allowing it to command attention and structure the viewer's encounter with the grave.

In the context of marital or family plots, representational choices may also reproduce existing social hierarchies. Photographs depicting couples frequently emphasize unity and continuity, sometimes masking asymmetries of age, status, or experience. When one partner's image is present and another absent, or when a youthful image stands in for a long life, the resulting representation shapes how relationships are remembered and interpreted. The photograph thus extends social arrangements into the realm of memory, reinforcing patterns of authority that persist beyond death.

The politics of representation become especially visible when photographs disrupt expectation. Images of children, the very young, or those who died prematurely intensify emotional response and complicate narrative closure. Similarly, photographs that portray religious initiation, military service, or occupational identity foreground particular affiliations as defining features of the self. These representations do not simply commemorate; they instruct viewers in how the deceased should be understood within the broader cultural order.

Importantly, these representational decisions are not static. As cultural values shift, the meanings attached to cemetery photographs evolve. What once conveyed honor or virtue may later appear restrictive or incomplete. Yet the photograph remains, continuing to shape interpretation long after the context of its selection has faded. Memory, once externalized in material form, acquires a durability that outlasts the intentions of its creators.

By examining selection and representation within cemetery photographs, the processes through which memory is managed become visible. Remembrance emerges not as a transparent reflection of the past, but as an active construction shaped by authority, omission, and cultural narrative. The cemetery photograph stands at the intersection of memory and power, revealing how societies negotiate identity, continuity, and meaning in the face of loss.

Section V: Endurance, Decay, and the Limits of Memory

The cemetery promises endurance. Stone suggests permanence, metal implies resilience, and the act of marking a grave carries an implicit expectation of longevity. Yet the material reality of cemeteries reveals a more fragile truth. Markers weather, inscriptions erode, photographs fade or fracture, and entire sections of burial grounds are altered, relocated, or forgotten. Memory, when entrusted to material form, gains durability but not immortality. The tension between endurance and decay is central to understanding how societies manage remembrance over time.

Photographs are especially vulnerable to this tension. Exposed to sun, moisture, temperature shifts, and physical impact, they deteriorate more rapidly than stone or metal. Images cloud, faces blur, and details dissolve into abstraction. Ironically, as photographic clarity diminishes, interpretive openness often increases. A partially obscured image invites projection, allowing viewers to fill gaps with imagination and association. Decay does not erase meaning; it transforms it, shifting memory from specificity toward suggestion.

This transformation underscores a fundamental limitation of material memory: no object can preserve meaning unchanged. As cultural contexts shift, the frameworks through which photographs are read also evolve. Clothing once legible as everyday attire becomes historical costume; symbols once widely understood lose resonance; facial expressions take on new interpretations. The photograph endures, but its language changes. Memory persists not as a fixed record, but as a living dialogue between artifact and observer.

The endurance of cemetery photographs also depends upon continued engagement. Graves that are visited, cleaned, and repaired remain legible sites of memory. Those neglected slip gradually into anonymity. Broken frames go unreplaced, images detach from stone, and names fade into illegibility. This uneven maintenance reflects broader social patterns: family dispersal, demographic change, economic constraint, and shifting attitudes toward burial and mourning. Memory endures unevenly, shaped by circumstance as much as intention.

Yet even in neglect, cemetery photographs retain significance. Their very deterioration testifies to the passage of time and the limits of remembrance. A faded face signals not only an individual life now distant, but the waning of those who once remembered that life intimately. In this way, decay becomes part of the narrative of memory rather than its failure. The photograph marks not only presence, but loss layered upon loss.

The limits of material memory do not negate its value. On the contrary, they reveal why societies continually renew commemorative practices. As older forms erode, new markers emerge: replacement stones, digital archives, genealogical databases, and virtual memorials. These innovations reflect the same underlying impulse that produced cemetery photographs—the desire to anchor memory outside the self, to resist erasure through material means.

By acknowledging endurance and decay together, the cemetery can be understood not as a failed archive, but as a dynamic system of remembrance. Its materials do not freeze memory in time; they invite continual reinterpretation. In this sense, the limits of memory are not endpoints but conditions of its persistence. The cemetery remains a place where meaning is neither fully secured nor wholly lost, but perpetually negotiated at the edge of time.

Section VI: Memory at the Threshold

The cemetery, when understood as a borderland, reveals memory not as a passive archive of the past but as an active practice sustained through material form, interpretation, and repetition. Photographs, situated within this space, externalize remembrance while simultaneously inviting continual re-engagement by the living. They do not resolve the tension between life and death; they manage it. In doing so, they make visible the human effort to hold presence and absence in productive relation.

Across the cemetery landscape, memory is stabilized through selection, encounter, and endurance, yet never secured against change. Images are chosen, gazes are met, meanings are projected, and materials decay. Each of these processes contributes to a dynamic system in which remembrance persists by adaptation rather than permanence. The work of memory unfolds not in spite of loss, but through it—shaped by cultural expectation, personal experience, and the limits imposed by time.

Understanding photographs as material memory technologies clarifies how societies negotiate continuity at moments of rupture. The cemetery does not simply commemorate the dead; it organizes the living response to death. Through visual presence, spatial arrangement, and ritualized encounter, it provides a framework for acknowledging mortality while sustaining social and emotional coherence. Memory, in this context, becomes a shared labor rather than an individual possession.

This chapter has traced how memory is externalized, activated, curated, and transformed within the cemetery borderland. In doing so, it establishes a conceptual foundation for examining memory under conditions of movement, uncertainty, and constraint. When death occurs away from home, beyond established ritual spaces, and under pressure that permits little pause for mourning, the strategies through which memory is managed become especially visible.

Chapter Four

Crossing the Border: Use of Photographs in the American Midwestern Cemetery

Section I - The Cemetery as Borderland

In the American Midwest, cemeteries are often embedded within working landscapes—bordered by fields, county roads, small towns, and the visible routines of everyday life. These burial grounds do not announce themselves as separate worlds so much as quiet interruptions within them, places where the living pass regularly and the dead remain visibly present. It is within this context that photographs appear on grave markers, operating as threshold objects that complicate the boundary between presence and absence. As Roland Barthes observed, the photograph holds together life and death in a single frame, capturing a moment that will never occur again and, in doing so, confronting the viewer with both vitality and finality at once.

These cemeteries occupy a space that is neither fully of the living nor entirely of the dead. It exists as a borderland—material, cultural, and psychological—where the binary oppositions that structure human understanding of existence are held in sustained proximity. Life and death, presence and absence, sacred and profane, material and immaterial converge within its bounds. The cemetery is not simply a place of disposal, nor merely a site of remembrance; it is a constructed environment through which societies negotiate the most profound rupture in human experience: the separation of the living from the dead.

Human cultures have always required a physical locus for death. Birth demands no such structure, as the living body itself occupies space and insists upon recognition. Death, by contrast, removes the body from the social world while leaving memory, attachment, and identity unresolved. The cemetery emerges as a response to this rupture, providing a tangible framework through which absence can be rendered present and loss made intelligible. By situating the dead within a defined landscape, societies impose order on what would otherwise remain unbounded and destabilizing.

Within this environment, the photograph takes on particular significance. Embedded in stone and set among graves, it does not merely mark identity; it reintroduces presence into a space structured around absence. The photograph collapses temporal distance, allowing the living to encounter the dead not as abstraction, but as a once-living body suspended in time. In doing so, cemetery photographs intensify the borderland quality of the space itself, doubling the threshold where life and death, memory and materiality, meet.

This encounter does not remain purely visual. In the cemetery, the photograph is encountered as a physical object—glazed, cracked, weathered, sometimes faded or partially obscured. Its surface bears the marks of exposure, maintenance, and neglect. These material conditions matter, because they situate the photograph not outside the cemetery's logic, but within it, subject to the same forces of time and environment as stone and soil.

As a material artifact, the cemetery reflects an external system of meaning constructed through cultural symbols, spatial organization, and ritual practice. Headstones, pathways, inscriptions, iconography, and plantings collectively form a language that communicates shared assumptions about identity, continuity, and the afterlife. Yet this external system does not operate independently. It is activated only through the interpretive engagement of the living, who bring to the cemetery their own memories, expectations, and embodied responses to death. Meaning emerges through the interaction of these internal and external systems, rather than residing solely in either.

The borderland quality of the cemetery is therefore not limited to geography. It is equally cognitive and emotional. Visitors experience the cemetery through sensory engagement—sight, touch, sound, and movement—while simultaneously processing loss, memory, and self-awareness. The act of standing before a grave requires an individual to negotiate personal mortality while confronting the trace of another's life. This encounter situates the cemetery as a liminal space, one that suspends ordinary social time and permits reflection on transitions that resist full articulation.

Within this liminal environment, material objects take on heightened significance. Ordinary items—stone, metal, wood, images—are imbued with symbolic weight through their placement and context. Among these objects, the photograph occupies a distinctive position. Unlike names or dates, photographs assert the visual presence of the deceased as they once were among the living. When introduced into the cemetery landscape, photographs disrupt the expected distance between life and death, inserting vitality, personality, and immediacy into a space otherwise marked by stillness and finality.

Understanding the cemetery as a borderland allows for an examination of how material culture functions as a mediator between worlds. It reveals how societies manage memory not as a passive repository of the past, but as an active, negotiated process shaped by environment, ritual, and perception. In this space, memory is stabilized through material form while remaining vulnerable to interpretation, decay, and transformation. The cemetery thus stands as both a site of continuity and a reminder of impermanence—a place where meaning is continually made, challenged, and renewed.

Section II: Photographs as Material Memory Technologies

Among the material objects incorporated into the cemetery landscape, the photograph occupies a singular and powerful role. Unlike inscriptions, symbols, or iconographic motifs, the photograph presents an indexical trace of the living body. It does not merely signify identity; it asserts presence. In doing so, the photograph functions as a technology of memory—an externalized mechanism through which the living stabilize, negotiate, and transmit remembrance across time.

Photographs differ from other funerary markers in that they originate outside the cemetery. They are created within the realm of the living, often long before death occurs, and for purposes unrelated to mourning. Portraits commemorate milestones, relationships, and moments of vitality. When later introduced into the cemetery, these images undergo a profound transformation. Removed from their original context and embedded within a funerary setting, they acquire new meaning through juxtaposition with death, absence, and ritualized remembrance.

This transformation is not passive. The photograph does not simply illustrate the deceased; it actively reshapes the experience of the cemetery encounter. Where names and dates abstract identity, the photograph particularizes it. The viewer is confronted not with a symbolic stand-in for the dead, but with a recognizable human face—one that once occupied the same social and physical world as the living observer. The photograph collapses temporal distance, creating a momentary convergence between past vitality and present absence.

As a material artifact, the photograph operates through both external and internal systems of meaning. Externally, it conveys culturally legible information: gender, age, social status, religious affiliation, ethnicity, and historical period. Clothing, posture, props, and photographic style situate the image within broader social narratives. Internally, the photograph activates subjective response. Memory, imagination, empathy, and identification emerge through the viewer's own experiences and emotional frameworks. Meaning arises through the synthesis of these systems rather than through either alone.

The photograph's power within the cemetery is heightened by its embodied nature. Unlike text, which requires literacy and interpretive translation, the photograph engages the senses directly. Vision initiates recognition before cognition intervenes. The immediacy of this encounter renders the photograph particularly effective as a mnemonic device, capable of eliciting affective response even in viewers with no personal connection to the deceased. In this way, photographs extend remembrance beyond familial boundaries, inviting communal participation in memory.

Importantly, the photograph also destabilizes the cemetery's expected visual grammar. Cemeteries traditionally communicate death through absence—through the stillness of stone and the finality of inscription. The introduction of photographic images interrupts this logic by reintroducing signs of life. Faces gaze outward. Eyes meet those of the visitor. The dead appear, paradoxically, animated within a space devoted to repose. This visual disruption compels the viewer to confront the unresolved tension between life and death that the cemetery is designed to manage.

As technologies of memory, cemetery photographs do not preserve meaning unchanged. They are subject to reinterpretation, decay, and shifting cultural frameworks. Weather erodes images, photographic styles age, and social conventions evolve. Yet this vulnerability does not diminish their function. Rather, it underscores the dynamic nature of memory itself. Remembrance is not fixed; it is continually renegotiated through material form, context, and perception.

By situating photographs within the cemetery borderland, societies externalize memory in a form that is both durable and contingent. The photograph becomes a site of encounter where personal recollection, cultural narrative, and material presence intersect. In this role, it serves not merely as decoration or identification, but as an active participant in the ongoing management of memory at the boundary between life and death.

Section III: Encounter, Interpretation, and the Work of Memory

The encounter between viewer and photograph within the cemetery is neither neutral nor incidental. It is an interpretive event shaped by bodily presence, cultural knowledge, and personal history. Unlike images encountered in domestic or archival settings, cemetery photographs are experienced in situ, within a landscape explicitly marked by death. Confirmation of mortality precedes interpretation. The viewer knows, before any conscious analysis begins, that the person represented is no longer living. This knowledge frames the encounter and conditions the meanings that follow.

Interpretation unfolds through the interaction of external cultural codes and internal cognitive and emotional responses. Clothing, hairstyle, photographic format, and compositional conventions situate the image within a recognizable social and historical framework. These elements provide the viewer with an initial orientation, allowing the photograph to be read within shared systems of meaning. Yet this external legibility does not exhaust the image's significance. The photograph simultaneously invites an inward turn, prompting memory, imagination, and empathetic projection that exceed culturally prescribed interpretation.

This dual process aligns with the distinction between collective comprehension and personal affect. The photograph communicates through recognizable signs, but it also elicits responses that are idiosyncratic and often ineffable. A viewer may be drawn to a particular image without fully articulating why, sensing a resonance that resists rational explanation. Such responses arise not from the photograph alone, but from the convergence of image, setting, and the viewer's own experiential archive. The cemetery amplifies this convergence by situating interpretation within a space already charged with emotional and existential significance.

The body plays a central role in this interpretive process. Movement through the cemetery, the act of stopping before a grave, the orientation of the viewer's gaze, and the physical proximity to the photograph all contribute to meaning-making. The encounter unfolds temporally rather than instantaneously. Initial recognition may give way to prolonged attention, followed by reflection, discomfort, or identification. In this way, memory is not simply recalled; it is actively produced through embodied engagement with material form.

Cemetery photographs also introduce an asymmetry of vision. The depicted subject appears to gaze outward, meeting the eyes of the living observer. This visual exchange disrupts the customary separation between the living and the dead by creating the illusion of mutual presence. The viewer becomes aware of being seen, even as they look. This reversal intensifies self-awareness and situates the observer within the scene of mortality. The photograph thus functions not only as a site of remembrance, but as a mirror through which the living confront their own temporal position.

Importantly, the meanings generated through these encounters are not fixed. They shift according to the viewer's relationship to the deceased, cultural familiarity, and emotional state. A photograph may evoke tenderness in one observer and unease in another. For family members, the image may reactivate intimate memories; for strangers, it may provoke curiosity, empathy, or avoidance. The same photograph can operate differently across time, as personal circumstances and cultural attitudes toward death evolve. Memory, in this context, is not preserved intact but continually reconfigured through repeated encounters.

The interpretive work performed at the cemetery therefore extends beyond the individual image. It encompasses the viewer's negotiation of loss, identity, and belonging within a broader cultural framework. By engaging photographs in this setting, individuals participate in a collective practice of remembrance that bridges private experience and public space. The cemetery becomes a site where memory is neither wholly personal nor entirely communal, but produced through their intersection.

Through these encounters, photographs mediate the ongoing relationship between the living and the dead. They invite reflection without closure, recognition without resolution. In doing so, they reveal memory as an active process—one that requires participation, interpretation, and repetition. The cemetery photograph does not simply recall a life once lived; it compels the living to continually renegotiate the meaning of life, death, and continuity within the borderland they share.

Section IV: Selection, Authority, and the Politics of Representation

The photograph displayed within a cemetery is rarely a neutral or self-evident artifact. Its presence reflects a series of choices made by the living—choices shaped by grief, memory, cultural expectation, and power. The individual represented in the image is most often not the individual who selected it. Instead, the photograph functions as a posthumous representation constructed by survivors, revealing as much about those who remember as about the one remembered.

Selection is therefore an act of authority. Families choose images that align with culturally sanctioned narratives of identity: youth, respectability, marital unity, religious devotion, military service, or familial role. These choices stabilize memory by privileging particular moments over others, effectively condensing a life into a single visual statement. What is omitted—illness, aging, conflict, ambivalence—disappears from the public record, replaced by an image that conforms to collective ideals of how a life should be remembered.

This process of selection underscores the cemetery photograph's function as a representational negotiation rather than a documentary truth. The image does not claim to show the deceased as they were in totality; it presents the deceased as they are meant to be seen. In this sense, cemetery photographs operate as curated memories, shaped by social norms and emotional needs. The authority to choose becomes an authority to define identity beyond death.

Power is further embedded in the placement and orientation of photographs. Images positioned prominently on headstones, often above inscriptions or names, assert visual dominance within the funerary landscape. The gaze of the deceased—fixed, frontal, and enduring—meets the visitor repeatedly, reinforcing presence through repetition. This visual hierarchy grants the image a form of agency, allowing it to command attention and structure the viewer's encounter with the grave.

In the context of marital or family plots, representational choices may also reproduce existing social hierarchies. Photographs depicting couples frequently emphasize unity and continuity, sometimes masking asymmetries of age, status, or experience. When one partner's image is present and another absent, or when a youthful image stands in for a long life, the resulting representation shapes how relationships are remembered and interpreted. The photograph thus extends social arrangements into the realm of memory, reinforcing patterns of authority that persist beyond death.

The politics of representation become especially visible when photographs disrupt expectation. Images of children, the very young, or those who died prematurely intensify emotional response and complicate narrative closure. Similarly, photographs that portray religious initiation, military service, or occupational identity foreground particular affiliations as defining features of the self. These representations do not simply commemorate; they instruct viewers in how the deceased should be understood within the broader cultural order.

Importantly, these representational decisions are not static. As cultural values shift, the meanings attached to cemetery photographs evolve. What once conveyed honor or virtue may later appear restrictive or incomplete. Yet the photograph remains, continuing to shape interpretation long after the context of its selection has faded. Memory, once externalized in material form, acquires a durability that outlasts the intentions of its creators.

By examining selection and representation within cemetery photographs, the processes through which memory is managed become visible. Remembrance emerges not as a transparent reflection of the past, but as an active construction shaped by authority, omission, and cultural narrative. The cemetery photograph stands at the intersection of memory and power, revealing how societies negotiate identity, continuity, and meaning in the face of loss.

Section V: Endurance, Decay, and the Limits of Memory

The cemetery promises endurance. Stone suggests permanence, metal implies resilience, and the act of marking a grave carries an implicit expectation of longevity. Yet the material reality of cemeteries reveals a more fragile truth. Markers weather, inscriptions erode, photographs fade or fracture, and entire sections of burial grounds are altered, relocated, or forgotten. Memory, when entrusted to material form, gains durability but not immortality. The tension between endurance and decay is central to understanding how societies manage remembrance over time.

Photographs are especially vulnerable to this tension. Exposed to sun, moisture, temperature shifts, and physical impact, they deteriorate more rapidly than stone or metal. Images cloud, faces blur, and details dissolve into abstraction. Ironically, as photographic clarity diminishes, interpretive openness often increases. A partially obscured image invites projection, allowing viewers to fill gaps with imagination and association. Decay does not erase meaning; it transforms it, shifting memory from specificity toward suggestion.

This transformation underscores a fundamental limitation of material memory: no object can preserve meaning unchanged. As cultural contexts shift, the frameworks through which photographs are read also evolve. Clothing once legible as everyday attire becomes historical costume; symbols once widely understood lose resonance; facial expressions take on new interpretations. The photograph endures, but its language changes. Memory persists not as a fixed record, but as a living dialogue between artifact and observer.

The endurance of cemetery photographs also depends upon continued engagement. Graves that are visited, cleaned, and repaired remain legible sites of memory. Those neglected slip gradually into anonymity. Broken frames go unreplaced, images detach from stone, and names fade into illegibility. This uneven maintenance reflects broader social patterns: family dispersal, demographic change, economic constraint, and shifting attitudes toward burial and mourning. Memory endures unevenly, shaped by circumstance as much as intention.

Yet even in neglect, cemetery photographs retain significance. Their very deterioration testifies to the passage of time and the limits of remembrance. A faded face signals not only an individual life now distant, but the waning of those who once remembered that life intimately. In this way, decay becomes part of the narrative of memory rather than its failure. The photograph marks not only presence, but loss layered upon loss.

The limits of material memory do not negate its value. On the contrary, they reveal why societies continually renew commemorative practices. As older forms erode, new markers emerge: replacement stones, digital archives, genealogical databases, and virtual memorials. These innovations reflect the same underlying impulse that produced cemetery photographs—the desire to anchor memory outside the self, to resist erasure through material means.

By acknowledging endurance and decay together, the cemetery can be understood not as a failed archive, but as a dynamic system of remembrance. Its materials do not freeze memory in time; they invite continual reinterpretation. In this sense, the limits of memory are not endpoints but conditions of its persistence. The cemetery remains a place where meaning is neither fully secured nor wholly lost but perpetually negotiated at the edge of time.

Section VI: Memory at the Threshold

The cemetery, when understood as a borderland, reveals memory not as a passive archive of the past but as an active practice sustained through material form, interpretation, and repetition. Photographs, situated within this space, externalize remembrance while simultaneously inviting continual re-engagement by the living. They do not resolve the tension between life and death; they manage it. In doing so, they make visible the human effort to hold presence and absence in productive relation.

Across the cemetery landscape, memory is stabilized through selection, encounter, and endurance, yet never secured against change. Images are chosen, gazes are met, meanings are projected, and materials decay. Each of these processes contributes to a dynamic system in which remembrance persists by adaptation rather than permanence. The work of memory unfolds not in spite of loss, but through it—shaped by cultural expectation, personal experience, and the limits imposed by time.

Understanding photographs as material memory technologies clarifies how societies negotiate continuity at moments of rupture. The cemetery does not simply commemorate the dead; it organizes the living response to death. Through visual presence, spatial arrangement, and ritualized encounter, it provides a framework for acknowledging mortality while sustaining social and emotional coherence. Memory, in this context, becomes a shared labor rather than an individual possession.

This chapter has traced how memory is externalized, activated, curated, and transformed within the cemetery borderland. In doing so, it establishes a conceptual foundation for examining memory under conditions of movement, uncertainty, and constraint. When death occurs away from home, beyond established ritual spaces, and under pressure that permits little pause for mourning, the strategies through which memory is managed become especially visible.

Section VII – Photographs as the Threshold

Photographs do not all ask the same kind of attention. Some images invite understanding through familiarity. They present themselves as legible, composed, and socially intelligible. Others resist this mode of reading. They interrupt rather than explain, drawing the viewer into a moment that feels disproportionate to the image itself. The difference between these two responses is not a matter of taste or sensitivity, but of structure.

What occurs in these moments resists full articulation.

Barthes described this distinction as the difference between *studium* and *punctum*. Studium refers to the cultural, historical, and social field in which an image can be understood. It is the part of the photograph that can be read: the uniform that signals military service, the wedding dress that signifies union, the child posed to suggest innocence or continuity. Studium operates through shared codes. It allows the viewer to recognize what the image is meant to represent and why it might matter within an established system of memory.

Punctum, by contrast, does not operate through recognition. It emerges unexpectedly, often from a detail that seems incidental or unintended. A hand held too tightly, a gaze that does not align with the pose, a fracture in the image surface, or the knowledge that the photographed body is already dead. Punctum is not assigned by the viewer, nor is it contained within the photograph as a stable feature. It arises in the encounter between image and observer, marking the moment when meaning exceeds intention.

This distinction is particularly relevant when photographs are embedded in stone and placed within cemeteries. These images are not private keepsakes; they are public artifacts of remembrance. Their studium is carefully curated. Clothing, posture, and framing work together to stabilize identity and render the dead socially legible. The photograph reassures by presenting a life as coherent, recognizable, and complete.

Yet these same images are also vulnerable to punctum. Time alters them. Porcelain cracks. Faces fade. Context is lost. In some cases, the image records not a living subject but a body already beyond life. What was meant to preserve continuity begins to expose fragility. The photograph no longer simply signifies who the person was supposed to be. It confronts the viewer with what cannot be stabilized.

Understanding punctum and studium does not mean choosing one over the other. Both are always present, though not equally. Studium allows memory to function as a social practice. Punctum unsettles that practice, reminding the viewer that remembrance is never complete, never fully controlled. In cemetery photographs, this tension is unavoidable. The image is asked to do cultural work, but it cannot entirely suppress the bodily reality it contains.

The interpretations that follow do not attempt to resolve this tension. They attend to it. Each photograph will be approached not as an illustration of an individual life, but as an encounter shaped by both studium and punctum: by what the image is designed to communicate and by what it reveals despite that design. The aim is not to assign meaning, but to observe how meaning is produced, interrupted, and sometimes undone in the act of looking.

Photographs used in cemeteries are meant to remind the visitor that the person commemorated was once alive. For the young, where life was cut short, images of a boy playing with a beloved toy or of a Jewish boy at his Bar Mitzvah often carry greater impact—greater punctum—than a formal portrait alone. These photographs do not merely present a likeness; they interrupt the viewer with evidence of a life in motion, a future imagined but never completed.

References to pivotal moments in an adult's life function in a similar way, whether those moments occurred recently or decades earlier. A photograph of a woman in her wedding dress marks a turning point that may have taken place fifty years before her death, just as an image of a man in military uniform recalls a period of service long past. In each case, the photograph anchors memory to a moment of transformation rather than to the condition of death itself.

Then there are photographs that function as explicit links between the living and the dead. An image of a young man in a police uniform holding his infant child records a moment of ordinary continuity; the officer was killed in the line of duty the following year. Another photograph, showing a young mother with her child, serves as a reminder of two lives lost within a day of each other to disease and buried together in the same grave. In both cases, the photograph does not simply commemorate an individual death, but preserves a relationship interrupted rather than completed.

Photographs that depict death are relatively rare in cemetery contexts because they disrupt the primary function of commemorative imagery, which is to affirm that the person depicted once belonged among the living. Most cemetery photographs work to stabilize memory by presenting vitality, role, or relationship—images that make the dead socially legible

by anchoring them to moments of participation in life. A photograph that shows death directly resists this stabilizing function. It interrupts the visual grammar that seeks continuity rather than finality.

When death itself is depicted, the photograph no longer reassures. It confronts the viewer with a body that cannot be folded back into narratives of future, service, or relational progression. Such images refuse the comfort of studium. They do not invite recognition through shared cultural codes in the same way that portraits of soldiers, brides, or children do. Instead, they force an encounter with absence made visible, with a body that is present but no longer capable of participation. In this way, photographs of death expose the limits of photographic memory as a technology of consolation.

For this reason, images of death tend to appear only where the disruption they cause cannot be avoided—most often in cases of infant mortality or sudden loss, where the boundary between life and death is itself the subject being marked. In these instances, the photograph does not function to preserve identity so much as to acknowledge rupture. It records not a life remembered, but a loss that cannot be assimilated into familiar commemorative forms. The rarity of such images underscores their power: they remain exceptions precisely because they resist the work that cemetery photographs are usually asked to perform.

However, such photographs do exist, and in some cases they are the only visual record of the deceased. This is particularly true for infants and young children, whose lives ended before the routines of portraiture or family documentation had fully begun. In these instances, the photograph does not commemorate a life as it was lived, but marks the brief fact of existence itself. The image stands in for what could not be accumulated—no sequence of moments, no progression of roles, no visible future—only the confirmation that the child was here and is now gone.

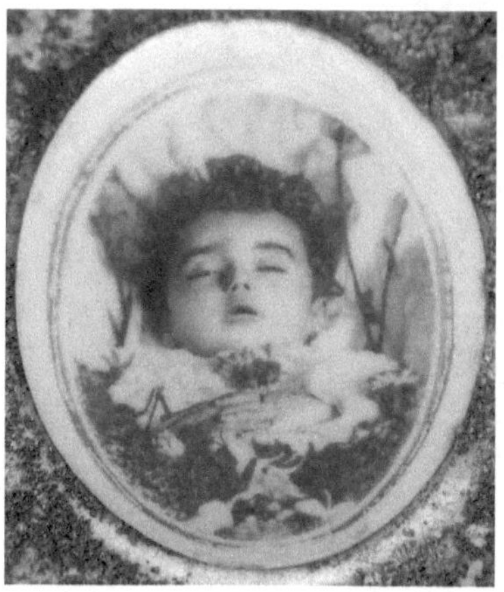

There is, however, a particular category of cemetery photograph that unsettles this threshold rather than mediating it: the image of the deceased in the coffin. Unlike portrait photographs, which function to recall the living body and momentarily resist absence, the coffin photograph confirms death with an unmistakable finality. It does not suspend the viewer between life and loss; it anchors them firmly on one side of the divide. The stillness of the body, the enclosure of the coffin, and the unmistakable signs of cessation foreclose the imaginative work that portrait photographs invite. Rather than collapsing temporal distance, these images fix it. They do not gesture toward continuity but toward termination, transforming the photograph from a bridge into a boundary. Within the cemetery, where photography often serves to reintroduce presence and soften the rupture between the living and the dead, the coffin image performs the opposite function.

The inclusion of this photograph interrupts the photograph's usual role as a technology of remembrance and instead becomes a visual confirmation of irreversibility, reminding the viewer not of who this person was among the living, but of what has been definitively lost.

Images of this kind are uncommon in contemporary American cemeteries. Their rarity is not incidental. They resist the photograph's more familiar role as a mediator between presence and absence, offering instead a confrontation that many communities appear unwilling to sustain.

Taken together, these photographic choices reveal not individual preference, but shared boundaries of comfort. The cemetery photographs do not resolve the tension they introduce. They hold it. Each image participates in an effort to stabilize memory by fixing identity, relationship, and meaning in material form, yet each also remains vulnerable to interruption—by decay, by context, by the knowledge the viewer brings to the encounter. The cemetery promises continuity, but the photographs reveal how contingent that promise is. What they preserve is not the past itself, but an ongoing negotiation between what can be remembered, what must be inferred, and what resists containment altogether.

In this way, the cemetery does not function as a repository of settled meaning, but as a site of repeated crossing. The living return, look again, and reinterpret what they see through altered circumstances and accumulated loss. Photographs embedded in stone assert presence, yet they also expose absence, reminding the viewer that memory endures not through permanence but through engagement. The border between life and death is never fully sealed. It is approached, marked, and revisited through material forms that invite recognition while withholding closure. What remains is not resolution, but relation—a sustained encounter at the threshold where memory continues its work.

The following chapter turns to a unique setting. Along the Oregon Trail, death accompanied migration with relentless frequency, forcing emigrants to adapt burial practices, memorialization, and remembrance in transit. Read through the lens established here, those practices can be understood not simply as expedient responses to hardship, but as deliberate efforts to preserve dignity, continuity, and meaning at the threshold between life and death.

Chapter Five

Oregon Trail: Oh, Bury Me Not on the Lone Prairie

Section I – The Responsibility of the Living

The human corpse serves as one of the most fundamental and compelling symbols of death. As the most immediate representation of human mortality, the care, treatment, and disposal of the body have long formed the focal point of spiritual belief, religious practice, and cultural identity. Mortuary rituals—including the preparation of the corpse, the selection of burial locations, and the marking of graves—offer a uniquely revealing lens through which to examine how societies understand death, memory, and the obligations owed to the dead.

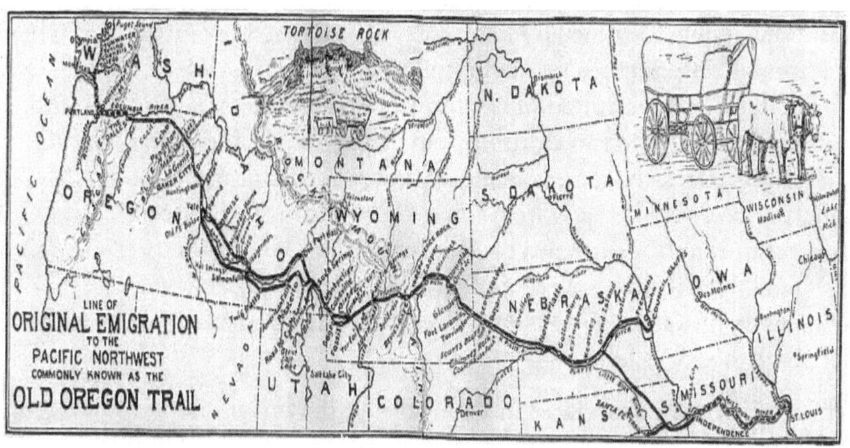

The westward migration along the Oregon Trail provides an exceptional context for examining these beliefs under conditions of sustained crisis. Stretching more than two thousand miles across plains, deserts, and mountain ranges, the Trail exposed emigrants to disease, exhaustion, accident, and environmental extremes that resulted in death with striking regularity. Unlike death within established communities, death along the Trail occurred in transit, far from home, family burial grounds, and familiar ritual spaces. Yet emigrants consistently recorded their experiences in diaries, journals, letters, and memoirs, leaving behind a remarkably detailed record of how burial customs were adapted when time, tools, and safety were in short supply.

These personal narratives—numbering in the thousands—provide an unusually rich archive of ordinary Americans whose lives are otherwise underrepresented in the historical record. While much of nineteenth-century history privileges political leaders, military figures, or economic elites, the Trail accounts preserve the voices of farmers, small business owners, wives, mothers, children, and extended family groups confronting death as a routine and unavoidable feature of migration. Scholars such as Merrill J. Mattes and John D. Unruh Jr. have demonstrated the value of these sources for understanding overland travel and social organization, yet comparatively little attention has been paid to what these records reveal about mortuary practice and cultural continuity under extreme conditions.

This chapter argues that burial practices documented along the Oregon Trail reveal which mortuary customs were deemed essential even when traditional observances proved impractical or impossible. Despite differences in denomination, region of origin, and social background, emigrants responded to death in remarkably consistent ways. These shared practices reflect a common Western European cultural inheritance and a broadly held nineteenth-century American understanding of death and proper mourning. Under the pressures of the Trail, burial rituals were not abandoned; rather, they were selectively modified to preserve dignity, reverence for the dead, and a sense of moral order.

The care of the corpse and the marking of gravesites along the Oregon Trail thus functioned as acts of cultural preservation as much as practical necessity. In confronting death under extreme circumstances, emigrants collectively engaged in an unwritten effort to sustain civility, humanity, and communal responsibility. Examining these adaptations offers insight not only into life and death along the Trail, but into broader processes of cultural resilience, continuity, and meaning-making when survival itself was uncertain.

Section II - The Oregon Trail

Early in the period of westward migration, most wagon trains relied on experienced guides to navigate the treacherous route west. In these earliest years, relatively few deaths occurred along the Trail, a fact that contributed to a misleading perception of safety. The apparent success of early wagon trains, combined with optimistic portrayals of the journey in popular emigrant guidebooks—most notably those by

Lansford Hastings and Francis Parkman—encouraged large numbers of settlers to head west ill-prepared for the realities they would encounter.

Although mid-nineteenth-century maps often labeled much of the region traversed by the Trail as the "Great American Desert," emigrants frequently underestimated the physical, emotional, and spiritual challenges of the journey. The Oregon Trail stretched approximately 2,170 miles across open prairie, rugged mountain ranges, and arid deserts. While Independence, Missouri is commonly identified as the official starting point, Council Bluffs, Nebraska and St. Joseph, Missouri also served as major points of departure, connecting with the main route farther west. In present-day Idaho, the Trail divided, with one branch leading south toward the Sacramento Valley in California and the primary route continuing northwest to Oregon City.

The opening of the Oregon Trail in 1843 marked the removal of the last significant geographic barrier to sustained westward migration. In the decades following the Lewis and Clark expedition, American trappers, traders, and explorers gradually penetrated the Rocky Mountains and the far reaches of the Louisiana Purchase, often entering territory contested by British, Russian, and Spanish interests. British influence in the Pacific Northwest was particularly strong through the Hudson's Bay Company, which established forts and trading posts along the coast.

Recognizing the strategic importance of an American presence in the region, President Thomas Jefferson persuaded John Jacob Astor to invest in westward expansion through the Pacific Fur Company. Astor's 1811 expedition, led by Wilson Price Hunt, laid early groundwork for American commercial activity in the Pacific Northwest. Competition between British and American fur interests intensified during and after the War of 1812 and continued intermittently for several decades. However, these early ventures remained largely commercial and transitory, failing to establish a permanent American population in the region.

Sustained settlement became possible only after the development of a route suitable for families and wagons. In 1834, Nathaniel Wyeth and Jason Lee, building upon geographic knowledge acquired from Native Americans, fur traders, and explorers, helped establish the first practical overland trail for American settlers to the Pacific Northwest. The route, originating near St. Joseph, Missouri, extended westward across the continent and became known as the Oregon Trail.

Migration remained limited until John C. Frémont mapped the route in 1842, making it accessible to a broader population. With the Trail now visible and increasingly navigable, the federal government actively promoted westward expansion through the ideology of Manifest Destiny. Encouraged by government enthusiasm, romanticized accounts of the journey, and letters from early settlers, emigrants sold their property, gathered supplies, purchased guidebooks, and set out for the West.

For many, however, the promise of opportunity masked the dangers of the journey. Disease, particularly cholera, time constraints imposed by seasonal weather, unfamiliar terrain, and frequent accidents led to a rising death toll along the Trail. As migration increased, so too did the presence of graves lining the route, transforming the Trail into both a pathway of hope and a corridor of loss. It was within this environment—defined by movement, uncertainty, and recurring death—that emigrants were forced to adapt longstanding burial customs to conditions that allowed little margin for error.

Section III - The Recorders

Emigrants traveling the Oregon Trail prior to the completion of the Transcontinental Railroad in 1869 produced thousands of diaries, journals, and letters documenting their experiences. Many of these texts survive and are now publicly accessible, offering a rare and valuable record of daily life along the Trail as experienced by a broad cross section of nineteenth-century Americans. Together, these writings preserve observations not only of geography and weather, but of illness, death, burial, and the emotional responses that accompanied them.

These first-person accounts vary considerably in tone and detail, reflecting both individual temperament and culturally defined expectations regarding the expression of grief. Men, in particular, tended to record death in brief, factual terms, often focusing on the cause of death and the physical location of the grave while omitting any reference to personal emotion. Virgil Pringle, for example, noted the accidental death of a young boy with stark efficiency: "Mr. Collins' son George, about 6 years old, fell from the wagon and the wheels ran over his head, killing him instantly; the remainder of the day occupied in burying him at the place where we left the river." Weeks later, another death appears with similar restraint: "Bury Mrs. Bounds, who died the day before, wife of J. B. Bounds."

Even when male diarists offered more elaborate descriptions, emotional response was rarely articulated. Pringle's account of the death of Mrs. Keyse demonstrates this pattern. He carefully recorded her age, illness, and the presence of a Presbyterian clergyman who conducted the burial and delivered a sermon at the graveside, yet offered no commentary on his own reaction. The entry concludes with a precise description of the grave's location beneath an oak tree near the road, underscoring the priority given to recordkeeping over reflection.

Other male diarists reveal subtle variations in this approach, particularly when the deceased was a woman or child, individuals for whom nineteenth-century social norms prescribed a heightened sense of responsibility and protection. Nicholas Carriager's journal initially records several deaths with minimal detail, including that of a boy whose name he does not even preserve. However, when Redwood Easton's wife died, Carriager noted not only the timing of her death but also the exact placement of her grave relative to the encampment, the road, and the riverbank. As familiarity among traveling companions increased, later deaths—particularly those involving women and children—were described with greater specificity. Yet as exhaustion mounted and the end of the journey approached, entries again became terse, reflecting both physical fatigue and emotional attrition.

Women's accounts, by contrast, consistently demonstrate greater attention to the rituals surrounding death and burial, as well as to the emotional toll of loss. Often functioning as what scholars have described as ritual caretakers, women recorded details of grave preparation, clothing, memorialization, and mourning that rarely appear in male-authored texts. Sarah Mousley recounted a death precipitated by emotional shock rather than physical injury, describing how an elderly woman died after witnessing her husband narrowly escape harm. The incident reveals an understanding of death as inseparable from emotional experience, a perspective that recurs throughout women's Trail narratives.

Even young girls documented death with remarkable sensitivity. Twelve-year-old Virginia E. B. Reed recorded the burial of her grandmother with careful attention to decency, noting the construction of a coffin, the carving of a headstone, and the planting of flowers at the grave. Her letter conveys not only the physical acts of burial but the enduring absence felt by the family, particularly the quiet moment of returning to the wagon and finding the grandmother's bed empty. Such passages illustrate how women and girls preserved continuity with established mourning practices even while adapting to the constraints imposed by the Trail.

Together, these records form the foundation for understanding burial practices along the Oregon Trail. While men and women differed in how they recorded death, their accounts collectively reveal a shared concern for dignity, remembrance, and proper treatment of the dead. The consistency with which burial location, grave marking, and ritual care appear across these narratives underscores the importance of mortuary customs as a stabilizing force amid the uncertainty and danger of westward migration.

Section IV - Death Along the Oregon Trail

During the height of westward migration, death became a persistent and visible presence along the Oregon Trail. Disease, accident, environmental exposure, and exhaustion claimed lives with unsettling regularity, transforming large stretches of the route into what many emigrants described as a corridor of graves. Among these threats, cholera proved the most lethal during the early stages of the journey, particularly along the Platte River, where contaminated water sources and crowded conditions accelerated its spread.

Cholera struck with terrifying speed. An emigrant who appeared healthy in the morning could be gravely ill by afternoon and dead before nightfall. One traveler recorded how two men, stricken only hours earlier, died before midnight despite immediate medical attention and the efforts of their companions. Another diarist described encountering a small white tent sheltering a man in the final stages of the disease, with a grave already dug beside him so that burial could proceed without delay. Such accounts underscore not only the prevalence of death, but the practical urgency with which emigrants were forced to respond.

Guidebooks emphasized the importance of timing, warning emigrants to begin their journey early in the spring to avoid being trapped by snow in the mountains. Despite this advice, many travelers departed late or followed alternative recommendations suggesting a slower pace to preserve livestock. These delays often proved fatal. Once emigrants recognized that survival depended upon maintaining momentum, even funeral observances were abbreviated. Burials were conducted swiftly so that wagon trains could resume travel before falling dangerously behind schedule.

Environmental hazards compounded the risks of disease. Prairie fires could outrun galloping horses, rivers swelled suddenly with seasonal rains, blizzards struck without warning in higher elevations, and potable water became scarce across long stretches of the Trail. Food shortages affected both humans and animals, and accidents involving wagons, livestock, and firearms were commonplace. Together, these dangers ensured that death was not an isolated occurrence but an expected possibility at nearly every stage of the journey.

As fatalities mounted, burial became a routine necessity rather than an extraordinary event. Graves appeared so frequently along certain portions of the Trail that emigrants likened the route to a battlefield or cemetery. While some diarists recorded these deaths with emotional restraint, others conveyed the cumulative psychological toll of witnessing repeated loss. The omnipresence of death forced emigrants to confront mortality not as an abstract inevitability, but as a daily companion.

Despite these conditions, burial practices retained recognizable structure. The consistency with which emigrants documented grave locations, conducted brief services, and marked burial sites reflects an enduring commitment to honoring the dead. Even as death occurred with increasing frequency, emigrants sought to impose order and meaning through ritual, using burial as a means of asserting humanity in the face of relentless danger. These practices formed the foundation upon which further adaptations in corpse care and grave protection would develop as the journey continued westward.

Section V - Caring for the Dead

Even before setting out on the journey west, many emigrants anticipated the possibility of death along the Trail. Some families included burial clothing, winding sheets, or even specific types of wood intended for coffins among their provisions, a precaution that reflects both the expectations of danger and the importance placed on proper burial. In practice, however, circumstances along the Trail often rendered these preparations unusable. Hasty deaths, loss of supplies, lack of tools, or the presence of strangers unfamiliar with a family's intentions frequently resulted in burials that departed from established plans.

As a result, many emigrants were buried in the clothing they wore at the time of death. Although this practice diverged from nineteenth-century norms, it was not viewed as a neglect of duty so much as an unavoidable compromise. One diarist described carefully arranging a young man's body in his everyday garments, noting with particular tenderness how natural and peaceful he appeared. The passage reflects a desire to preserve dignity even when ideal preparations were impossible, revealing how emotional care substituted for ritual completeness.

Grave goods, traditionally included to reflect the identity or occupation of the deceased, also accompanied some burials along the Trail. Tools, personal items, or symbols of trade occasionally remained with the body, particularly when the individual was buried by close companions. In other instances, however, valuables were removed—sometimes as an act of necessity, sometimes as a form of compensation for those who provided care or burial. The line between respectful removal and grave robbing often blurred under Trail conditions, where survival depended on limited resources and immediate decisions.

Exposure and the threat of scavenging animals posed additional challenges. Shallow graves, frozen or sun-hardened ground, and limited time for digging meant that bodies were often vulnerable to disturbance. Several emigrants recorded encountering graves where wolves or coyotes had uncovered remains, an experience that deeply unsettled those who later passed the site. Such encounters heightened awareness of the fragility of Trail burials and intensified concern for the protection of newly interred bodies.

Despite these constraints, emigrants consistently demonstrated attentiveness to the physical care of the dead. Bodies were washed when possible, arranged with care, and wrapped in blankets or cloth if shrouds were unavailable. Even when burial took place quickly, the acts surrounding the corpse—however abbreviated—served as an assertion of respect and moral obligation. These practices reveal that caring for the dead remained a priority not because of strict adherence to tradition, but because it affirmed shared values of humanity and decency in an environment that otherwise threatened to erode both.

The compromises evident in corpse care along the Oregon Trail did not signal cultural abandonment. Rather, they reflect a pragmatic adaptation of established mortuary customs to extreme conditions. The dead were still recognized as deserving of attention, protection, and remembrance, even when circumstances dictated that such care take unfamiliar or incomplete forms.

Section VI - Protecting the Gravesite

While the immediate care of the corpse was a primary concern, the protection of the gravesite quickly emerged as an equally urgent priority for emigrants along the Oregon Trail. Time constraints, environmental conditions, and the ever-present threat of disturbance meant that burial did not end the responsibility owed to the dead. Ensuring that a grave remained intact—at least for as long as circumstances allowed—became a significant measure of whether a burial was considered successful.

The conditions of the Trail often made deep graves impossible. In regions where the ground was frozen, sun-baked, or densely packed with stone, emigrants resorted to alternative methods to shield the body. Rock cairns were commonly constructed in the most barren stretches of the Trail, serving both as protection against scavenging animals and as visible markers of burial. One emigrant described bodies sewn into blankets and buried beneath carefully stacked stones, with a substantial cairn erected above the grave. These structures, though rudimentary, represented deliberate efforts to secure the body when traditional burial methods were impractical.

Scavenging animals posed a persistent threat. Wolves and coyotes, drawn by shallow graves and the scent of decomposition, frequently disturbed burial sites. Emigrants recorded encounters with exposed bones and scattered clothing, experiences that reinforced the importance of concealment and protection. Such sights were deeply unsettling, not only for what they revealed about the vulnerability of the dead, but for what they suggested about the possible fate of loved ones left behind along the Trail.

Concerns over grave disturbance extended beyond natural scavengers. Emigrants feared that graves might be opened in search of clothing or personal effects, and in some regions this fear was reinforced by observation. As a result, burial strategies increasingly emphasized concealment. Graves were sometimes placed beneath wagon paths so that repeated travel would obscure their location. In other instances, livestock were corralled over fresh graves to disguise disturbed soil and mask scent. Wagons were occasionally burned over gravesites, both to conceal the burial and to prevent future discovery.

Despite the necessity of concealment, reverence for the gravesite remained central. Passing emigrants often avoided driving wagons over known graves and repaired damaged markers when encountered. Bones found exposed were sometimes reburied by later travelers, reflecting an unwritten code of grave etiquette observed along much of the Trail. These acts suggest that even among strangers, responsibility for the dead extended beyond the immediate burial party.

Grave placement itself carried symbolic weight. Whenever possible, emigrants selected sites near streams, beneath trees, or on elevated ground overlooking the Trail. Such locations offered both practical protection and a measure of aesthetic or spiritual comfort. Yet the ideal location was often sacrificed to necessity. In these cases, the effort invested in safeguarding the body took precedence over scenic considerations, underscoring the primacy of protection over sentiment.

The measures taken to protect gravesites along the Oregon Trail reveal the depth of concern emigrants held for the dead long after burial. These efforts—often labor-intensive and emotionally taxing—demonstrate that burial was understood not as a single act, but as an ongoing obligation shaped by environment, danger, and collective responsibility.

Section VII - Rituals of Internment

In established communities throughout nineteenth-century America, burial rituals were intimate affairs governed by well-defined social and religious expectations. Funerals typically took place in the home of the deceased and were attended only by family members and close acquaintances. Care of the body was entrusted to relatives—most often women—who washed and prepared the corpse, closed the eyes and mouth, and wrapped the body in a winding sheet or shroud.

Mourning followed prescribed conventions of dress, behavior, and duration, reinforcing both familial bonds and communal order.

Along the Oregon Trail, these expectations were difficult, and often impossible, to maintain. The mixing of wagon trains, the frequent absence of extended family, and the necessity of rapid burial fundamentally altered the nature of funerary observance. Death occurred among strangers as often as among kin, and burial frequently took place at the roadside or near encampments rather than within consecrated or familiar spaces. As a result, funerals along the Trail became communal events out of necessity rather than choice.

Despite these constraints, emigrants sought to preserve recognizable elements of ritual whenever circumstances allowed. Clergy traveling with wagon trains sometimes conducted brief services at gravesides, offering prayers or sermons before burial. Even when no minister was present, moments of collective pause, silence, or spoken remembrance often marked the internment. These abbreviated rituals functioned as acknowledgments of loss and as affirmations of shared values among the living.

The presence of strangers at funerals, while contrary to social norms in the States, became an accepted feature of Trail life. Attendance was no longer a marker of personal relationship but of shared circumstance. One observer noted that individuals who did not even know the name of the deceased nevertheless participated in the burial, later recalling the event as a defining moment of the journey. Notably, this suspension of social boundaries did not diminish the perceived seriousness of the ritual; rather, it expanded the circle of responsibility.

Time constraints exerted the greatest influence on internment practices. Wagon trains rarely remained in place for extended periods, and delays increased the risk of disease, accident, or entrapment by seasonal weather. As a result, burial services were often brief and conducted with minimal ceremony. One emigrant described how a child was buried beside a stream during a short halt in travel, the clods of earth falling quickly upon a coffin-less body before the train moved on. Such accounts underscore the painful necessity of recognizing loss while continuing forward.

The emotional toll of these truncated rituals was significant. Parents were often forced to leave children behind, spouses to bury partners, and families to part from loved ones without the comfort of extended mourning or return visits. Yet even in these moments, emigrants demonstrated a commitment to acknowledging death through ritual, however abbreviated. The act of stopping, digging a grave, and marking the place—even briefly—served as a vital assertion of humanity in a landscape that permitted little pause for grief.

The rituals of internment along the Oregon Trail thus reveal a profound tension between cultural expectation and environmental reality. Funerary customs were neither abandoned nor rigidly preserved; instead, they were reshaped to accommodate the demands of survival. In doing so, emigrants reaffirmed the social and moral significance of burial, even as they redefined its form.

Section VIII - Left Behind

Death along the Oregon Trail carried a burden that extended beyond loss itself: the fear of being left behind, both literally and symbolically. Unlike death within established communities, where graves remained accessible to family and memory, death on the Trail often meant permanent separation from loved ones and from known places of mourning. The absence of embalming practices and the impossibility of transporting bodies over long distances ensured that burial along the route was final, a reality that weighed heavily on emigrants throughout the journey.

For those who fell ill, the prospect of dying on the plains inspired deep anxiety. Many emigrants expressed the hope of surviving long enough to reach California or Oregon, not only for opportunity but to avoid burial in an unfamiliar and isolated landscape. Louisa Lithgrow, who grew dangerously ill during the journey, voiced this fear openly. When she died before reaching her destination, her burial was conducted with exceptional care. Family members dug a deep grave, constructed a vault from wagon boards, and secured a tombstone transported from miles away. The time and labor devoted to her burial reflect an effort to mitigate the anguish of leaving a loved one behind in an otherwise anonymous place.

The emotional toll of departure following burial is a recurring theme in Trail narratives. Emigrants often described the moment of resuming travel as particularly painful, marked by silence and restrained grief. One traveler recalled covering a mother's grave with wild roses to soften the harshness of stone, an act that symbolized both devotion and farewell. Such gestures suggest an attempt to preserve tenderness in circumstances that demanded emotional endurance.

For surviving family members, guilt frequently accompanied departure. The inability to return, revisit, or tend graves compounded feelings of helplessness. Some attempted to compensate through careful grave placement, selecting sites near streams, beneath trees, or in locations perceived as less desolate. Others promised markers or memorials to be erected later, though many of these intentions were never fulfilled due to distance, cost, or the difficulty of relocation.

In rare instances, family members returned years later in an effort to recover the bodies of loved ones buried along the Trail. These efforts were seldom successful. Graves were difficult to locate, markers deteriorated rapidly, and landscapes changed. As a result, most Trail burials remained permanent, their precise locations known only through diary entries written by strangers who happened to pass by.

The fear of being left behind thus shaped both emotional response and burial behavior along the Oregon Trail. The emphasis placed on marking graves, choosing protective or meaningful locations, and performing even abbreviated rituals reflects a desire to counter isolation through remembrance. In this way, burial practices served not only the dead, but the living—providing a measure of psychological continuity in a journey defined by irreversible forward movement.

Section IX - Grave Markers

The marking of graves along the Oregon Trail represented one of the most visible and enduring efforts by emigrants to preserve memory in an otherwise transitory landscape. While burial itself was often hurried, the act of marking a grave signaled an intention that the deceased not be forgotten, even if their resting place lay far from family and home. In many cases, grave markers served not only as memorials but also as warnings and records for those who followed.

In keeping with early nineteenth-century American burial customs, the most common marker used along the Trail was a wooden board inscribed with the name, age, and date of death of the deceased. When materials and time permitted, these boards were carefully carved, sometimes including the individual's place of origin or cause of death. One emigrant observed that nearly every day's travel revealed graves marked by boards or flat stones, "rudely carved by the hand of affection," bearing testimony to lives cut short along the route.

Stone markers were less common due to their weight and the difficulty of carving, but when available they offered greater durability. In a few instances, families or traveling companions constructed substantial stone markers or cairns that have survived long after wooden markers decayed. The headstone of George Winslow, who died of cholera after his wagon train waited several days for his recovery, stands as a rare example of an early Trail grave preserved through deliberate effort. Such markers reflect a conscious choice to invest time and labor in memorialization despite the risks of delay.

When neither wood nor stone was readily available, emigrants improvised. Wagon tongues, wheels, rocks, wildflowers, and brush were used to mark graves, transforming everyday objects into symbols of remembrance. These makeshift markers were especially vulnerable to weather, livestock, and passing traffic, and many disappeared within days or weeks of placement. As a result, countless graves were rendered invisible soon after burial, their locations preserved only in written accounts.

Proximity to settlements occasionally allowed emigrants to obtain commercially produced tombstones, particularly later in the migration period. These markers provided a sense of permanence and connection to established burial traditions. However, such opportunities were rare, and most Trail graves remained marked by temporary or improvised means.

Ironically, some of the most enduring records of Trail burials are not physical markers at all, but diary entries written by fellow emigrants—often strangers—who recorded the presence of a grave as they passed. These written observations preserved names, locations, and circumstances long after material markers vanished. In this way, the collective documentation of the Trail functioned as an informal memorial landscape, sustaining remembrance through narrative when physical traces failed.

The impermanence of grave markers along the Oregon Trail underscores the tension between intention and reality faced by emigrants. While they sought to honor the dead through visible memorials, environmental conditions and the demands of migration frequently erased these efforts. Yet the act of marking a grave, however briefly, affirmed the value of individual lives within a journey defined by movement and loss.

Section X - Conclusion

The process of westward migration required more than physical endurance and logistical planning; it demanded the transport and preservation of cultural values under conditions that repeatedly threatened their erosion. Among the most revealing of these values were the beliefs and practices surrounding death. Along the Oregon Trail, emigrants encountered mortality with a frequency and immediacy that forced them to reconsider how burial, mourning, and remembrance could be carried out when time, safety, and resources were severely limited.

Rather than abandoning mortuary customs, emigrants adapted them. Burial practices documented in diaries, journals, and letters reveal a selective preservation of what was deemed essential: care of the corpse, protection of the grave, acknowledgment through ritual, and some form of memorialization. These elements persisted even as funerary observances were shortened, graves concealed, and markers improvised. The consistency of these adaptations across emigrant groups suggests a shared cultural framework rooted in Western European and nineteenth-century American traditions, one flexible enough to endure extraordinary hardship.

The modifications observed along the Trail were shaped primarily by environmental constraints and the relentless necessity of forward movement. Disease, particularly cholera, demanded swift response; seasonal weather imposed unforgiving deadlines; and the dangers of delay carried consequences that could claim additional lives. Within this context, burial became an act negotiated between reverence and survival. Emigrants balanced emotional obligation with practical necessity, revealing a moral calculus that prioritized dignity without compromising collective safety.

Equally significant is the role burial practices played in sustaining the living. The fear of being left behind—isolated from family, memory, and civilization—haunted emigrants as much as death itself. Acts of care, protection, and marking served not only to honor the dead, but to alleviate the psychological burden borne by survivors. Even when graves quickly vanished from the landscape, the act of burial affirmed continuity, humanity, and responsibility within a journey defined by loss and impermanence.

Ultimately, the burial customs of the Oregon Trail illuminate the resilience of cultural meaning under extreme conditions. They demonstrate how societies negotiate continuity amid disruption and how ritual, even when abbreviated or altered, remains central to human responses to death. By examining these adaptations, this chapter contributes to a broader understanding of cultural persistence among ordinary Americans, revealing how deeply held values endure—not despite adversity, but through the ways communities respond to it.

Chapter Six

Disturbing the Dead: Practices at the Edge of Memory, Respect, and Belief

Section I - The Boundary We Pretend Exists

The dead are often spoken of as settled, their stories closed, their bodies secured by ritual and stone. Burial is meant to mark an ending, not only of life but of obligation. Once interred, the dead are said to belong to memory rather than to the present, to reverence rather than to use. This assumption undergirds much of how modern cultures imagine their relationship to death: that there exists a clear boundary between the living and the dead, and that crossing it is both rare and transgressive.

Yet history suggests otherwise. The boundary is neither firm nor consistently respected. It shifts according to need, profit, curiosity, fear, and convenience. The dead are disturbed far more often than cultural narratives admit, and not only through acts that appear extreme or illicit. Disturbance occurs whenever bodies, names, or presumed voices are accessed without consent, whether that access is physical, symbolic, or interpretive. What changes across time is not the act itself, but the language used to justify it.

In cemeteries, this justification often takes the form of progress. Roads must be widened. Cities must expand. Graves must be moved for the sake of development, hygiene, or public good. The remains are relocated, cataloged, sometimes reburied, sometimes stored, sometimes simply displaced. These actions are framed as practical necessities rather than moral decisions. The dead are not consulted. Their descendants, when they exist and can be found, are frequently treated as obstacles rather than stakeholders. Disturbance is rendered invisible by bureaucratic language, and the violence of displacement is softened by euphemism.

At other times, the justification is knowledge. Bodies are exhumed for study, measurement, classification, or proof. This has occurred most visibly in the histories of medicine and anthropology, where graves—particularly those of the poor, the institutionalized, the enslaved, and the colonized—were treated as repositories of data rather than as sites of mourning. The dead became objects through which the living sought answers, often about themselves. What mattered was not the integrity of the body, but the utility of its parts.

There is also disturbance driven by profit, though it is rarely named as such. Human remains have long circulated through private collections, museums, and traveling exhibitions. Bones have been bought, sold, displayed, and traded under the guise of education or preservation. Even when intentions were described as respectful, the underlying logic remained extractive. The dead were valued not for who they had been, but for what they could provide.

These practices are often presented as relics of a less ethical past, yet they persist in modified forms. The relocation of cemeteries for construction, the storage of remains in institutional archives, and the delayed repatriation of Indigenous bodies all testify to the ongoing instability of burial as a guarantee of rest. The promise that the dead will be left alone is conditional, contingent upon their continued inconvenience to no one with authority.

What is less often acknowledged is that disturbance does not require physical contact. Access to the dead can also occur through symbolic means, through claims of communication, interpretation, or representation. In these cases, the body remains intact, but the boundary is crossed nonetheless. The dead are spoken for, spoken through, or spoken to, often without agreement about who has the right to do so.

This symbolic disturbance is frequently framed as benign, even comforting. Practices that claim to mediate contact with the dead are described as forms of healing, closure, or curiosity. They are allowed space within cultural life precisely because they do not appear to threaten physical order. Yet they raise parallel questions about consent, authority, and ownership. Who may claim access to the dead's voice? Who decides whether such access is legitimate? And what happens when those claims challenge sanctioned narratives about memory and control?

The anxiety surrounding these practices reveals a contradiction. On the one hand, cultures insist that the dead are beyond reach, their stories complete. On the other, they repeatedly seek to retrieve something from them—knowledge, reassurance, warning, legitimacy. This retrieval is rarely neutral. It is shaped by gender, class, race, and belief, as well as by broader cultural comfort with ambiguity. Some forms of access are normalized, even celebrated, while others are pathologized or criminalized.

What unites these varied disturbances is not their method but their function. Each represents a moment in which the dead are rendered available to the living under conditions defined by power. Whether through shovel, séance table, mass-produced board, or reflective surface, the dead are drawn back into the present and made to serve a purpose. The ethical question is not whether such access is possible, but who controls it and why.

This chapter does not seek to adjudicate belief. It does not ask whether communication with the dead is real, fraudulent, or imagined. Such debates obscure the more pressing issue, which is cultural permission. The concern here is not metaphysical truth, but social logic. Which disturbances are tolerated, which are condemned, and which are quietly absorbed into everyday practice reveal far more about a culture's relationship to memory than about the dead themselves.

By examining grave witching alongside practices such as Ouija boards, mediumship, and scrying, it becomes possible to see disturbance as a spectrum rather than an anomaly. Physical violation and symbolic access are not opposites but variations on the same impulse: the refusal to let the dead remain entirely beyond reach. The boundary exists, but it is porous by design, opening when the living find reason enough to cross it.

Section II — What Is Taken

Grave witching occupies a peculiar place in the cultural imagination. It is remembered as illicit, furtive, and morally suspect, a practice carried out at night or in secrecy, driven by desperation, superstition, or greed. In popular retellings, it appears as an aberration rather than as a symptom, an act so clearly transgressive that it reassures the living of their own ethical distance. Grave witchers are cast as villains precisely so the broader system of disturbance can remain unexamined.

Historically, however, grave witching did not emerge in isolation. It developed within a context in which the dead had already been rendered available. Medical schools required bodies. Anatomical knowledge demanded specimens. Scientific progress was framed as urgent and necessary, and the legal supply of cadavers was limited. The result was not a crisis of ethics but a logistical problem, one that was solved by redirecting attention toward those least able to resist. The poor, the institutionalized, the incarcerated, and the socially marginal became the primary targets, their graves treated as provisional rather than sacred.

What distinguishes grave witching from other forms of disturbance is not the violation itself, but the absence of institutional cover. Unlike sanctioned disinterment, which is accompanied by paperwork, permits, and professional language, grave witching lacked the veneer of legitimacy. It exposed too clearly the underlying assumption that some bodies mattered less than others. The outrage it provoked was therefore selective. The act was condemned, but the demand that made it profitable was rarely interrogated with the same intensity.

This selectivity is instructive. Cultural condemnation did not center on the harm done to the dead or to their families, but on the breach of order. Graves were not to be opened by unauthorized hands. Authority, not sanctity, was the line that had been crossed. When similar disturbances occurred under the auspices of science or civic necessity, the moral language softened considerably. The same body could be disturbed without scandal if the disturbance could be framed as useful.

Grave witching also reveals how burial itself functioned as a conditional promise. For those whose social position granted them visibility, burial offered relative security. Family plots, marked graves, and ongoing visitation created layers of protection, not because the dead were inherently respected, but because their disturbance would be noticed. For others, burial was provisional. The absence of markers, the isolation of pauper cemeteries, and the invisibility of institutional dead made exhumation both easier and easier to justify. The dead were not only unprotected; they were assumed to be available.

The language used to describe grave witching often emphasizes theft, but what was taken was not always material in the narrow sense. Bodies were removed, certainly, but so too were identities. Names were stripped away, replaced by numbers or labels. Context was erased. Once disinterred, the dead ceased to belong to a particular life or community and instead entered a system of abstraction. They became examples, specimens, resources. The violence lay not only in the act of removal, but in the transformation that followed.

This abstraction mirrors patterns seen elsewhere in the management of memory. When bodies are removed from their original resting places, they are severed from the narratives that gave them meaning. What remains is a fragment that can be reinterpreted at will. In this sense, grave witching is not merely an act of physical disturbance but an early form of narrative control. The dead are stripped of their stories so that new stories may be imposed.

Public reactions to grave witching often focused on the spectacle of violation rather than on the conditions that enabled it. Newspaper accounts emphasized outrage, fear, and moral decay, framing the practice as a threat to communal values. Yet these reactions rarely extended to a broader reconsideration of how the dead were treated once removed from their graves. The violation was seen as complete at the moment of exhumation, rather than as ongoing through use, display, and erasure.

This framing allowed societies to condemn grave witching without addressing the more uncomfortable question of why bodies were needed in the first place. Scientific progress, medical education, and institutional authority were granted moral exemption, even when they relied on the same assumptions about disposability. The dead, once disturbed, were expected to serve silently, their consent presumed or deemed irrelevant.

What grave witching ultimately exposes is not a lack of respect for the dead, but a hierarchy of respect. Some graves were inviolable. Others were negotiable. The distinction was not spiritual but social. It rested on visibility, power, and the likelihood of protest. Disturbance, in this context, was not an accident or a failure of values, but an extension of existing inequalities beyond death.

Seen this way, grave witching is less a dark footnote than an early signal. It demonstrates how quickly the promise of rest can be overridden when competing interests assert themselves. It also reveals how easily moral boundaries shift when the dead are rendered voiceless and interchangeable. The outrage directed at grave witchers functioned as a kind of containment, allowing societies to displace responsibility onto individuals while preserving the broader structures that made such practices possible.

In the chapters that follow, disturbance will take other forms, less overt and often more socially acceptable. The body will not always be moved, but access will still be claimed. Authority will be asserted not through force, but through interpretation. The dead will continue to be disturbed, not because boundaries have disappeared, but because they were never as firm as they appeared.

Section III — Mediated Access

As practices like grave witching came under increasing scrutiny and regulation, cultural interest in the dead did not diminish. It shifted. The desire for access did not disappear when physical disturbance became more difficult to justify or conceal. Instead, it found forms that appeared less violent, less invasive, and therefore more acceptable. The boundary between the living and the dead remained porous, but the means of crossing it changed. Where bodies could no longer be taken without consequence, voices were sought instead.

This transition marks an important moment in the cultural management of death. Physical exhumation is unmistakably disruptive. It leaves visible traces, provokes outrage, and invites legal intervention. Symbolic access, by contrast, can be framed as harmless or even benevolent. It requires no disturbed soil, no broken markers, no displaced remains. The dead are approached through objects, gestures, and interpretations that leave burial intact while still claiming connection. The appearance of respect is preserved, even as the boundary is crossed.

The emergence and popularization of devices such as the Ouija board exemplify this shift. Marketed as a game, a novelty, or a parlor diversion, the board translated communication with the dead into a controlled and repeatable activity. Its structure imposed order on uncertainty. Letters were arranged neatly. Responses were constrained to predetermined options. Contact, if it occurred, did so within a framework that emphasized rules, turns, and moderation. Whatever anxiety the practice evoked was contained by familiarity and domesticity.

The commercial success of the Ouija board depended not on belief, but on accessibility. It required no specialist, no spiritual authority, and no explicit commitment to faith. Anyone could participate, and participation could be dismissed as play if discomfort arose. This ambiguity was crucial. It allowed engagement with the dead to enter the home without threatening social norms. The dead became approachable without becoming disruptive. Communication was framed not as intrusion, but as curiosity.

This domestication of access altered the moral landscape. What would have been condemned as violation if enacted through physical means was reframed as entertainment when mediated through an object. The dead were no longer at risk of being taken apart or displaced, only consulted. Yet this consultation still assumed availability. The question of consent remained unresolved. The dead were presumed willing to respond, eager even, their silence interpreted not as refusal but as absence.

Mediumship occupied a more complex position within this landscape. Unlike the Ouija board, which dispersed authority among participants, mediums claimed a particular capacity to hear, see, or transmit messages from the dead. This claim placed them at the center of debates about legitimacy and fraud, belief and deception. Yet these debates often obscured the social function mediumship served. Mediums did not merely offer communication; they offered interpretation. They translated uncertainty into narrative, grief into coherence.

The cultural reception of mediums was deeply shaped by gender. Many prominent mediums were women, operating in a space that permitted emotional sensitivity while denying formal authority. Their proximity to the dead was tolerated precisely because it was framed as intuitive rather than intellectual, experiential rather than analytical. This framing allowed mediumship to flourish while also ensuring it could be dismissed when convenient. The authority to speak for the dead was extended and withdrawn selectively, reinforcing existing hierarchies rather than challenging them.

What mattered was not whether mediums were believed, but how belief was managed. When mediumship provided comfort without disrupting dominant narratives, it was often indulged. When it threatened established power or offered alternative interpretations of history, it was more likely to be ridiculed or suppressed. The dead could be consulted, but only within limits. Their messages were acceptable insofar as they affirmed the living order.

Scrying occupies a different register of mediated access. Unlike devices or intermediaries that claim direct communication, scrying emphasizes perception rather than dialogue. Meaning is sought not through words, but through surfaces. Water, glass, mirrors, and polished stone become sites of attention, their reflective qualities inviting interpretation. The practice does not presume that the dead will speak plainly. Instead, it assumes that meaning must be discerned, that what is seen will be partial, distorted, or symbolic.

This distinction is significant. Scrying acknowledges uncertainty rather than resolving it. It accepts that access to the dead, if it exists at all, will not be straightforward. The surface does not deliver answers; it offers possibilities. Interpretation becomes central, and responsibility shifts to the observer. What is seen cannot be separated from how it is seen.

Because of this emphasis on perception, scrying has often been treated with suspicion. It lacks the structure of a board, the authority of a medium, or the reassurance of fixed responses. It resists commodification, even when objects are sold to facilitate it. The practice foregrounds ambiguity in a culture that prefers clarity. Yet it also reveals something essential about symbolic access to the dead: that meaning is not extracted so much as constructed.

Across these practices, a pattern emerges. As physical disturbance became increasingly regulated, symbolic disturbance expanded. The dead were left in place, but their presence was invoked, interpreted, and repurposed. Access shifted from the body to the narrative, from material remains to imagined voices and images. This shift did not resolve ethical questions; it reframed them. The issue was no longer whether the dead should be left undisturbed, but who had the right to interpret their silence.

The relative acceptance of these practices reflects a broader cultural comfort with mediated access. When the dead are encountered through objects, performances, or interpretive acts, the encounter can be managed. It can be limited in time, framed as voluntary, and absorbed into existing rituals. Disturbance becomes less visible, and therefore less troubling. Yet the underlying assumption remains the same: that the dead are available to the living when the living find reason enough to seek them.

This availability is not evenly distributed. Just as certain graves were more vulnerable to physical disturbance, certain dead are more frequently invoked symbolically. Marginalized lives are more easily spoken for, their presumed voices aligned with narratives imposed upon them. Authority determines not only who may access the dead, but which dead are considered accessible. Silence is interpreted selectively, and meaning is assigned accordingly.

By the time mediated access becomes commonplace, the boundary between the living and the dead has not been restored. It has simply been redrawn. The shovel is replaced by the planchette, the séance table, the reflective surface. Disturbance continues, less visibly but no less consequential. The dead remain unsettled, not because they are restless, but because the living continue to require something from them.

Section IV — Who May Speak

As symbolic access to the dead became more common, questions of authority moved to the foreground. It was no longer enough to ask whether the dead could be reached; the more pressing issue became who was permitted to claim that reach, and under what conditions their claims would be taken seriously. Belief alone was insufficient. Access had to be regulated, not through proof, but through credibility, respectability, and alignment with existing power structures.

This regulation did not operate uniformly. Some forms of access were tolerated, even encouraged, while others were ridiculed, criminalized, or quietly marginalized. The distinction was rarely based on the nature of the practice itself. Instead, it rested on who was speaking, what they were saying, and whether their interpretations threatened established narratives. Authority over the dead mirrored authority among the living.

Mediumship provides a clear illustration of this dynamic. While mediums claimed the ability to transmit messages from the dead, their legitimacy was always provisional. Acceptance hinged on context. In private settings, among family members seeking comfort, mediumship could be indulged as therapeutic or harmless. In public or institutional contexts, it was far more likely to be framed as deception or hysteria. The same act could be read as healing or fraudulent depending on who observed it and what was at stake.

Gender played a decisive role in these assessments. Women were often positioned as natural intermediaries, their emotional sensitivity framed as an asset rather than a liability, but this positioning came with limits. The authority granted to women as mediums was contingent and easily revoked. Their proximity to the dead was tolerated only so long as it remained personal and apolitical. When claims extended beyond consolation into interpretation of history, injustice, or responsibility, skepticism hardened quickly.

This pattern reflects a broader discomfort with voices that challenge sanctioned memory. The dead, when permitted to speak at all, are expected to confirm what the living already believe. Messages that reinforce prevailing moral frameworks are welcomed. Those that complicate or contradict official narratives are dismissed as unreliable, the product of imagination rather than insight. The question of truth becomes secondary to the question of usefulness.

The management of belief thus functions as a form of containment. By framing certain practices as irrational or unserious, institutions maintain control over which interpretations circulate publicly. This does not eliminate symbolic access to the dead; it channels it. Popular forms of engagement are permitted precisely because they are easy to dismiss. Their ambiguity protects dominant narratives from challenge, allowing engagement without consequence.

Skepticism, in this context, operates selectively. It is not directed equally at all claims about the dead. Official histories, monuments, and sanctioned commemorations are rarely subjected to the same level of doubt, even though they too rely on interpretation and omission. The authority to speak for the dead is assumed when it aligns with power, questioned only when it emerges from outside established channels.

This asymmetry reveals that the issue is not belief, but control. The problem is not that the dead might be misrepresented, but that they might be represented differently. Alternative voices introduce instability into narratives that depend on closure. They reopen questions that institutions have worked to settle. As a result, access to the dead becomes a contested space, policed not through evidence but through credibility.

The language used to discredit unsanctioned access often emphasizes rationality and progress. Practices are labeled superstitious, backward, or unscientific, reinforcing a boundary between legitimate knowledge and unacceptable belief. Yet this boundary is porous. Many practices once dismissed later become absorbed into acceptable discourse once they can be reframed, studied, or controlled. What changes is not the practice itself, but who governs its interpretation.

The dead occupy a paradoxical position within this system. They are invoked constantly, yet rarely allowed autonomy. Their voices are imagined, filtered, or silenced according to present needs. When their presumed messages align with existing values, they are embraced as evidence of continuity or moral order. When they disrupt, they are discounted as noise. The dead are granted presence without agency.

This dynamic extends beyond explicit claims of communication. It is visible in how remains are displayed, how graves are interpreted, and how symbols are deployed. The authority to assign meaning to the dead's presence or absence rests with institutions that present their interpretations as neutral or factual. Alternative readings are marginalized, not because they lack coherence, but because they lack sanction.

What emerges across these practices is a hierarchy of speech. Some are permitted to speak for the dead openly, their narratives amplified through museums, monuments, and textbooks. Others may speak only in private, their interpretations confined to personal belief or dismissed as eccentric. The dead themselves remain silent, their presumed consent irrelevant. Access is granted not to them, but to those who can manage the consequences of speaking in their name.

This hierarchy does not eliminate disturbance. It refines it. By regulating who may speak and what may be said, cultures maintain the appearance of respect while continuing to extract meaning from the dead. Disturbance becomes less about physical intrusion and more about narrative control. The dead are left in their graves, but their stories are continually rearranged.

In this way, symbolic access to the dead functions as both concession and containment. It allows engagement while limiting impact. It acknowledges the dead's presence without granting them authority. The boundary remains intact in form, even as it is crossed in practice. What appears as restraint is, in fact, a different mode of control.

Section V — Surfaces and Seeing

Across the practices considered so far, a subtle shift has been taking place. The focus has moved steadily away from the dead as physical presence and toward the conditions under which meaning is perceived. Bodies were first disturbed, then voices were sought, then authority was negotiated. What remains, beneath these changes, is the question of how the living come to believe they are seeing something at all. Access to the dead, whether material or symbolic, ultimately depends on surfaces.

Scrying makes this dependency explicit. Unlike practices that promise communication or revelation, scrying offers only reflection. The surface does not speak. It does not instruct or command. It waits. What appears within it is inseparable from the act of looking. The observer brings expectation, fear, memory, and desire to the surface, and these elements shape what is perceived. The dead, if they are present at all, are present indirectly, refracted through the conditions of attention.

This indirectness has often been treated as a weakness, a sign that scrying lacks substance or reliability. Yet it is precisely this quality that reveals something essential about how disturbance operates. The dead do not need to be extracted from the ground or summoned by name in order to be disturbed. They can be unsettled through interpretation alone. When meaning is imposed upon absence, when silence is made to signify, the boundary is crossed without visible trace.

Reflective practices expose the role of the living more clearly than other forms of access. They offer no external authority to absorb responsibility. There is no medium to blame, no device to mediate intention. The surface returns what is brought to it, altered only by distortion and light. In this way, scrying does not merely facilitate access to the dead; it implicates the observer in the act of meaning-making. What is seen cannot be separated from who is seeing.

This implication is uncomfortable, which may explain why reflective practices occupy a marginal position in cultural hierarchies of legitimacy. They resist regulation because they resist standardization. There are no fixed outcomes, no verifiable messages, no clear boundary between insight and projection. As a result, they cannot be easily absorbed into systems that prefer control over ambiguity. Their value lies not in what they reveal, but in what they expose about the act of looking itself.

The same dynamic operates, less overtly, in other forms of symbolic disturbance. When the dead are spoken for, displayed, or interpreted, a surface is always involved. It may be a photograph, a name etched in stone, a curated exhibit, or a story repeated until it hardens into fact. These surfaces present themselves as transparent, but they are not neutral. They frame what can be seen and what must remain out of view. The disturbance occurs not only in the act of access, but in the shaping of perception.

What distinguishes reflective practices is that they refuse to conceal this shaping. The surface remains visible. The act of interpretation cannot be disguised as discovery. The observer is confronted with their own role in producing meaning, and this confrontation destabilizes the comfort of distance. The dead are no longer passive objects of inquiry. They become mirrors through which the living encounter their own assumptions.

This encounter alters the moral terrain. If disturbance is understood solely as physical violation, responsibility can be assigned to specific acts and actors. If disturbance includes symbolic access and interpretive control, responsibility becomes diffuse. It resides not only in institutions or individuals, but in habits of seeing that are widely shared and rarely examined. The dead are unsettled not by extraordinary transgression, but by ordinary acts of interpretation repeated without reflection.

Within this framework, the boundary between reverence and violation becomes increasingly difficult to maintain. Acts intended to honor the dead may nonetheless appropriate their presence for purposes they did not choose. Commemoration, when unexamined, can function as a form of disturbance, fixing meaning in ways that foreclose alternative narratives. The dead are preserved, but their complexity is reduced. They are remembered, but only in the forms that serve present needs.

Reflective practices complicate this process by refusing closure. They do not offer definitive meaning. They invite return rather than resolution. In doing so, they challenge the assumption that memory must be settled in order to be respected. They suggest instead that uncertainty may be a more ethical stance, one that acknowledges the limits of access rather than attempting to overcome them.

The discomfort provoked by such practices is instructive. It reveals a cultural preference for managed memory over open-ended engagement. Disturbance is tolerated when it produces usable narratives, but resisted when it exposes the instability of meaning itself. The dead are permitted to speak only when their speech can be contained.

By foregrounding surfaces and seeing, this section brings the chapter back to its central concern. Disturbance is not confined to moments of overt violation. It occurs whenever the dead are rendered available to interpretation without consent, whenever silence is made to answer questions it was never asked. The methods vary, but the impulse remains consistent. The living continue to require something from the dead, and they continue to find ways to take it.

As the chapter moves toward its close, the focus will shift once more, not to a new practice, but to the cumulative effect of these disturbances. What emerges, across physical and symbolic access alike, is a pattern in which the dead are never entirely left alone. They persist not as autonomous presences, but as sites upon which the living rehearse authority, anxiety, and meaning. The boundary holds only so long as it is not tested, and history shows that it is tested often.

Section VI — What Is Never Settled

Across the practices traced here, disturbance appears less as an exception than as a condition. Whether enacted through the removal of bodies, the mediation of voices, or the interpretation of surfaces, access to the dead is repeatedly claimed under circumstances shaped by need and authority. The methods differ, the justifications shift, but the underlying assumption remains consistent: that the dead are not entirely beyond reach, and that their presence can be made to serve the living in ways that appear necessary, benign, or inevitable.

What varies most is not the act of disturbance itself, but the cultural language surrounding it. Physical violation is condemned when it lacks authorization, tolerated when it is framed as progress, and forgotten when its consequences are absorbed into institutional routine. Symbolic access is embraced when it comforts, dismissed when it unsettles, and regulated when it threatens to complicate sanctioned narratives. In each case, the dead are positioned as available but not autonomous, present but not self-determining.

This availability is often described as care. Disturbance is softened by claims of respect, curiosity, healing, or remembrance. Yet care, when defined solely by the needs of the living, becomes indistinguishable from appropriation. The dead are invoked, interpreted, or displayed without agreement about what constitutes consent or restraint. Their silence is taken as permission, their absence as openness. The boundary that burial is meant to establish persists more as symbol than as protection.

What becomes visible through this accumulation is a pattern of unsettledness that does not originate with the dead themselves. It originates with the living. The refusal to leave the dead alone reflects not restlessness on the other side of the boundary, but uncertainty on this one. The dead are returned to repeatedly because they are imagined as repositories of meaning that the present cannot generate on its own. They are asked to justify, to explain, to reassure, to confirm. When they cannot, or do not, speak clearly enough, interpretation fills the gap.

This interpretive impulse carries consequences. Once the dead are positioned as sources of meaning, their representation becomes a site of power. Decisions about how they are remembered, which voices are amplified, and which practices are dismissed shape not only the past but the ethical possibilities of the present. Disturbance, in this sense, is cumulative. Each act of access builds upon those that came before, reinforcing habits of seeing that make further access seem natural.

The persistence of these habits suggests that disturbance is not merely tolerated, but necessary to certain forms of social order. Systems that rely on managed memory cannot afford to let the dead remain fully opaque. Silence introduces instability. Ambiguity resists closure. To function smoothly, memory must be shaped, directed, and contained. Disturbance provides the means by which this shaping occurs, even when it is denied or displaced.

At the same time, the discomfort that surrounds unsanctioned practices indicates that the boundary has not disappeared entirely. Outrage at grave violation, skepticism toward mediums, and unease with reflective practices all point to an awareness that something is at stake. The dead are not simply raw material. There remains an intuition, however inconsistently applied, that they deserve limits. The conflict lies not between belief and disbelief, but between competing understandings of responsibility.

This tension leaves the dead in an unresolved position. They are neither fully protected nor fully exploited, neither wholly absent nor wholly present. They persist as figures through which the living negotiate questions of authority, legitimacy, and meaning. Disturbance, then, is not a singular act to be condemned or defended, but an ongoing negotiation that reveals where power settles and where it frays.

By tracing disturbance across physical and symbolic forms, this chapter does not seek to collapse differences between practices. It seeks instead to make visible the continuity that allows them to coexist. The dead are unsettled not because they demand attention, but because attention is continually taken. The boundary between the living and the dead is crossed not in moments of excess alone, but in ordinary acts of interpretation repeated without acknowledgment.

What follows in the broader arc of this book will move away from individual practices and toward the structures that formalize them. The concern will no longer be how access occurs, but how it is normalized, staged, and defended. The dead will recede again, not into rest, but into background, their disturbance absorbed into larger systems of memory and power. The traces remain, though often unnoticed, shaping what can be seen and what is allowed to remain unseen.

Here, at least, the unsettledness has been named. Not resolved, not corrected, but recognized as a condition produced by the living rather than by the dead. Burial promises rest, but memory rarely keeps that promise intact. The ground closes, the stone is set, and the boundary is declared, yet the work of disturbance continues, quietly and persistently, wherever meaning is demanded from those who can no longer refuse.

Chapter Seven

My Precious Little Boy: Attachment, Grief, and the Expansion of Remembrance

Section I – Family Pets as Fictive Kin

The first thing that becomes apparent when walking through a pet cemetery is not the emotion itself, but the language through which that emotion is expressed. The markers speak differently than those found in human burial grounds, and the difference is not subtle. Names are rarely formal. Dates feel secondary to relationships. The stones are less concerned with documenting a life span than with preserving a bond. What emerges almost immediately is a grammar of intimacy that resists the conventions normally governing public expressions of grief.

Many headstones identify the mourners as Mom and Dad, and the animals buried beneath them as sons and daughters. This is not occasional or idiosyncratic phrasing, but a recurring pattern that appears across decades, regions, and socioeconomic boundaries. The consistency of this language matters. It signals that these terms were not chosen impulsively at the moment of loss, but reflect roles that had been lived daily over years. The cemetery does not introduce the relationship; it records it.

In human cemeteries, language often feels constrained by social expectations. Titles are formalized, relationships reduced to legally or biologically recognized categories, and emotional expression filtered through phrases that are widely accepted and rarely questioned. Even profound love is often rendered cautiously, as if grief must remain contained to be respectable. Pet cemeteries do not appear to operate under the same restrictions. The stones speak plainly, using the same words people used while the animal was alive, without adjusting tone or vocabulary to suit an imagined public audience.

This difference exposes something important about how kinship is actually practiced rather than officially defined. The use of parental language is especially revealing. To call oneself a parent is not simply to express affection. It is to claim responsibility, obligation, and moral accountability for another life. Parenting is a role defined by care, protection, routine, and the assumption of a future that extends beyond the present moment. When people identify themselves as

Mom or Dad in relation to an animal, they are not borrowing sentiment; they are naming a role they already inhabited.

The grief that follows the death of such an animal is shaped by that role. Parents are not meant to outlive their children, and this expectation is so deeply embedded in cultural consciousness that it often goes unspoken. When it is violated, the result is not only sorrow but disorientation. The future that had been assumed dissolves. Daily routines abruptly lose their purpose. Identity itself becomes unstable, because the role of parent does not disappear simply because the child is gone. The pet cemetery captures this rupture without attempting to soften it.

Many epitaphs express guilt, regret, and self-reproach in language that closely mirrors the grief associated with child loss. Statements about failing to protect, not doing enough, or wishing for one more moment are common. Outside the context of pet loss, such expressions would be immediately recognized as the language of parental bereavement. Their presence here clarifies that the grief is not excessive or misplaced, but internally consistent with the relationship that existed.

Anthropology offers a useful framework for understanding this consistency through the concept of fictive kin. Fictive kinship describes relationships that function as family without biological or legal ties, relationships structured by obligation, care, loyalty, and shared identity. Godparents, adopted relatives, clan members, and chosen families all fall within this category. Pet cemeteries demonstrate that animals are frequently incorporated into these kinship systems in ways that are emotionally and practically indistinguishable from human family roles.

What makes pet cemeteries particularly revealing is the absence of apology. The stones do not defend the relationship or attempt to justify the depth of grief. They do not anticipate criticism or minimize loss. Within the boundaries of the cemetery, the relationship is treated as self-evident. The memorial does not argue that the animal mattered; it proceeds from the assumption that this was already understood.

This stands in sharp contrast to how grief over animals is often treated in broader social contexts, where it is frequently minimized, redirected, or framed as something that should resolve quickly. Phrases such as "it was just a dog" or "you can get another one" reflect an underlying discomfort with acknowledging the depth of attachment that often exists. Pet cemeteries quietly resist that minimization by preserving evidence of grief in a form that cannot be easily dismissed.

Taken collectively, these memorials form a cultural record of how people actually live with animals. They reveal kinship structures that exist alongside officially recognized family systems and sometimes challenge their boundaries. The cemetery becomes a place where those relationships are allowed to be named without correction, where grief does not need to be scaled down to meet external expectations, and where love is permitted to remain exactly as large as it was in life.

In this way, pet cemeteries function less as marginal spaces and more as corrective ones. They show what is often excluded from formal narratives of kinship and mourning, preserving relational truths that might otherwise remain private or unspoken. The stones do not editorialize or exaggerate. They simply record what was lived, and in doing so, they make visible a form of family that has always existed, even when it was not officially acknowledged.

Section II – Memory Lasts a Lifetime

Another feature of pet cemeteries that becomes apparent over time, rather than at first glance, is the persistence of care. Many graves are not only marked but actively tended long after the animal's death, sometimes decades later. Flowers appear on stones that date back twenty years or more, their freshness indicating recent visits rather than inherited neglect. Artificial arrangements are replaced when they fade. Small tokens are rearranged. The ground is cleared of leaves. These are not gestures of momentary remembrance, but evidence of an ongoing relationship maintained across time.

This persistence complicates common assumptions about grief, particularly the expectation that mourning should diminish predictably or resolve altogether. In human contexts, long-term tending of a grave is often understood as normal, even admirable, especially when the deceased was a child or close family member. In pet cemeteries, the same behaviors are sometimes viewed as excessive or sentimental when observed from the outside. Yet the actions themselves are identical. What differs is not the practice of remembrance, but the social permission granted to it.

The repeated care of these graves suggests that the bond does not end with death, nor does it gradually lose relevance as years pass. The flowers are not there because the loss is unresolved, but because the relationship continues to be acknowledged. The act of tending becomes a way of maintaining connection, much as one might do for a human family member whose grave is visited regularly. The passage of time does not erase kinship; it reframes it.

This is especially evident in pet cemeteries where multiple graves appear together, arranged deliberately as family plots. These groupings are rarely accidental. Animals who lived together, arrived at different times, or died years apart are buried side by side, their stones positioned in ways that reflect household relationships rather than chronological order. Parents rest beside children. Longtime companions are reunited in death. New animals are placed carefully among earlier ones, extending the family plot forward rather than closing it.

The existence of these family plots reinforces the reality that pets are not remembered as isolated losses, but as members of an enduring family system. The cemetery becomes a spatial representation of household continuity, mapping relationships that once existed in shared living spaces onto a landscape of remembrance. In this way, pet cemeteries mirror human burial practices more closely than is often acknowledged, particularly those traditions that emphasize lineage, proximity, and collective identity.

The presence of flowers on long-established graves also challenges the notion that attachment to animals is transient or replaceable. The idea that one pet simply substitutes for another is contradicted by the careful differentiation evident in these memorials. Each stone names a specific individual. Each grave carries its own markers, dates, and expressions of affection. Even when newer animals are buried nearby, earlier ones are not displaced or forgotten. The family expands rather than resets.

This continuity highlights a key aspect of fictive kinship: its durability. Relationships structured as kin do not dissolve simply because they lack biological ties. They persist through memory, ritual, and ongoing acknowledgment. The repeated placement of flowers functions as a ritual reaffirmation of belonging, signaling that the deceased remains part of the family narrative rather than a closed chapter.

There is also a temporal layering visible in these cemeteries that deepens their emotional complexity. A single visit might reveal fresh flowers on a grave from the early 2000s, faded tokens on one from the

1980s, and newly placed stones for animals buried only weeks earlier. This layering collapses time, allowing multiple moments of grief to coexist in the same space. The cemetery becomes not just a record of loss, but a living archive of attachment across generations of animals and caregivers.

In some cases, the same names appear repeatedly across stones, accompanied by qualifiers such as "the second," "junior," or affectionate variations that distinguish one animal from another while preserving continuity. This practice reflects a desire not to replace, but to carry forward. The name becomes a lineage marker, linking past and present members of the household in a shared symbolic thread.

What emerges from these observations is a picture of mourning that is neither fleeting nor pathological, but structured, intentional, and relational. The ongoing care of graves and the formation of family plots indicate that pet cemeteries function as sites of sustained kinship maintenance. They are places where bonds are not expected to fade quietly, but are allowed to endure visibly and without explanation.

In this sense, the pet cemetery does not merely commemorate loss; it preserves family structure. It allows relationships formed in life to retain coherence in death, offering a space where grief can evolve without being erased. The flowers placed year after year are not signs of being unable to move on, but markers of a relationship that continues to be honored as real, meaningful, and complete.

Section III – Companion vs. Commodity

The persistence of care and the deliberate construction of family plots in pet cemeteries leads inevitably to a broader realization about how unevenly animals are valued within the same cultural framework. These burial grounds make visible a divide that usually remains implicit, one that governs how animals are categorized, treated, and remembered. Some animals are granted full kinship status, while others are denied even individual recognition, despite belonging to the same species or sharing similar capacities for attachment and suffering.

Within a single culture, dogs may be buried with engraved stones and tended graves, while other dogs are bred for labor, confined, or euthanized without ceremony once their usefulness ends. Cats may be mourned as children in one household and exterminated as pests in another. Horses may be revered companions or disposable tools. Livestock may be raised with care and familiarity, yet their deaths marked only by accounting records rather than ritual. The pet cemetery does not resolve these contradictions, but it exposes them by drawing a sharp line between animals who cross into fictive kinship and those who remain classified as resources.

What determines which animals are remembered in this way is not species alone, but relationship. Animals who are named, spoken to, depended upon emotionally, and integrated into daily routines undergo a transformation in status. They cease to be interchangeable representatives of a category and become specific individuals whose absence is felt as a rupture. The cemetery records this transformation not through theory, but through practice. Each stone affirms that a particular life mattered enough to be named, marked, and revisited.

This relational distinction carries moral weight. The act of memorialization signals that an animal was owed something beyond basic care, that its life created obligations that did not end at death. The ongoing tending of graves reinforces this sense of responsibility, suggesting that kinship entails remembrance as well as care. In this context, grief is not merely an emotional response but a moral one, shaped by the recognition that a bond existed which cannot be undone or replaced.

Pet cemeteries therefore occupy a complicated position within broader conversations about animals and ethics. They demonstrate that people are capable of extending profound moral consideration across species lines, yet they also reveal how selectively that consideration is applied. The same society that produces these cemeteries also supports systems that depend on the instrumental use of animals on a massive scale. The cemetery does not condemn this divide, but it quietly documents its existence.

The discomfort many people feel toward intense grief for animals may stem from this tension. To acknowledge the depth of attachment recorded in pet cemeteries is to confront the arbitrariness of the boundaries we draw. If one animal can be mourned as a child, what justifies the dismissal of another as disposable? The stones do not pose this question explicitly, but their presence makes it difficult to avoid.

Importantly, pet cemeteries do not suggest that all animals should be treated identically or remembered in the same way. Rather, they show how meaning is generated through relationship. Kinship is not assigned universally; it is built through shared life, mutual dependence, and emotional investment over time. This does not erase the moral complexity of how animals are used in other contexts, but it clarifies why some losses are felt more deeply than others.

The cemetery thus becomes a site where private moral worlds are made public. Each grave reflects a household's internal hierarchy of value, revealing which lives were woven into the fabric of daily existence and which remained outside it. Taken together, these individual choices form a collective portrait of how people negotiate the place of animals in their lives, often in ways that diverge sharply from official or economic classifications.

What emerges is not a coherent ideology, but a lived reality marked by inconsistency and contradiction. Pet cemeteries capture this reality without attempting to smooth it over. They allow deeply personal valuations to coexist side by side, creating a landscape that mirrors the uneven moral terrain of human–animal relationships more honestly than abstract debates ever could.

By preserving these relationships in stone, pet cemeteries ensure that the animals buried there are not absorbed back into anonymity. They remain distinct, remembered not for what they provided, but for who they were within a particular family. In doing so, the cemetery affirms that kinship, once established, carries a claim on memory that does not easily fade, even when it crosses boundaries that society prefers to keep firmly in place.

Section IV – Grief and the Meaning of Loss

Pet cemeteries also function as spaces where grief is permitted to exist without correction, a role that becomes clearer when contrasted with the limited tolerance often shown toward mourning animals in everyday social life. Outside these fenced grounds, grief for a pet is frequently subjected to subtle forms of regulation. It is measured against unspoken standards of proportionality, expected to resolve quickly, and often redirected toward reassurance rather than acknowledgment. Within the cemetery, those pressures fall away. The relationship does not need to be justified, explained, or minimized in order to be honored.

This permission matters because grief is not only an emotional response but a social experience shaped by what is allowed to be expressed. When mourning is constrained, it does not disappear; it is simply carried in quieter, more isolated ways. Pet cemeteries offer an alternative structure, one in which grief is given a physical location and a visible form. The act of visiting, tending, and remembering becomes a sanctioned practice rather than a private indulgence. In this sense, the cemetery does not intensify grief but stabilizes it, giving it a place to settle rather than forcing it inward.

The rituals observed in these spaces mirror those associated with human loss. Visitors speak aloud to the deceased, recount recent events, apologize for absences, and reaffirm bonds that feel unchanged despite death. These behaviors are not signs of denial but expressions of continuity. They reflect an understanding of relationship that does not end abruptly at the moment of loss, but transitions into a different form. The cemetery supports this transition by providing a setting in which such expressions are neither questioned nor interrupted.

Over time, these practices shape how grief is carried across a lifetime. The repeated visits, the seasonal placement of flowers, and the careful maintenance of family plots allow mourning to evolve without being erased. Grief becomes something integrated rather than resolved, a component of personal history rather than an open wound. This integration is particularly important for losses that carry parental weight, where identity itself has been altered by the death of a dependent being.

Pet cemeteries also create a quiet community of shared recognition. While visitors may not speak to one another, the presence of others engaged in similar acts of remembrance reduces isolation. The knowledge that one is not alone in mourning an animal as family provides a form of validation that is often absent elsewhere. Each tended grave affirms that such grief is not singular or aberrant, but part of a broader, if rarely acknowledged, human experience.

The physical design of these cemeteries reinforces this sense of legitimacy. Pathways, markers, benches, and gates mirror those found in human burial grounds, signaling that what occurs here belongs within established traditions of mourning. The similarity is not accidental. It situates animal loss within familiar cultural frameworks, granting it a gravity that might otherwise be denied. At the same time, the informality of language and decoration allows for a level of emotional honesty that human cemeteries sometimes restrict.

In allowing grief to be expressed fully, pet cemeteries also reveal how much emotional labor is involved in caring for animals during life. The intensity of mourning reflects the depth of daily involvement that preceded it: feeding, medical decisions, training, play, and comfort during illness or aging. These forms of care require attention, sacrifice, and emotional investment, all of which contribute to the strength of the bond. When the animal dies, the sudden absence of these routines leaves a void that is both practical and emotional. The cemetery becomes a place where that absence can be acknowledged rather than ignored.

The long-term tending of graves further underscores that grief does not operate on a simple timeline. Years may pass, new animals may join the household, and life may continue in visible ways, yet the bond represented by a particular grave remains intact. The flowers placed decades later do not indicate an inability to move forward, but a willingness to remember honestly. They mark a relationship that mattered enough to be carried across time without being diminished.

Through this lens, pet cemeteries emerge as essential cultural spaces rather than sentimental anomalies. They provide a structure for mourning that aligns with lived experience rather than prescribed norms. They allow grief to exist in proportion to attachment, not in accordance with social hierarchy. In doing so, they preserve a form of emotional truth that might otherwise be forced into silence.

As places where grief is permitted to unfold without constraint, pet cemeteries challenge narrow definitions of whose lives are grievable. They do not demand agreement or universal application, but they quietly insist that the bonds they commemorate were real, sustained, and deserving of remembrance. Within their boundaries, loss is allowed to take the shape it needs, and that allowance becomes one of their most important functions.

Section V – Kinship, Memory, and Moral Responsibility

Taken as a whole, pet cemeteries reveal something quietly radical about how people construct kinship, memory, and moral responsibility. They do not argue for a philosophical position or attempt to redefine animals in abstract terms. Instead, they document how relationships were actually lived, and how those relationships continue to matter after death. The cemetery becomes a record of insistence, a refusal to let bonds that shaped daily life be reduced or erased simply because they crossed species boundaries.

What these spaces ultimately preserve is not sentiment, but relational truth. The stones, flowers, and family plots attest to lives that were woven into households through routines of care, mutual dependence, and emotional presence. These animals were not peripheral. They shaped schedules, influenced decisions, and anchored people during periods of illness, grief, loneliness, and transition. Their deaths therefore mark not only the loss of a being, but the collapse of a structure that once organized parts of everyday life.

The language used in these cemeteries makes clear that memory itself is relational. People remember animals as who they were to them, not as representatives of a category. A dog is not recalled as a dog, but as a son who waited by the door, a daughter who slept at the foot of the bed, a presence that understood tone and routine with a fluency that required no translation. The cemetery safeguards that specificity, resisting the tendency to generalize or diminish the loss.

In doing so, pet cemeteries also expose how selective remembrance always is. Every culture draws boundaries around whose lives are publicly mourned and whose are allowed to disappear without ceremony. These boundaries are not fixed; they shift with context, relationship, and power. Pet cemeteries show one way those boundaries are quietly redrawn, not through protest or policy, but through ordinary acts of care carried forward into death. A grave, a name, a flower placed years later all signal that a life claimed space in someone's moral universe.

This insistence on remembrance does not deny the contradictions inherent in how animals are treated more broadly. People who lovingly tend pet graves may still participate in systems that exploit or instrumentalize other animals. The cemetery does not resolve that tension, but it does make it visible. It records moments where relationship overrode abstraction, where a particular life mattered enough to be mourned fully, even if others were not granted the same recognition.

What emerges from these spaces is not a demand for consistency, but an acknowledgment of complexity. Human relationships with animals are layered, uneven, and often contradictory. Pet cemeteries do not pretend otherwise. Instead, they offer a place where one form of relationship is honored without being required to stand in for all others. They allow people to tell the truth about who mattered to them, even when that truth does not align neatly with broader cultural narratives.

In this sense, pet cemeteries function as quiet acts of resistance against erasure. They refuse the idea that love must conform to socially sanctioned hierarchies in order to be legitimate. They preserve evidence of kinship that might otherwise be dismissed as excessive, irrational, or sentimental. The care invested in these spaces over decades affirms that remembrance itself is a moral act, one that asserts the continuing significance of a bond rather than allowing it to be overwritten by time.

Ultimately, pet cemeteries remind us that grief follows relationship, not status. The depth of mourning reflects the depth of attachment, and attachment is shaped by proximity, care, and shared life rather than by species alone. These cemeteries exist because people needed a place where that reality could be acknowledged without qualification. They stand as quiet testimony to the human capacity to extend kinship beyond prescribed limits and to insist, through memory and ritual, that those relationships were real and enduring.

In the end, the people who place the stones do not seek permission. They do not ask whether such grief is appropriate or whether such bonds should count. They simply believe that their loved ones should be tended and remembered, marking lives that they were family and continue to be carried that way, long after death has made silence possible.

Section VI – Pet Cemeteries and Remembrance

There is also something important to be said about the way pet cemeteries normalize remembrance over time, rather than treating memory as something that must gradually recede. In many areas of life, grief is expected to follow an arc: acute pain, gradual softening, eventual closure. Pet cemeteries complicate that narrative by showing how remembrance can remain active without being pathological. The flowers placed on decades-old graves are not expressions of unresolved loss so much as evidence that love does not expire on a schedule.

This challenges a cultural assumption that healing requires forgetting, or at least quieting attachment to the point where it no longer demands expression. In the context of fictive kinship, however, forgetting would represent not recovery but rupture. To stop remembering would mean to deny the relationship itself, something few people seem willing to do. Instead, memory is allowed to evolve into a form that is steady rather than overwhelming, carried through small, repeated acts rather than dramatic displays of grief.

The cemetery provides a structure for this kind of remembrance. It offers a place where memory can be externalized and revisited without explanation. The physicality of the grave allows grief to be grounded, preventing it from becoming diffuse or isolating. For many people, this grounding appears to be essential, particularly when the loss occurred under circumstances that involved difficult decisions, prolonged illness, or perceived failure. The ability to return to a specific place, marked by a name and a date, offers a sense of continuity that private memory alone may not provide.

Pet cemeteries also reveal how remembrance can coexist with new attachments rather than competing with them. The presence of newer graves alongside older ones, or the careful placement of multiple animals within a shared family plot, suggests that love is not treated as a finite resource. Earlier bonds are not displaced by later ones. Instead, they are incorporated into a larger narrative of family life that expands over time. The cemetery becomes a visible map of that expansion, charting how relationships accumulate rather than replace one another.

This accumulation of memory has implications for how people understand responsibility and care. When animals are remembered as kin, their lives are integrated into personal histories in ways that shape future choices. Decisions about adopting new animals, caring for them in old age, or facing eventual loss are informed by previous experiences that remain emotionally present. The cemetery thus influences not only how loss is processed, but how future relationships are approached.

The sustained attention given to these graves also suggests that remembrance itself is a form of care that continues beyond death. Just as feeding, grooming, and medical care structured the relationship in life, tending the grave becomes a way of maintaining that ethic of care afterward. This continuity reinforces the idea that kinship does not end at death, but shifts in form. The animal is no longer physically present, but the relationship remains active through memory, ritual, and acknowledgment.

In this way, pet cemeteries serve as sites where people practice an expanded understanding of family that is flexible enough to accommodate loss without erasing connection. They allow individuals to honor relationships that may not be recognized or validated elsewhere, providing a space where the meaning of those bonds is preserved rather than negotiated. The persistence of these practices over decades indicates that they meet a genuine human need, one that is not adequately addressed by existing cultural frameworks.

By observing how people interact with these spaces over time, it becomes clear that pet cemeteries are not about holding on to grief, but about carrying love forward in a form that remains tangible. They provide a language and a place for remembering that resists simplification. In doing so, they affirm that some relationships, once formed, do not diminish simply because the world expects them to.

Section VII – A Lifetime of Unconditional Love

Over the course of a lifetime, loss accumulates, and pet cemeteries quietly record that accumulation in ways that feel both intimate and expansive. The family plots that emerge over decades are not simply collections of graves, but timelines of attachment, marking periods of life defined by the animals who were present within them. Childhood pets, companions during years of work or caregiving, animals who witnessed illness, divorce, solitude, or aging all take their place in the ground, creating a parallel history that runs alongside more conventional milestones.

For many people, these animals provided continuity during times when human relationships were unstable or unavailable. They offered daily presence without condition, grounding routines that anchored identity when other roles were in flux. When such animals die, the loss intersects not only with grief, but with memory of who one was during that period of life. Visiting a grave years later becomes a way of revisiting that earlier self, acknowledging both what has changed and what has endured.

This is particularly evident in older visitors, whose interactions with pet cemeteries often reflect an awareness of limited time ahead. Some speak aloud about nearing reunions, framing their own eventual deaths as moments of reconnection rather than final separation. Others arrange family plots with deliberate foresight, ensuring that future animals will rest beside earlier ones, and that the story of care will continue beyond their own lifespan. These acts suggest that remembrance is not only backward-looking, but anticipatory, shaping how people imagine continuity even as loss becomes more frequent.

Pet cemeteries also reveal how identity is shaped by relationships that fall outside traditional recognition. To have been someone's caregiver, protector, or parent to an animal is to have occupied a role that may not be visible elsewhere, yet remains central to how many people understand themselves. The maintenance of these graves affirms those identities long after the daily routines that sustained them have ended. The cemetery becomes a place where those roles are preserved rather than relinquished.

In acknowledging these bonds, pet cemeteries resist a narrowing of grief that would confine mourning to socially sanctioned categories. They allow people to remember honestly, without ranking loss according to external hierarchies. The depth of care visible in these spaces suggests that what ultimately matters is not whether a relationship fits conventional definitions, but whether it shaped a life in meaningful ways.

As sites of memory, pet cemeteries do not ask to be interpreted or defended. They stand as evidence of relationships that mattered enough to be carried forward, tended, and named. The flowers placed year after year, the careful arrangement of family plots, and the language carved into stone all insist on the same truth: kinship is not determined solely by blood or law, but by lived connection.

In the end, pet cemeteries remind us that remembrance itself is an act of love, one that extends beyond death without needing justification. They show how people choose to honor those who shaped their lives, even when those choices exist at the margins of cultural comfort. Within their quiet boundaries, grief is allowed to remain proportionate to attachment, memory is allowed to persist, and family is defined not by species, but by care.

Chapter Eight

The G.A.R. and The Making of Separate But Equal

Section I - Ritual Before Law

The mechanisms that govern remembrance do not remain confined to the dead. What had been sorted quietly in the cemetery would soon be sorted explicitly in law.

Segregation did not enter American life solely through statutes or court rulings. Long before "separate but equal" became legal doctrine, it was rehearsed, normalized, and made to feel customary through ritual. One of the most influential arenas in which this occurred was commemoration—specifically, the organized remembrance of the Civil War dead.

The Grand Army of the Republic (G.A.R.), founded in 1866, positioned itself as both guardian and interpreter of Union memory. It was a fraternal organization, but it functioned as something more consequential: a cultural authority on sacrifice, loyalty, and national belonging. Through its ceremonies, burial practices, and memorial standards, the G.A.R. helped establish what forms of remembrance were considered proper, dignified, and patriotic.

These decisions mattered because remembrance is not passive. The way a society honors its dead teaches the living how to organize value. Processions, headstone inscriptions, monument placement, and the choreography of public mourning all operate as instruction. They establish expectations about who may be honored collectively, who must be honored separately, and who may be acknowledged only abstractly. Once these expectations are set, they become difficult to question—not because they are explicitly defended, but because they are repeated.

Ritual carries authority precisely because it resists interruption. Memorial Day observances, for example, were not merely moments of reflection; they were annual performances of order. Veterans marched in formation. Wreaths were laid according to rank and affiliation. Speeches followed predictable scripts of sacrifice and unity. Within these carefully managed spaces, deviation appeared inappropriate. To object to arrangement was to risk appearing disrespectful, not dissenting.

In this way, ritual performs a kind of quiet governance. It establishes boundaries without announcing them as rules. It shapes behavior without requiring enforcement. When separation is enacted within ceremonies of honor, it does not present itself as exclusion. It presents itself as decorum.

This distinction is critical. Law invites challenge; ritual discourages it. Legal decisions can be appealed, repealed, or revised. Rituals, by contrast, are absorbed. They are learned through participation and reinforced through repetition until they feel inherited rather than imposed. By the time separation appears in statute, it has often already been rehearsed so thoroughly in public life that it no longer feels like a choice.

The G.A.R. understood this instinctively. By anchoring remembrance in ceremony, it helped translate social hierarchy into emotional order. Reverence became a stabilizing force, smoothing contradictions that might otherwise have provoked conflict. In this environment, segregation did not need to justify itself. It needed only to be observed.

Section II - Veterans, Authority, and Moral Capital

The influence of the Grand Army of the Republic rested less on formal power than on moral capital. Union veterans occupied a privileged position in postwar American society, their service framed as both sacrifice and salvation. They were widely regarded as the men who had preserved the nation, and that perception granted them an authority that extended well beyond their numbers.

G.A.R. posts were not marginal organizations. They functioned as civic centers, particularly in small towns and growing cities where veterans often became visible leaders. Meetings were social as well as ceremonial. Posts organized parades, coordinated Memorial Day observances, raised funds for monuments, and participated in public decision-making about how the war would be remembered. In many communities, G.A.R. halls were among the most respected public spaces, and the organization's endorsement carried weight in local affairs.

This authority was reinforced through proximity to grief. Veterans were not abstract symbols of sacrifice; they were men who had buried comrades, carried wounds, and returned home marked by loss. Their claims to moral standing were rarely challenged openly. To question a veteran's authority was to risk appearing ungrateful or disloyal, particularly in a nation still defining itself through the memory of civil conflict.

Within this context, the G.A.R. became an informal arbiter of legitimacy. Who marched together, who spoke from the platform, and who was recognized publicly as a comrade were decisions that communicated belonging. These choices were not framed as political acts, but they had political consequences. When inclusion was granted, it appeared as honor. When withheld, it was often explained as propriety.

African American Union veterans entered this landscape with a legitimate claim to recognition. Their service had been essential to Union victory, and their participation in the war was frequently cited in Northern rhetoric as proof of the conflict's moral purpose. Yet the authority that elevated white veterans also insulated them from scrutiny when that rhetoric faltered. The G.A.R.'s moral capital allowed it to manage contradiction quietly.

As posts multiplied and expanded into the South, the organization's role as memory custodian became more complex. G.A.R. leaders were often expected to maintain local stability as well as national narrative. Decisions about membership, meeting attendance, and ceremonial participation were shaped not only by ideology, but by perceived necessity. Authority, once established, tends to prioritize continuity over consistency.

This dynamic matters because moral capital can be spent in more than one direction. It can be used to challenge injustice, but it can also be used to smooth over conflict. In the case of the G.A.R., the latter often prevailed. Separation, when enacted by an organization widely associated with sacrifice and patriotism, acquired a veneer of legitimacy. It did not need to announce itself as exclusion. It could present as stewardship.

By the early 1890s, this accumulation of authority meant that the G.A.R.'s internal arrangements were rarely questioned from outside. The organization's practices appeared settled, customary, and beyond dispute. What remained unresolved, however, were the tensions within its own ranks—tensions that would soon force separation to move from informal practice to structured policy.

Section III — Fracture Within the Ranks

By the early 1890s, the Grand Army of the Republic was no longer able to manage racial tension through quiet custom alone. What had once been handled informally through seating arrangements, social cues, or selective participation began to surface as an explicit institutional problem. The cause of this shift was not abstract ideology, but lived pressure within the organization itself, as established practices proved insufficient to contain growing demands for inclusion.

African American veterans of the Union Army increasingly asserted their right to full participation within G.A.R. posts. Their claims were direct and grounded in service. They had worn Union blue, endured the same campaigns, and borne the same losses as their white counterparts. Many sought not symbolic acknowledgment, but practical inclusion: the right to attend meetings, vote on post business, hold office, and participate fully in commemorative rituals.

These demands exposed a contradiction the G.A.R. could no longer postpone. The organization's public identity rested on a narrative of Union victory tied to emancipation. Yet its internal practices increasingly reflected the racial hierarchies of the society in which it operated. For white veterans, particularly those who had relocated to the South, this contradiction was not theoretical. Integrated posts risked social backlash, economic consequence, and local instability.

As these pressures intensified, segregation within the G.A.R. began to formalize. Some posts quietly discouraged Black participation by restricting meeting access or limiting ceremonial roles. Others moved more decisively, establishing separate posts for Black veterans while maintaining nominal allegiance to the same national organization. On paper, membership remained intact. In practice, equality fractured along local lines.

This arrangement was presented as pragmatic rather than ideological. Separation was framed as a way to preserve harmony, protect the organization's standing, and avoid confrontation. Yet pragmatism did not resolve the underlying tension. It displaced it, allowing the organization to function without confronting the implications of its own practices.

Black veterans recognized the distinction immediately. Separate posts meant reduced influence, diminished visibility, and exclusion from the symbolic center of remembrance. Participation without proximity carried little weight. To be honored apart was to be reminded that honor itself was conditional, contingent on access to shared ritual and authority.

Within the G.A.R., these divisions produced increasing discomfort. White members who embraced segregation struggled to reconcile it with the organization's founding rhetoric. Those who opposed it found themselves in the minority, constrained by local realities and institutional inertia. National leadership hesitated to intervene decisively, wary of provoking schism in an organization built on unity and shared sacrifice.

What had once been managed through custom was becoming too visible to ignore.

The result was a growing sense of instability. The G.A.R. had become large, influential, and symbolically powerful, yet internally conflicted. Its rituals projected cohesion even as its membership fractured. Preserving the organization's public narrative required a way to stabilize practice without reopening internal debate.

That need created an opening. Segregation, if left as a matter of choice, demanded justification, and justification invited conflict. What the G.A.R. required was not consensus, but clarity, a mechanism that could transform contested practice into settled order.

The conflict within the ranks did not demand innovation. It demanded permission.

What the G.A.R. revealed at this stage was not ideological confusion, but institutional fatigue. The organization did not lack moral language or historical justification; it lacked a mechanism that would allow its existing practices to continue without constant renegotiation. Ritual could establish separation, but ritual alone could not stabilize it indefinitely.

Section IV — Northern Memory Meets Southern Reality

The internal divisions within the Grand Army of the Republic did not exist in isolation. They unfolded within a South still deeply invested in its own memory of the war, a memory shaped by defeat, resentment, and careful reconstruction. Former Confederate states were not neutral ground, and every public ritual, every parade, and every veterans' meeting took place under the scrutiny of communities that had not accepted the moral narrative of Union victory, even if they had accepted its political outcome.

For white Union veterans who relocated southward, this created a delicate balancing act. They arrived bearing the authority of victory and the symbolism of emancipation, yet they lived among populations that remained hostile to both. Integrated G.A.R. posts risked provoking local opposition and social friction, not only from former Confederates but from white Southerners invested in maintaining racial hierarchy. The presence of Black veterans as equals in commemorative space was perceived less as reconciliation than as escalation, introducing tensions that extended beyond the organization itself.

This situation exposed a vulnerability within Northern memory as it was practiced rather than proclaimed. The Union had framed the war as a moral struggle, fought to preserve the nation and end slavery, and that narrative depended in part on the visible recognition of Black service. Yet when Black veterans sought full participation within G.A.R. posts, particularly in Southern communities, their inclusion threatened the stability Northern veterans hoped to secure. What had functioned as a moral claim in abstraction increasingly appeared as a logistical problem in practice, one that required negotiation rather than affirmation.

Southern observers were attentive to this contradiction. In some Confederate veterans' organizations, Black men who had served the Confederacy, often in support roles and later claimed as soldiers, were permitted limited association. These gestures did not represent racial equality, but they carried symbolic weight within the postwar memory economy. They allowed Southern groups to argue that even they could acknowledge Black participation, while the victorious North struggled to align its commemorative practices with its professed ideals.

The comparison proved rhetorically effective. It cast the Union's moral narrative as selective and self-serving, reinforcing Southern skepticism toward claims that emancipation had been the war's central purpose. For the G.A.R., this dynamic extended beyond embarrassment. It raised questions about legitimacy, authority, and consistency that the organization was ill equipped to answer internally.

Public exclusion of Black veterans risked confirming Southern accusations of hypocrisy, while full inclusion threatened to destabilize local relationships and fracture posts from within. The G.A.R.

increasingly found itself negotiating between two audiences, one that expected moral coherence and another that demanded racial separation. Each audience exerted pressure, and neither could be fully satisfied without cost.

Within this environment, segregation began to appear less as an injustice requiring debate than as a practical arrangement to be managed. Separate posts, separate meetings, and separate ceremonial roles allowed the organization to project unity while accommodating local expectations. These measures offered temporary stability, but they remained precarious so long as they rested on discretionary choice exercised by individual posts.

Choice carried consequences. Decisions invited scrutiny, and scrutiny invited conflict, particularly when those decisions exposed the moral tensions the organization sought to contain. What the G.A.R. increasingly lacked was a framework that could remove the burden of justification from local leadership. Post commanders needed a way to explain separation without reopening debates about the war's meaning or the organization's obligations.

They required an authority capable of absorbing responsibility for the arrangement and rendering it unremarkable. The tension between Northern memory and Southern reality made clear that ritual alone could no longer sustain the organization's position. Its practices had moved ahead of its explanations, and what had begun as informal custom now required confirmation that lay beyond individual discretion.

At this point, the problem was no longer how to justify separation, but how to remove it from debate altogether.

That confirmation would not emerge from within the ranks. It would arrive from outside the organization, carrying with it the weight of law rather than memory.

Section V — Plessy v. Ferguson as Institutional Relief

When the Supreme Court issued its decision in *Plessy v. Ferguson* in 1896, it did not introduce segregation into American life, nor did it resolve the moral contradictions already embedded within it. What the decision offered instead was stabilization. Practices that had been enacted unevenly through custom, ritual, and local discretion were given a legal frame that rendered them ordinary rather than contested.

For organizations like the Grand Army of the Republic, *Plessy* functioned less as instruction than as permission—a means of converting strained practice into settled order.

For organizations such as the Grand Army of the Republic, this distinction carried significant weight. The doctrine of "separate but equal" did not require institutions to invent new arrangements so much as it validated those already in place. It relieved organizations of the ongoing obligation to justify separation repeatedly, allowing them to point to law rather than to custom, necessity, or preference. What had been an internal problem of governance could now be aligned with an external standard.

Within the G.A.R., the timing aligned closely with mounting internal strain. By the mid-1890s, posts across the South were attempting to balance competing pressures: the desire to preserve Union memory, the need to maintain local stability, and the increasingly insistent demands of Black veterans for full participation. Each decision carried consequence. Inclusion risked backlash from surrounding communities, while exclusion demanded explanation to members and invited internal dispute. Neither approach offered durability.

The *Plessy* decision altered this balance by affirming segregation as constitutionally permissible. In doing so, it supplied a language of compliance that shifted moral agency away from local decision-making. Separation no longer required debate within posts or justification to membership. It could be framed instead as adherence to established legal principle. Black veterans could remain members of the G.A.R. in name, preserving the organization's national narrative of loyalty and sacrifice, while being excluded from meetings, ceremonies, and shared spaces at the local level.

The contradiction inherent in this arrangement did not vanish under these conditions. It was instead absorbed into institutional routine. A distinction emerged between abstract membership and embodied participation, one that allowed the G.A.R. to claim inclusivity at the organizational level while permitting segregation to govern lived experience. Law functioned as a buffer in this process, insulating the institution from the need to reconcile its public identity with its internal practices.

It is important to note that *Plessy* did not mandate segregation within voluntary organizations such as the G.A.R.. It rendered segregation defensible. That difference clarifies the decision's function as institutional relief rather than directive. Posts were not compelled to segregate; they were permitted to do so without consequence, a permission that carried substantial practical effect.

Once separation was sanctioned in this way, the burden of proof shifted. Those who objected to segregation were now required to argue against established law rather than against discretionary practice. What had previously been a matter of internal negotiation became framed as compliance. Debate narrowed, and resistance carried increased cost, both socially and institutionally.

Through this shift, *Plessy* contributed to stabilizing the G.A.R.'s internal divisions by removing them from the realm of choice. Segregation could be enacted consistently across posts without appearing arbitrary or hypocritical. Organizational rituals such as parades, memorial services, and cemetery observances could proceed uninterrupted, projecting cohesion even as participation remained unequal.

The decision also resolved a persistent optics problem for the G.A.R. in the South. Separation could now be presented not as Northern hypocrisy, but as alignment with national standard. The moral narrative of Union victory remained publicly intact, even as its implications were quietly constrained in practice.

This pattern, in which law formalizes practices institutions have already adopted in order to resolve internal contradiction, recurs throughout the management of memory. Legal authority does not always initiate cultural change. Often, it arrives to consolidate arrangements already in motion, converting contested choices into background conditions.

For the G.A.R., *Plessy v. Ferguson* did not settle questions of racial equality. It settled questions of organizational stability. By codifying separation, the Court enabled the organization to continue functioning as a guardian of Union memory without confronting the unresolved legacies of the war itself, allowing segregation to recede from explanation and become part of the institutional landscape.

Section VI — Separation Without Schism

Once segregation was legally sanctioned, it no longer needed to announce itself. Within the Grand Army of the Republic, separation ceased to function as a point of active contention and instead became a condition of ordinary operation. The organization did not fracture under this shift, but adjusted to it, incorporating separation into its routines without the appearance of rupture.

This adjustment unfolded gradually and with little overt conflict, which contributed to its effectiveness. White G.A.R. posts continued their activities with minimal visible disruption. Meetings proceeded according to schedule, Memorial Day observances followed established scripts, and parades traced familiar routes through public space. The outward form of unity remained intact, reinforced through repetition and display. At the same time, Black veterans were increasingly confined to parallel structures, including separate posts, separate gatherings, and separate commemorative roles that reproduced the appearance of inclusion while withholding its substance.

What mattered most in this process was not the existence of separation itself, but the manner in which it was presented. Segregation did not register as a rupture within the G.A.R.'s organizational life. It appeared instead as order, embedded quietly into the rhythms of institutional practice.

Cemeteries provided one of the clearest sites through which this order became visible. Burial practices translated organizational decisions into spatial arrangements that required no explanation. Segregated sections, distinct plots, and variations in monument style communicated hierarchy through placement rather than proclamation. Once established, these arrangements rarely drew comment. They were maintained through routine processes such as maintenance schedules, procession routes, and the choreography of remembrance. To a casual observer, the cemetery appeared unified, its internal divisions discernible only through sustained attention.

This spatialization of memory carried particular significance because it rendered separation into landscape. Boundaries, once drawn, no longer required defense. They needed only to be preserved. Each ceremony reenacted the arrangement, and each visit reaffirmed it. Over time, separation came to feel less like a decision and more like inheritance, something encountered rather than chosen.

Within the G.A.R., this produced a form of organizational stability that obscured inequality without resolving it. Black veterans were not expelled, nor was their service formally denied. They remained part of the Union's abstract memory, acknowledged in rhetoric and occasionally in print. Yet their exclusion from shared space ensured that their presence did not unsettle the organization's emotional equilibrium or disrupt the narratives its rituals sustained.

The distinction between recognition and proximity shaped this outcome. By allowing Black veterans to belong in name while remaining absent in practice, the G.A.R. avoided open conflict. Its moral capital remained largely intact, and its public rituals continued without interruption. The costs of segregation were displaced away from the institution itself and absorbed by those relegated to its margins.

As time passed, this arrangement reinforced itself. New members entered an organization where separation was already normalized. Younger veterans absorbed expectations implicitly, learning the boundaries of participation without formal instruction. The absence of debate signaled resolution, even as the underlying inequities persisted.

In this way, separation endured without producing schism or reconciliation. Once stabilized, segregation no longer depended on hostility or overt enforcement. It required maintenance rather than justification. Within the G.A.R., as within other institutions responsible for managing memory, that maintenance was accomplished through routine. Choices that had once demanded explanation were now embedded in practice, already inscribed in space, movement, and habit, and therefore no longer required articulation.

Section VII — Memory Codified

The history of the Grand Army of the Republic's internal divisions reveals a pattern that extends beyond veterans' organizations or the late nineteenth century. What might initially appear as a legal story is more accurately understood as a cultural one. Law did not create segregation within the G.A.R. so much as it formalized arrangements that ritual, space, and custom had already rendered operational.

The sequence by which this occurred is significant. When separation is enacted first through ceremony, habit, and spatial arrangement, it acquires legitimacy before it acquires legality. By the time law intervenes, its function is less to impose order than to stabilize it. *Plessy v. Ferguson* did not resolve moral contradiction within the G.A.R.. It resolved institutional strain, allowing memory organizations to continue functioning without confronting the implications of their own practices.

Once codified, segregation no longer required ongoing explanation. It became embedded in infrastructure, taking form in meeting halls, procession routes, cemetery layouts, and commemorative calendars. These systems reproduced themselves quietly over time. They instructed new participants without explicit guidance and preserved hierarchy without argument. The absence of visible conflict signaled resolution, even as inequity remained present within the structure itself.

This process helps clarify why memory operates as such an effective site of social regulation. Remembrance appears backward-looking, oriented toward what has already occurred, yet the organization of memory shapes expectations in the present. It teaches who belongs together, who may be honored alongside whom, and whose presence must be managed carefully to preserve order. When memory is arranged spatially and ritualized through repetition, its lessons are absorbed rather than debated.

The G.A.R. chapter demonstrates that segregation did not require universal agreement in order to endure. It required routinization. Once separation was woven into acts of reverence, it could be maintained without hostility and defended without speech. Memory assumed the work that policy alone could not accomplish, reinforcing arrangements through practice rather than proclamation.

This pattern appears repeatedly in other contexts. Burial practices along the Oregon Trail, shaped initially by necessity rather than ideology, illustrate how improvised arrangements harden into tradition. What begins as pragmatism often becomes precedent, and over time those precedents acquire authority simply through persistence.

Attending to how memory is codified through ritual, repetition, and space makes visible the mechanisms by which social orders survive their own contradictions. What is remembered together, what is remembered apart, and what is permitted to fade entirely are not incidental outcomes. They are shaped through practice, stabilized through repetition, and maintained without requiring continual justification.

Chapter Nine

Women and the Shape of Memory

Section I - Memory Without Monuments

The history of cultural memory is often told through what endures visibly—stone, text, architecture, and institution. Monuments rise. Archives expand. Names are preserved through repetition and citation. Yet much of what societies remember does not survive in this way. It is carried instead through practice, instruction, and continuity that leaves little physical trace, and women's memory work has historically occupied this second register.

Excluded from formal authority, women rarely controlled the mechanisms that produce public remembrance. They did not commission monuments or author official histories. Their contributions were more often embedded in systems rather than attributed within them, with knowledge passing through hands, classrooms, households, and informal networks rather than through title or inscription. This difference has consequences for how memory appears.

When women shape memory, they tend to do so relationally rather than declaratively. Their work emphasizes transmission over proclamation and continuity over permanence. What is preserved is not a single authoritative account, but a way of thinking, teaching, or organizing knowledge that can be carried forward without requiring recognition of its source. This does not make women's memory work weaker; it makes it harder to see.

Fields dominated by women—education, home economics, social reform, librarianship, nursing, early psychology—have often been dismissed as secondary or derivative. Yet these disciplines shaped everyday life, professional standards, and cultural norms far more directly than many fields considered foundational. Their influence persists precisely because it was absorbed into practice rather than enshrined as theory. The absence of monuments is therefore not the absence of impact.

Women's contributions to cultural memory are frequently invisible not because they failed to endure, but because they endured too well. Once absorbed into systems of knowledge, they no longer appeared exceptional. Their origins faded as their effects became ordinary. This pattern mirrors others traced throughout this book. Memory does not disappear when it is denied public recognition; it relocates and adapts to available structures. When formal avenues are closed, it survives through form rather than declaration.

Understanding the shape of women's memory work requires shifting attention away from what is named and toward what persists. It requires reading continuity where attribution is missing and influence where authorship has been stripped away. Women have always shaped cultural memory; the difference is that they have rarely been allowed to sign it.

Section II - Scholarship as Shelter

When women have shaped cultural memory most effectively, they have often done so by working within disciplines that offered limited protection but broad reach. Scholarship became a form of shelter, not because it conferred authority, but because it allowed continuity. Within these spaces, women could preserve knowledge that was otherwise vulnerable to dismissal, distortion, or disappearance.

This shelter was rarely secure. Fields that women built or sustained were frequently categorized as secondary, domestic, or applied, and their intellectual labor was framed as supportive rather than foundational. Yet these same fields shaped how culture understood itself at the most intimate levels: education, ritual, symbolism, ethics, and daily practice.

Patricia Monaghan's work exemplifies this pattern without standing apart from it. Writing at the intersection of mythology, women's studies, and cultural history, she produced frameworks that preserved women-centered symbolic knowledge at a moment when such material was either marginalized or fragmented across disciplines. Her scholarship did not seek monumentality; it sought coherence. Symbols were gathered, contextualized, and made legible again, not as relics, but as living systems of meaning.

This approach was not unique to Monaghan, nor was it anomalous. Women working in adjacent fields—folklore, anthropology, home economics, religious studies, education—often performed similar labor. They stabilized knowledge by organizing it, teaching it, and translating it across audiences. Their work endured not because it was canonized, but because it was used.

Scholarship, in this sense, functioned less as a platform than as a vessel. It carried memory forward even when attribution was stripped away. Concepts entered circulation while names faded. Frameworks persisted while their architects were softened, reframed, or quietly sidelined.

The protective quality of this work lay in its adaptability. Women's scholarship often crossed boundaries that more rigid disciplines resisted. It moved between academic and public audiences, between theory and practice, between archive and lived experience. This flexibility allowed memory to survive institutional neglect, even as it made authorship easier to detach.

Once absorbed into broader discourse, ideas no longer required their originators to remain visible. Symbolic systems, pedagogical methods, and interpretive lenses became part of the intellectual environment. Their persistence was taken as evidence of inevitability rather than labor.

This is the paradox of scholarship as shelter. It preserves memory by embedding it so thoroughly that it becomes difficult to trace. What survives does so at the cost of recognition. The work endures. The worker recedes.

Women's influence on cultural memory has often followed this path. Their scholarship did not announce itself as authoritative, yet it shaped what later authorities would cite, adapt, or assume. The shelter held. The names did not.

Section III - Transmission Over Attribution

Where women have been denied authority over archives, they have exercised influence through transmission. Knowledge moved not through formal citation or institutional recognition, but through teaching, mentorship, and repetition across generations. What mattered was not that a name was attached to an idea, but that the idea continued to function.

This form of memory work privileges continuity over ownership. Concepts are passed hand to hand, absorbed into practice, and adapted to new contexts without requiring acknowledgement of origin. Within this system, survival takes precedence over recognition. Memory endures because it is useful, not because it is credited.

This pattern is especially visible in disciplines shaped by women. Pedagogical methods, ethical frameworks, and interpretive lenses are often inherited rather than referenced. Students learn how to see before they learn who taught them to see, and the labor that shaped that vision remains present in form even as authorship fades.

Mentorship plays a central role in this process. Women have often taught women—sometimes formally, often informally—creating chains of transmission that operate alongside official curricula. These networks do not require permanence of institution. They rely on presence, repetition, and trust. Knowledge moves through conversation, example, and shared practice.

The effectiveness of this model lies in its resilience. Because transmission does not depend on formal recognition, it is less vulnerable to exclusion. When women are pushed out of institutions or disciplines are redefined to minimize their contributions, the knowledge itself does not vanish. It reappears elsewhere, carried by those who learned it.

At the same time, this resilience carries a cost. Transmission without attribution makes memory difficult to defend. Ideas that circulate without names are easily appropriated, reframed, or dismissed. Their origins become ambiguous. Their authority is diluted even as their influence persists.

This dynamic explains why women's intellectual labor is so often described as diffuse. The diffusion is not accidental. It is the result of a system in which visibility is restricted, but continuity is possible. Women's work survives by becoming embedded, not by being acknowledged.

Transmission also shapes the ethical posture of memory. When knowledge is passed through relationship rather than decree, it carries obligation rather than command. Students inherit not just information, but responsibility—to use, adapt, and carry forward what they have been given. Memory becomes a shared burden rather than a proprietary claim.

This form of inheritance stands in contrast to monumental memory, which asserts permanence through inscription and authority. Transmission accepts impermanence in exchange for survival. It allows memory to move, change, and persist without relying on recognition from systems that have historically withheld it.

Understanding this mechanism clarifies why women's contributions to cultural memory are both pervasive and difficult to trace. They are not absent. They are everywhere, carried quietly through practice rather than proclaimed through authorship.

Section IV - Respectability as Camouflage

For much of modern history, women's intellectual labor has survived by aligning itself with respectability. This alignment was rarely chosen freely. It emerged as a strategy for persistence in environments where overt authority was inaccessible or actively denied. By operating within fields deemed acceptable—domestic, moral, pedagogical—women were able to continue shaping cultural memory without provoking the resistance that more visible power invites. Respectability offered cover.

Disciplines associated with care, education, or everyday life were permitted space because they were not perceived as sites of influence. Home economics, for example, was framed as practical instruction rather than cultural engineering, even as it standardized norms of nutrition, hygiene, and family structure that shaped generations. Teaching was treated as service rather than scholarship, despite its role in determining what knowledge would be carried forward and how it would be understood.

This framing mattered. Work labeled respectable could circulate widely without being scrutinized as ideological. It appeared neutral, helpful, and apolitical. In reality, it carried values, assumptions, and interpretive frameworks that quietly reorganized social understanding. Memory entered culture through habit rather than proclamation.

Respectability also softened resistance to women's authority. When influence arrived disguised as instruction or care, it was less likely to be challenged. This allowed women to occupy positions of continuity—teachers, librarians, editors, researchers—where they controlled access to information even if they did not control its formal validation.

At the same time, camouflage exacted a cost. To remain acceptable, women's work often had to downplay ambition, theory, or critique. Ideas were presented as common sense rather than intervention. Innovation was framed as refinement. Authority was exercised indirectly, through structure rather than declaration.

This indirectness contributed to later erasure. Work that appeared merely practical was rarely preserved as intellectual history. Its architects were remembered, if at all, as facilitators rather than originators. The camouflage that enabled survival also obscured authorship.

Yet camouflage does not negate agency. It reveals adaptation. Women learned to shape memory in ways that avoided confrontation with systems designed to exclude them. They embedded influence within routine, pedagogy, and practice. Over time, what had been introduced cautiously became foundational. Respectability allowed memory to settle into place.

This pattern mirrors others traced throughout the book. When direct authority is unavailable, power migrates to form. It expresses itself through repetition, normalization, and expectation. Respectability, in this context, functions not as compliance, but as strategy.

By understanding respectability as camouflage, the persistence of women's influence becomes clearer. What survived did so not because it was harmless, but because it appeared so. Memory was preserved by learning how to pass unnoticed.

Section V - When Memory Loses Its Name

When women succeed in shaping systems that endure, their work often becomes invisible precisely because it has succeeded. Memory does not disappear, but attribution does, leaving structure without signature and practice without provenance.

This is one of the paradoxes of women's intellectual labor. The more fully it is integrated into daily life, institutional routine, or professional standard, the less likely it is to be remembered as authored work. Ideas become normalized. Methods become expected. Disciplines begin to appear inevitable rather than constructed. In this way, memory survives by shedding names.

Fields shaped by women frequently undergo this transition once they stabilize. What begins as deliberate intervention—designed curricula, organized bodies of knowledge, pedagogical frameworks—gradually hardens into background assumption. The work is no longer perceived as intellectual labor at all. It becomes "how things are done."

This loss of attribution is not the result of individual failure or neglect. It is structural. Systems are built to preserve outcomes, not origins.

Once a framework proves useful, the system no longer requires the presence of its architects. Their continued visibility would introduce contingency, reminding others that what exists could have been otherwise.

For women, this contingency is particularly threatening to institutional order. Acknowledging women as originators complicates narratives of authority, hierarchy, and expertise. It introduces questions the system does not need to answer in order to function. Memory resolves this tension by keeping the work and discarding the name.

The process is subtle. There is rarely a moment of erasure. Instead, attribution thins over time. References become generalized. Contributions are reframed as collaborative, supportive, or administrative. The language used to describe women's work shifts away from innovation and toward maintenance. What was once recognized as creation is later described as stewardship.

This shift has consequences for how women are remembered. Their presence recedes from record not because they were absent, but because they were embedded. Their influence becomes difficult to trace because it is everywhere. The very success of their labor ensures that it will no longer be marked as labor at all. What is preserved is function. What is lost is authorship.

This dynamic also reshapes how later generations understand the past. When systems appear fully formed, they invite origin stories that center power elsewhere. Women become participants rather than builders, facilitators rather than architects. Their role is remembered as supportive rather than directive, even when the historical record suggests otherwise.

The loss of names does not mean the loss of memory. It means memory has been absorbed into form. But this absorption comes at a cost. Without attribution, women's authority becomes harder to claim, defend, or extend. Their work can be revised, redirected, or dismantled without acknowledgment of what is being altered or whose labor is being undone.

Understanding this process is essential to understanding women's place in cultural memory. Women are not absent from history because they failed to leave a mark. They are difficult to see because the marks they left were incorporated so completely that they ceased to be recognized as marks at all. Memory does not forget them; it uses them.

Section VI - The Cost of Being Remembered Indirectly

There is a point at which women's memory work can no longer be protected by camouflage. When scholarship does more than stabilize existing norms—when it requires those norms to be rethought—the system's tolerance ends. At that point, memory does not simply thin. It resists.

This is where figures such as Jane Ellen Harrison, Marija Gimbutas, and Helen Diner come into view. All three worked in areas that cut close to the foundations of cultural authority: myth, religion, prehistory, and symbolic order. Their scholarship did not merely add material to existing frameworks; it questioned the frameworks themselves. They asked how religious meaning formed, whose stories were preserved, and what had been erased in the transition to patriarchal systems of power. In doing so, they exposed memory not as neutral inheritance, but as curated tradition, and that exposure carried a cost.

Harrison's work reshaped classical studies by insisting that ritual, myth, and communal practice—not elite philosophy alone—were central to understanding ancient religion. Her insights influenced the field profoundly, yet her authority remained conditional. She was cited, debated, and relied upon, but never allowed to fully reframe the canon she helped redefine. Her work survived, but often detached from the challenge it posed.

Gimbutas encountered a sharper version of the same resistance. Her research into Old European cultures and symbolic systems confronted deeply held assumptions about the origins of civilization, religion, and gendered power. Rather than engage fully with the implications of her findings, much of the field chose to discredit her methodology, label her speculative, or relegate her work to the margins. What could not be absorbed was instead dismissed.

Diner's scholarship followed a similar trajectory. Her work on myth and women's religious history offered alternative readings that unsettled linear, male-centered narratives. Like Harrison and Gimbutas, she contributed ideas that circulated unevenly—taken up in fragments, referenced selectively, and stripped of their more disruptive force.

Together, these women illustrate a critical boundary in women's relationship to cultural memory. When women build systems that can function within existing structures, their labor may be absorbed and anonymized. When women produce knowledge that requires those structures to change, memory responds differently. It does not simply forget. It constrains.

This constraint takes recognizable forms. Critique replaces engagement. Tone becomes the focus rather than substance. Work is labeled marginal, intuitive, or ideological rather than analytical. Authority is questioned not through direct refutation, but through doubt cast on legitimacy itself. The work remains visible enough to be known, but never stable enough to be foundational.

Being remembered indirectly comes at a cost beyond recognition. It limits what later scholars feel permitted to do with the work. Ideas survive without sponsorship. Frameworks circulate without endorsement. Influence persists, but authority does not.

For women, this creates a double bind. To be absorbed is to risk losing authorship. To resist absorption is to risk marginalization. Either way, memory is managed to protect the existing order. The difference lies in how visible that management becomes.

Harrison, Gimbutas, and Diner mark the point where management can no longer remain quiet. Their work makes the editing process visible by refusing to fit cleanly into inherited narratives. In doing so, it reveals that the issue is not women's capacity to produce knowledge, but the system's willingness to accommodate its consequences.

This is the cost of being remembered indirectly: not disappearance, but containment; not silence, but distortion. The work survives, but never on its own terms.

Section VII - Memory That Refuses Erasure

Despite the constraints placed upon it, women's memory work does not disappear. It persists in altered form, carried forward through structure, practice, and repetition even when recognition is denied. The absence of names does not signal the absence of influence; it signals that influence has been rendered ordinary.

This persistence is not accidental. Women's memory labor has survived precisely because it learned how to move through systems that did not fully acknowledge it. When monuments were unavailable, memory took relational form. When authority was denied, it embedded itself in pedagogy. When attribution thinned, transmission continued. What could not be preserved openly was preserved indirectly.

This indirect survival is both strength and limitation. It allows knowledge to endure beyond the individuals who produced it, but it also obscures the conditions under which that knowledge was created. Memory remains, but the story of how it came to be—who carried it, who shaped it, who paid the cost of sustaining it—becomes increasingly difficult to recover.

Yet erasure is never complete. The work leaves traces. Patterns emerge. Gaps invite attention. When systems rely on omission to maintain coherence, those omissions eventually become visible, not because they are named, but because their effects accumulate. Questions arise where explanations no longer suffice. Authority begins to look inherited rather than earned.

Women's presence in cultural memory often appears this way: not as a continuous narrative, but as pressure. Their influence surfaces in moments of instability, in fields that cannot quite explain their own foundations, in traditions that persist without clear origin. Memory does not forget them so much as struggle to account for them.

This chapter has traced how women have carried memory forward through scholarship, transmission, institutional labor, and strategic invisibility. It has also shown the cost of that endurance: loss of authorship, constrained authority, and partial recognition. What remains unresolved is not whether women shaped cultural memory, but why that shaping required silence.

That question cannot be answered by examining women alone. The mechanisms that demanded camouflage, that thinned attribution, and that constrained authority operate more broadly. They decide what parts of a life are relevant enough to preserve, which relationships count, which identities are assumed, and which contradictions must remain unspoken. Women's memory work makes these mechanisms visible because it has been forced to navigate them so persistently.

Memory that refuses erasure does not announce itself. It accumulates. It waits. It reappears where it is least convenient and most necessary. The fact that women's influence continues to surface, despite the systems designed to smooth it away, suggests that memory is never entirely manageable. The next chapter turns directly to those mechanisms of management: how lives are edited, how defaults replace evidence, and how history remembers people not as they were, but as they were allowed to be.

Chapter Ten

Allowed to Be Remembered, Forbidden to Be Known

Section I – The Danger of Selective Memory

Selective memory is routinely misrepresented as benign—a polite euphemism that disguises its real function. In public life, it is defended as restraint: a way of honoring achievement without intruding on privacy, preserving dignity without unnecessary detail. This defense is not merely misleading; it is dishonest. Selective memory does not operate as discretion. It operates as control.

At the cultural level, selective memory is not a failure of recall or a limitation of knowledge. It is a deliberate practice. Institutions decide what belongs in biographies, plaques, textbooks, archives, and commemorative narratives. Families decide which relationships are named and which are softened. Scholars decide which interpretations are permitted and which are dismissed as speculative. These decisions are not accidental. They reflect and enforce norms about respectability, legibility, and belonging.

Selective memory is not about forgetting. It is about editing.

The danger lies in the precision of that editing. Selective memory preserves enough truth to appear honest while excising what would disrupt dominant assumptions. Names remain. Achievements are celebrated. Relationships are acknowledged—but only in forms that align with heterosexual expectation. The result is not absence, but distortion. Lives are remembered in outline while their organizing realities are removed.

This practice is especially visible in the treatment of prominent gay and lesbian figures. Their public contributions are elevated while their intimate lives are rendered irrelevant, ambiguous, or politely unknowable. Long-term partnerships are reduced to "friendships." Shared households become conveniences. Emotional devotion is reframed as temperament. Sexual orientation—when it appears at all—is treated as incidental rather than constitutive. Heterosexuality remains the unspoken default, and queerness becomes optional.

This is not a matter of respecting historical difference or avoiding anachronism. Sexual orientation shaped lives long before it was named in modern terms. It structured attachment, risk, secrecy, companionship, and loss. To remove it from the narrative is not historical caution; it is historical falsification. What remains may appear coherent, but it explains very little.

Selective memory functions as a strategy of normalization and exclusion. It allows societies to benefit from queer lives while denying their truth. Achievement can be celebrated without challenging the frameworks that once constrained it. Legacy can be preserved without reckoning with exclusion. The past is kept comfortable by being rendered incomplete.

The ethical failure here is not the withholding of private detail. It is the treatment of entire dimensions of identity as expendable—discarded once they threaten the stability of dominant norms. When sexual orientation is erased, the resulting narrative does not become more respectful. It becomes complicit.

This chapter is not concerned with why individuals sometimes struggled to articulate their identities under conditions of constraint. It is concerned with what happens when erasure persists after recognition becomes possible. It examines selective memory not as a survival strategy, but as a cultural practice that continues to shape whose lives are allowed to be remembered in full.

Selective memory is not a flaw of recollection. It is a politics of remembrance. Its consequences are not abstract. They determine whose relationships count, whose histories are legible, and whose lives are permitted to exist without distortion.

Section II - Cultural Permission and Forbidden Memory

Selective memory does not arise spontaneously from individual limitation; it is produced and enforced by culture. Societies do not merely influence what can be remembered—they regulate it. Through language, institutions, family structures, and historical convention, cultures determine which lives are intelligible, which identities are speakable, and which forms of attachment are allowed to appear in public memory at all. What cannot be accommodated within these limits is not simply ignored; it is disciplined into silence.

Few aspects of identity have been more thoroughly managed through silence than sexual orientation. Gay and lesbian lives were not erased primarily through open confrontation, but through omission. They were left unnamed, unrecorded, and unacknowledged, creating the impression that they did not exist in meaningful numbers or forms. This absence was not accidental. It was essential to the maintenance of compulsory heterosexuality, which depends less on enforcement than on inevitability.

Compulsory heterosexuality functions by presenting itself as natural and universal. It does not require that alternative orientations be actively disproven; it requires only that they be rendered invisible or unintelligible. When heterosexuality is assumed rather than articulated, it becomes the default explanation for intimacy, attachment, and desire. Anything that does not conform to that explanation is reassigned a different meaning.

In this system, same-sex desire is not remembered as desire. It is remembered as friendship, admiration, loyalty, intensity, or confusion. Romantic attachment between women is reframed as emotional closeness. Lifelong partnerships between men are recorded as companionship or convenience. The language of intimacy is preserved, but its meaning is displaced. Memory adapts by substituting what is permitted for what is forbidden.

This substitution does not diminish the importance of sexual orientation; it underscores it. Being gay or lesbian is not a minor biographical detail that can be excised without consequence. It shapes how a person experiences the world—how they form attachments, navigate risk, interpret social cues, imagine futures, and locate themselves within communities. To erase sexual orientation is therefore to distort the architecture of a life. What remains may appear coherent, but it is incomplete.

The cultural demand for normality exerts pressure not only on public narratives, but on private ones. Families learn what can be spoken and what must be softened or avoided. Biographies are edited. Letters are curated. Stories are retold in ways that align with acceptable norms. Over time, these practices teach both individuals and communities how to remember selectively. What is not named gradually loses its place in shared memory, even when it shaped a life profoundly.

This process does not require malicious intent. Erasure is often justified as protection—of reputation, of family harmony, of historical dignity. Silence is framed as discretion or kindness. Yet the effect is cumulative. Each omission reinforces the idea that heterosexuality is the only meaningful framework through which lives can be understood. Each reframing teaches future generations what not to see.

Selective memory, in this context, becomes a cultural achievement. It allows societies to maintain the appearance of continuity and moral order while absorbing lives that do not fit their ideals. The cost of this coherence is borne by those whose experiences must be translated into acceptable forms or lost altogether.

This helps explain why recognition of sexual orientation so often occurs later in life, or retrospectively. The memories were always present, but they were stored without names. Without language, memory cannot organize itself into identity. It remains fragmented, surfacing as unease, intensity, or longing rather than clarity. Only when cultural permission expands—through visibility, community, or changing norms—do these memories return with coherence.

Forbidden memory does not announce itself as such. It appears as absence. As gaps in family stories. As biographical silences. As relationships that mattered deeply but were never fully explained. To notice these absences is not to impose modern categories on the past, but to recognize the power structures that shaped what could be remembered.

Understanding selective memory in this way shifts the question from individual psychology to cultural accountability. It asks not why people failed to know themselves sooner, but what conditions made knowing impossible. It reveals how normality is preserved not only through what is said, but through what is never allowed to be said at all.

In the sections that follow, this dynamic will be traced through families, literature, and historical record, where selective memory operates not as a flaw in recollection, but as a mechanism of cultural continuity—and, increasingly, as a site of correction.

Section III - Unspeakability and the Interior Cost of Cultural Erasure

Gay and lesbian erasure provides one of the clearest illustrations of how selective memory operates under cultural pressure. For much of modern history, queer lives were not merely discouraged; they were rendered unspeakable. The absence of language, representation, and future models did not prevent queer experience from occurring, but it profoundly shaped how that experience could be remembered. Desire, attachment, and recognition often appeared early, but without names.

Without mirrors. Without sanctioned narratives through which they could be understood.

In such conditions, memory cannot consolidate. The mind records what it can safely store—friendship, admiration, intensity, confusion—while postponing what has no place to land. Early attachments are remembered as closeness. Bodily responses are remembered as discomfort or fascination. Moments of recognition are remembered as anomalies rather than signals. This is not evidence of confusion, but of constraint.

What is often called "late realization" in gay and lesbian lives is better understood as delayed integration. The memory itself is not new. What is new is the interpretive frame that allows it to be recognized as what it was. When cultural conditions change—through visibility, community, safety, or language—the mind revisits what it could not previously hold. Memory returns not because it was hidden, but because it finally has permission.

This is why selective memory cannot be understood solely as an error to be corrected. It is a record of adaptation. It tells us not only what happened, but what was possible at the time it happened. What could be named. What could be spoken. What could be survived.

Selective memory does not mean that people remember only what they want. It means they remember what they are able to live with. As circumstances shift, as support appears, as language expands, memory reorganizes itself. The past does not change—but access to it does.

Selective memory, then, is not merely a feature of individual cognition. It is shaped by the conditions under which a life is lived. What is remembered depends not only on what occurred, but on what could be acknowledged without consequence. Experiences that threaten belonging, stability, or social intelligibility are often deferred until alternative frameworks emerge. Memory remains unintegrated until cultural conditions allow it to be named.

That permission does not arise solely within the self. It is granted—or withheld—by families, institutions, languages, and norms that determine what kinds of lives are legible. To understand selective memory fully, we must therefore move beyond the individual and examine the cultural forces that make certain memories livable and others forbidden.

Nowhere is this more visible than in the selective forgetting of identities that threaten cultural norms of normality.

Section IV - Selective Memory in Families, Literature and the Historical Record

Selective memory becomes most visible where personal lives intersect with collective storytelling. Families, literature, and history are not neutral containers of memory; they are curatorial spaces. What is preserved, emphasized, softened, or omitted reflects not only affection or forgetfulness, but the norms a culture seeks to protect. Nowhere is this clearer than in the handling of sexual orientation.

Within families, selective memory often operates through affection rather than hostility. Stories are told lovingly, but incompletely. A daughter's lifelong companion is remembered as a "close friend." A son who never married is recalled as devoted to his work, eccentric, or unlucky in love. These narratives are not usually invented out of malice. They arise from a shared understanding of what kinds of lives are safe to narrate across generations. To name queerness would require explaining it, defending it, or acknowledging that the family itself existed within a culture that offered limited choices. Silence is easier. Silence preserves harmony.

Over time, these omissions harden into fact. Younger generations inherit stories already edited, already normalized. The absence of sexual orientation becomes part of the family's self-understanding, and questioning it can feel like an accusation rather than an inquiry. Selective memory thus becomes intergenerational, teaching descendants not only what to remember, but how to remember.

Literature participates in this process in more complex ways. Texts often preserve what families cannot, but they do so indirectly. Same-sex desire appears in coded forms: intense friendships, aesthetic fixation, moral struggle, renunciation, or sudden narrative withdrawal. These elements are frequently treated as symbolic rather than literal, allowing readers to absorb them without confronting their implications. Critical traditions reinforce this tendency, privileging interpretations that align with dominant norms and dismissing others as anachronistic or speculative.

This is where selective memory and interpretation intersect. When heterosexuality is assumed as the default, literary analysis follows suit. Desire is redirected toward acceptable objects. Relationships that resist categorization are flattened into allegory. What cannot be named is treated as atmosphere rather than substance. Over time, these interpretive habits become institutionalized, shaping how texts are taught, anthologized, and remembered.

The historical record compounds these effects. Archives reflect the priorities of those who created and preserved them. Letters are destroyed. Diaries are edited. Official documents record marriages and births while ignoring partnerships that did not conform to legal recognition. The result is not a neutral absence, but a patterned one. Queer lives appear sporadically, often only where scandal, prosecution, or pathology forced them into visibility.

Yet even within these constraints, traces remain. Gaps, evasions, repetitions, and sudden silences signal what could not be fully recorded. Lifelong cohabitations without explanation. Intense correspondences that abruptly end. Biographical turns that are narrated without motive. These are not proofs, but they are not nothing. They are the residue of lives lived under conditions that required discretion.

Recognizing selective memory in these contexts does not mean rewriting the past to fit contemporary categories. It means acknowledging that the past was already shaped by powerful constraints. To read family stories, literature, or history without accounting for those constraints is not objectivity; it is compliance with inherited silence.

When forbidden memory begins to surface—through genealogical research, archival recovery, or new interpretive frameworks—it often feels disruptive. Established narratives are unsettled. Coherence is threatened. This discomfort is not a sign that something untrue has been introduced. It is a sign that something long excluded is being allowed back into view.

Selective memory, then, is not merely about what individuals forget. It is about how societies remember. It reveals the mechanisms by which normality is preserved and how entire dimensions of human experience are rendered peripheral or invisible. To notice selective memory at work is to begin the task of correction—not by filling every gap with certainty, but by refusing to treat absence as innocence.

Section V - Lives Remembered Selectively: When Names Remain but Truth Does Not

Selective memory becomes easiest to recognize when it attaches itself to real people. Abstract discussions of erasure can feel theoretical until one encounters the repeated pattern by which certain lives are preserved in outline but stripped of their interior truth. In these cases, names remain, accomplishments are recorded, and relationships are acknowledged—yet the central organizing feature of a life is quietly omitted.

One frequently cited example is **Jane Addams**, founder of Hull House and one of the most influential social reformers of the early twentieth century. Addams shared an intimate, decades-long partnership with **Mary Rozet Smith**, marked by emotional dependence, shared households, extensive correspondence, and mutual devotion. Their relationship shaped Addams's daily life, emotional world, and capacity for work. Yet for much of the twentieth century, this partnership was described in biographies as a close friendship or supportive companionship, as though such sustained intimacy between women required no further explanation.

The issue is not whether Addams would have used the word "lesbian"—she would not have. The issue is that removing sexual orientation from the narrative leaves her life structurally unintelligible. Her choices, attachments, and emotional priorities are flattened into abstraction. Selective memory preserves her public achievements while neutralizing the relational reality that made them possible.

A similar pattern appears in the life of **Willa Cather**. Cather lived for decades with **Edith Lewis**, sharing a household, daily routines, and emotional intimacy that persisted throughout her adult life. Letters and personal papers reveal intensity, protectiveness, and devotion. Yet for years, literary scholarship avoided naming the nature of this relationship, instead emphasizing Cather's independence, professionalism, or supposed aversion to intimacy altogether. The result was a portrait of a woman oddly detached from relational life, a distortion created not by lack of evidence but by interpretive refusal.

Male lives were shaped by the same mechanisms. **Bayard Rustin**, a central architect of the Civil Rights Movement, was routinely written out of leadership histories not because of lack of contribution, but because he was openly gay. His sexual orientation was remembered only as liability or scandal, while its role in shaping his political strategy, ethics, and vulnerability was ignored. Here, selective memory did not erase orientation entirely—it weaponized it, reducing a complex life to a risk factor rather than an organizing reality.

In other cases, erasure is quieter. **Emily Dickinson's** emotional and poetic attachments to women such as **Susan Gilbert Dickinson** were long reframed as heightened sentiment or literary convention. Letters containing language of longing and devotion were softened, edited, or explained away. The intensity was preserved, but its meaning was redirected. The result was a poet remembered for isolation rather than relational depth.

These examples span different genders, eras, and public roles, yet the pattern is consistent. Sexual orientation is either:

- omitted entirely
- reframed as friendship
- treated as incidental rather than constitutive
- or acknowledged only to neutralize its significance

In each case, selective memory serves the same function: it maintains the appearance of normality by ensuring that heterosexuality remains the default explanation, even when it explains very little.

What is lost in this process is not simply accuracy, but proportion. When sexual orientation is removed, lives become oddly shaped. Choices appear eccentric. Attachments seem excessive or inexplicable. Emotional commitments lack context. These distortions are then used to reinforce the very norms that produced them, creating a circular logic in which queerness is both erased and rendered unnecessary to understanding.

Restoring these dimensions does not require certainty about private acts or modern identity categories. It requires only the willingness to acknowledge that sexual orientation mattered—and that its omission was not neutral. Naming this pattern is not an act of retroactive labeling. It is an act of narrative repair.

These named lives demonstrate what this chapter has argued throughout: selective memory is not about forgetting everything. It is about remembering *just enough* to preserve coherence while leaving the most disruptive truths unspoken. When those truths are allowed back into view, the past does not collapse. It becomes more legible.

Section VI - When Forbidden Memory Is Named and What Changes

Once selective memory is recognized at work—once omissions are seen not as accidents but as structural choices—something important shifts. The past does not suddenly become transparent, nor do lives resolve themselves into neat categories. What changes is the frame through which evidence is read. Absence is no longer treated as innocence, and silence is no longer mistaken for irrelevance.

For individuals, naming forbidden memory often produces a reordering rather than a revelation. Experiences that once appeared disconnected begin to align. Attachments that felt excessive or inexplicable acquire proportion. The sense of having lived "around" something without touching it gives way to the recognition that the thing was always present, simply unacknowledged. What returns is not a new self, but a more accurate account of the one that has been lived.

This accuracy can be unsettling. It exposes how much effort went into sustaining normality—how many substitutions were made, how many explanations rehearsed. Yet it also relieves a long-standing cognitive tension. When memory is permitted to organize itself honestly, it no longer has to maintain parallel stories. The self is freed from collusion with its own erasure.

At the cultural level, the naming of forbidden memory proceeds unevenly. Some lives are reinterpreted with care; others are resisted fiercely. Charges of anachronism or projection often appear at this stage, serving as a last defense of inherited narratives. But acknowledging constraint is not the same as imposing identity. To say that sexual orientation shaped a life is not to claim that the person named it as such; it is to recognize that orientation mattered even when it could not be spoken.

What follows naming is not certainty, but responsibility. Biographies become more careful. Literary readings grow more attentive to pattern and omission. Family stories expand to include what was once bracketed off. This work does not flatten lives into single traits; it restores dimension. Choices make sense. Attachments clarify. Losses become legible.

Importantly, naming forbidden memory does not require completion. Some gaps remain. Some silences cannot be filled without speculation that exceeds evidence. The ethical task is not to replace one certainty with another, but to refuse the comfort of distortion. Precision, here, lies in acknowledging limits while correcting known omissions.

Across this chapter, selective memory has been traced from its adaptive role in individual lives to its function in sustaining compulsory heterosexuality across families, texts, and histories. What emerges is not a narrative of failure, but of endurance under constraint. People remembered what they could, when they could, in the forms available to them. That many memories return later is not evidence of instability; it is evidence that conditions have changed.

To name forbidden memory is to practice a different kind of attention—one that listens for what was silenced and asks why. It is an act of repair rather than accusation, restoration rather than revision. By allowing these memories into view, we do not dismantle the past; we read it more accurately. And in doing so, we make room for lives—past and present—to be understood in their full, human complexity.

Chapter Eleven

Who Gets to Be Human: Neanderthals, Sapiens and the Politics of Survival

Section I - Rethinking "Advancement" in Human History

The conventional story of human advancement rests on a deceptively simple premise: that the groups who survive, expand, and dominate must also be the most intelligent, the most capable, and the most fully human. This assumption underlies not only popular understandings of prehistory, but also many of the frameworks through which later historical encounters are interpreted. It equates continuity of presence with superiority of culture and treats disappearance as evidence of inferiority. Yet when examined across time, this logic proves unreliable. History repeatedly shows that survival often depends less on cultural depth than on orientation toward expansion, hierarchy, and force.

This pattern becomes visible when intelligence is decoupled from conquest and reattached to the practices that make social life durable: care for the vulnerable, symbolic engagement with death, ritual continuity, and long-term investment in place. These traits do not guarantee survival in moments of contact and competition. In fact, they may increase vulnerability when confronted by groups optimized for rapid growth and aggressive displacement. The result is a recurring historical phenomenon in which culturally dense societies are absorbed or overrun by more expansionist ones, and then redefined as primitive or obsolete by those who remain.

The Homo neanderthal–Homo sapiens encounter has long been framed as a story of evolutionary improvement, with Neanderthals cast as cognitively inferior precursors replaced by a more advanced species. This framing persists despite mounting evidence that Neanderthals possessed many of the hallmarks associated with complex social life: intentional burial, care for injured and elderly members, symbolic behavior, and stable, localized communities. Rather than resolving these contradictions, the dominant narrative tends to minimize them, preserving the assumption that replacement implies superiority.

A broader historical lens complicates that assumption. When similar dynamics occur in historically documented societies, the outcome is rarely interpreted as proof that the displaced culture lacked intelligence.

Instead, it is understood as the result of asymmetries in power, population, and willingness to use violence. Applying this lens to deep prehistory does not require romanticizing Neanderthals or vilifying Homo sapiens. It requires acknowledging that cultural sophistication and survival are not synonymous.

The key issue, then, is not whether Neanderthals were capable of complex thought, but why their disappearance has been taken as evidence that they were less human. The answer lies not in biology alone, but in a pattern of memory formation that favors the perspective of those who dominate. Cultures that persist gain the authority to define what counts as intelligence, progress, and humanity. Those that are absorbed or displaced lose that authority, even when their practices suggest a high degree of social and symbolic development.

This pattern can be traced clearly in later historical contexts, where the evidence is less ambiguous and the documentation more complete. The transition from Minoan to Mycenaean dominance in the Aegean, the absorption of Etruscan culture by Rome, and the displacement of Native American societies by European colonizers each demonstrate the same structural logic. In all three cases, the displaced culture exhibits deep investment in ritual, continuity, and care for the dead, while the conquering culture succeeds through militarization, hierarchy, and expansion. In none of these cases does conquest equate neatly with cultural or moral advancement.

By placing Neanderthals within this broader pattern, the question shifts from one of evolutionary ranking to one of historical process. The issue becomes how certain ways of being human are rendered invisible when they do not align with the traits that enable domination. The archaeological record, particularly evidence related to burial and social care, suggests that Neanderthals may have been culturally sophisticated in precisely the ways that history tends to undervalue.

This reframing does not argue that Neanderthals were superior to Homo sapiens in any absolute sense. Rather, it challenges the assumption that aggression, expansion, and narrative control are reliable measures of intelligence. It opens space to consider the possibility that Neanderthals, like later displaced cultures, practiced forms of social life that prioritized continuity over conquest. Such priorities leave deep material traces—especially in how the dead are treated—but they do not ensure survival when confronted by groups organized around different imperatives.

Understanding this distinction is essential before turning to specific historical parallels. Without it, comparisons risk being read as moral judgments rather than analytical tools. With it, the Minoans, Etruscans, and Native American societies can be examined not as analogies meant to provoke, but as concrete cases that illuminate how cultural depth and historical survival repeatedly diverge. These cases provide a framework for reconsidering Neanderthals not as failed ancestors, but as participants in a long human story in which the most enduring cultures are not always the ones that prevail.

Section II - The Minoans and the Vulnerability of Cultural Density

The Minoan civilization offers one of the clearest historical examples of how cultural sophistication and historical survival can diverge. Flourishing on Crete during the Bronze Age, the Minoans developed a society characterized by economic integration, symbolic richness, and ritual continuity. Their cities reveal advanced planning, complex drainage systems, and architectural forms oriented toward openness rather than defense. Palatial centers such as Knossos, Phaistos, and Malia functioned not only as administrative hubs but as ceremonial and economic nexuses, binding communities together through shared practice rather than centralized coercion.

Minoan material culture emphasizes movement, fertility, and relationship rather than conquest. Frescoes depict ritual processions, marine life, and athletic performance, conveying a worldview in which human activity is embedded within natural and ceremonial rhythms. Weapons are present, but they do not dominate the iconographic landscape. Fortifications, where they exist at all, are minimal compared to those of contemporaneous mainland societies. This absence is not evidence of naivety; it reflects a social orientation that prioritized stability, trade, and internal cohesion over militarized defense.

Burial practices further illuminate this orientation. Minoan mortuary traditions emphasize continuity and collective identity rather than individual glorification. Tholos tombs and communal burial spaces were reused across generations, reinforcing kinship ties and ancestral presence. The dead remained integrated within the social fabric, their memory sustained through ongoing ritual engagement rather than monumental display. This approach to death situates the Minoans firmly within a continuity-oriented cultural framework, one in which identity is maintained through relationship rather than domination.

When Mycenaean influence expands into Crete, the contrast in cultural priorities becomes stark. Mycenaean society was explicitly hierarchical and martial, organized around fortified citadels, warrior elites, and centralized authority. Their art emphasizes weapons, hunting, and power, and their architecture reflects an enduring concern with defense and control. Administrative practices, preserved in Linear B tablets, focus on inventory, tribute, and the management of resources, revealing a system optimized for extraction and enforcement.

The Mycenaean takeover of Crete did not involve the immediate eradication of Minoan culture. Instead, it followed a familiar historical pattern of absorption and overwriting. Minoan religious symbols, architectural forms, and administrative structures were selectively retained, while Minoan language and identity were displaced. Linear A disappeared, replaced by Linear B, which recorded an early form of Greek. The continuity of population and practice contrasts sharply with the discontinuity of narrative. What survived was reframed as a precursor rather than a coequal culture.

This transition is often explained through a combination of natural disaster, internal instability, and external pressure, but such explanations do not diminish the underlying dynamic. The Mycenaeans succeeded not because they were more symbolically or socially complex, but because they were better positioned to impose control during periods of stress. Their militarized structure allowed them to capitalize on disruption, transforming vulnerability into opportunity. Cultural density, which sustained the Minoans in stable conditions, became a liability under pressure.

The Minoan case is instructive because it demonstrates how a society can be deeply sophisticated without being resilient to conquest. Their investment in ritual, continuity, and relational identity produced a culture of remarkable coherence, but it did not translate into dominance. When the balance shifted, the qualities that defined Minoan life were absorbed rather than preserved, their origins gradually obscured by the narrative of the conqueror. The Mycenaean story becomes the foundation of later Greek identity, while the Minoans recede into the background as a formative but ultimately surpassed stage.

Seen through this lens, the Minoans resemble many other cultures that history labels as transitional or primitive despite evidence of complexity. Their displacement does not testify to inferiority, but to a mismatch between cultural priorities and the demands of violent competition. This mismatch appears repeatedly in human history, and recognizing it allows for a more nuanced understanding of cultural change. The Minoans were not replaced because they failed to be human in the fullest sense; they were replaced because their way of being human was not oriented toward survival through domination.

This pattern provides a critical bridge to reconsidering Neanderthals. Like the Minoans, Neanderthals appear to have been culturally dense, socially cohesive, and invested in continuity. Their disappearance need not be read as evidence of cognitive deficiency. Instead, it can be understood as part of a broader historical phenomenon in which cultures organized around care, ritual, and stability are vulnerable to those organized around expansion and force. The Minoan example grounds this possibility in well-documented history, preparing the way for further comparisons that reinforce the argument rather than relying on speculation alone.

Section III -The Etruscans and the Erasure of Cultural Memory

The Etruscans offer a particularly instructive case because their displacement occurred not in prehistory or at the margins of the historical record, but at the very foundation of what later defined itself as classical civilization. Unlike the Minoans, whose legacy survives largely through archaeology, the Etruscans lived alongside—and directly shaped—the culture that would ultimately absorb them. Their disappearance as a named people is therefore not a consequence of obscurity or collapse, but of narrative replacement enacted by a successor that inherited their achievements while denying their autonomy.

Etruscan society was urbanized, technologically advanced, and ritually elaborate. Their cities were carefully planned, their metallurgy and engineering sophisticated, and their trade networks extensive throughout the Mediterranean. Yet it is in their mortuary practices that the depth of their cultural orientation becomes most evident. Etruscan tombs were constructed as enduring domestic spaces for the dead, complete with architectural detail, painted walls, furnishings, and personal objects. These were not monuments to conquest or individual glory, but environments designed to sustain memory and kinship across generations. The dead were not removed from social life; they were housed within it.

This approach to burial reflects a worldview in which continuity mattered more than dominance. Identity was preserved through lineage, ritual repetition, and the maintenance of ancestral presence rather than through territorial expansion. The Etruscans invested heavily in symbolic systems that interpreted the relationship between humans, gods, and the natural world. Divination, augury, and ritual practice structured daily life, reinforcing a sense of order grounded in interpretation rather than enforcement. Power was dispersed among city-states rather than concentrated in a single imperial authority, further emphasizing stability over conquest.

Rome's rise occurred within this Etruscan-influenced world. Early Roman institutions, religious practices, and symbols of authority bear unmistakable Etruscan imprint. The fasces, the curule chair, ritual divination, aspects of urban planning, and even elements of political organization were adopted directly from Etruscan models. Rome did not displace the Etruscans because it was more culturally refined. It displaced them because it was structured for expansion. Roman society centralized authority, militarized citizenship, and oriented itself toward territorial control. These traits proved decisive as Rome extended its reach across the Italian peninsula.

The absorption of the Etruscans followed a familiar pattern. Their population was incorporated into Roman society, their practices selectively retained, and their language gradually supplanted by Latin. What disappeared was not the people themselves, but their ability to define their own history. Roman authors framed the Etruscans as enigmatic, decadent, or obsolete, recasting them as a prelude to Roman greatness rather than as a contemporaneous civilization with its own trajectory. This reframing served a political purpose. By situating the Etruscans safely in the past, Rome legitimized its dominance and naturalized its claim to cultural authority.

Burial practices again reveal the tension between cultural depth and narrative survival. Etruscan tombs remained visible and compelling long after Roman conquest, yet they were increasingly treated as curiosities rather than as evidence of an alternative way of organizing society. Roman burial practices, while evolving over time, emphasized civic identity and state affiliation more than familial continuity. The shift reflects a broader transformation in how social belonging was conceived, from relational networks anchored in ancestry to political identity anchored in citizenship and empire.

The Etruscan case demonstrates how a culture can be foundational without being remembered as such. Their contributions became inseparable from Roman civilization even as their name faded from prominence. This disappearance was not an accident of time; it was the outcome of power. Rome survived, expanded, and wrote the histories that defined Western antiquity. In doing so, it established a template for interpreting cultural succession as progress rather than as displacement.

This dynamic mirrors the Neanderthal narrative with striking clarity. Just as Neanderthals persist biologically within modern human populations while being labeled extinct, Etruscans persist culturally within Rome while being treated as vanished. In both cases, continuity is acknowledged only insofar as it supports the identity of the successor. The absorbed culture's own values—particularly those centered on care, ritual, and memory—are marginalized because they do not align with the traits that enabled conquest.

The Etruscans thus serve as a critical intermediary between deep prehistory and documented history. They show how erasure operates even when evidence of sophistication is abundant and proximity is close. Their fate underscores a central point of this chapter: cultural richness does not guarantee narrative survival. Those who prevail in conflict inherit not only land and people, but the authority to define what counts as civilization. Recognizing this pattern strengthens the case for reevaluating Neanderthals not as evolutionary failures, but as participants in a recurring human story in which the most enduring cultural values are often the first to be overwritten.

Section IV: Native American Societies and the Persistence of Erasure

The encounter between Native American societies and European colonizers provides the most visible and ethically charged example of the pattern traced throughout this chapter. Unlike the Minoans or the Etruscans, whose displacement lies at a distance that can soften its implications, the dispossession of Indigenous peoples in the Americas occurred within a historical frame that is extensively documented and continues to shape the present. It therefore offers a critical test of the argument that cultural sophistication and historical survival are not synonymous, and that the traits most closely associated with being deeply human are often those least rewarded by expansionist power.

Indigenous societies across North America were extraordinarily diverse, yet many shared structural characteristics that parallel those seen in Neanderthal, Minoan, and Etruscan contexts. Social organization was frequently grounded in kinship networks rather than centralized authority. Relationships to land emphasized stewardship and continuity rather than ownership and extraction. Ritual life was integrated into seasonal cycles, subsistence practices, and communal memory. Burial practices reinforced these values, situating the dead within ongoing relationships to place, ancestry, and the living community. Death was not a rupture to be managed administratively, but a transition embedded within the fabric of collective life.

European societies arrived with a markedly different orientation. Their expansion into the Americas was driven by demographic pressure, state-backed ambition, and economic systems predicated on accumulation and control. Hierarchical political structures, militarized enforcement, and legal frameworks designed to legitimate dispossession shaped colonial encounters from their inception. These traits proved devastatingly effective. Indigenous populations were decimated through violence, disease, and forced displacement, while surviving communities were subjected to policies of removal, assimilation, and cultural suppression. Yet as in earlier cases, disappearance was more narrative than biological. Indigenous peoples persisted, even as their presence was reframed as marginal or vanishing.

The treatment of Indigenous burial grounds reveals the depth of this erasure. Native graves were frequently disturbed, relocated, or appropriated, their sacred character subordinated to colonial claims of land use and scientific inquiry. Ancestral remains were excavated, cataloged, and displayed, stripped of relational meaning and reclassified as objects of study. European graves, by contrast, were protected, monumentalized, and eventually integrated into national commemorative landscapes. This asymmetry exposes how power determines whose dead are honored and whose are rendered expendable. Burial, once again, becomes a diagnostic marker of cultural valuation.

Narratives of civilization reinforced this imbalance. Indigenous societies were cast as primitive or static, their complex systems of governance, knowledge, and ritual dismissed as obstacles to progress. European domination was framed as inevitable advancement, obscuring the reality that conquest succeeded through organized violence and structural coercion rather than cultural superiority. The persistence of Indigenous knowledge, agricultural practices, ecological understanding, and genetic continuity stands in stark contrast to the story of disappearance promoted by colonial ideology. As with earlier examples, absorption and survival were reframed as extinction.

This dynamic completes the comparative arc of the chapter. In each case—the Minoans, the Etruscans, and Native American societies—the displaced culture exhibits sustained investment in continuity, ritual, and care, particularly in how the dead are treated. Each is overtaken by a group more willing and able to impose control through force, scale, and hierarchy. Each is subsequently redefined by the victor as less advanced in order to legitimize domination. The consistency of this pattern across time and context undermines any simple equation between conquest and intelligence.

Placed within this framework, the Neanderthal–Homo sapiens encounter appears less exceptional and more recognizably human. Neanderthals buried their dead, cared for the injured, and lived in socially cohesive groups oriented toward place and continuity. These traits align them with cultures history repeatedly marginalizes, not because they lack humanity, but because their form of humanity does not privilege expansion. Homo sapiens, like later conquerors, survived through numbers, mobility, and aggression, and in doing so acquired the authority to define what it meant to be human.

This does not invert a hierarchy so much as expose its construction. Intelligence, when measured solely by survival and dominance, reflects the capacity to overrun and erase. When measured by care, memory, and symbolic continuity, a different picture emerges—one in which Neanderthals, like the Minoans, the Etruscans, and Indigenous societies, exemplify a form of cultural depth that history routinely undervalues. Recognizing this pattern does not diminish Homo sapiens; it complicates the story we tell about ourselves.

The persistence of these dynamics into the modern era suggests that the question raised by Neanderthals is not confined to prehistory. It challenges contemporary assumptions about progress, civilization, and whose ways of being are deemed worthy of remembrance. By reading Neanderthals through the lens of later historical erasures, the archaeological record becomes less a story of evolutionary failure and more a mirror reflecting the long human tendency to mistake domination for advancement.

Section V: Reconsidering Neanderthals as a Human Precedent

When the comparative cases are placed side by side, the Neanderthal question resolves into a recognizable human pattern rather than an evolutionary anomaly. The Minoans, the Etruscans, and Native American societies were not displaced because they lacked complexity, intelligence, or symbolic depth. They were displaced because the forms of complexity they cultivated—ritual continuity, care for the dead, relational identity, and long-term investment in place—did not confer an advantage against groups organized for expansion, hierarchy, and force. In each case, conquest was followed by narrative control, and narrative control reshaped memory. Neanderthals occupy the same position in deep time.

The archaeological record suggests that Neanderthals lived within culturally dense worlds. Intentional burial, sustained care for injured and elderly individuals, and evidence of symbolic behavior indicate social structures oriented toward continuity rather than constant movement. These practices require foresight, obligation, and shared meaning. They are not the byproducts of brute survival. They are investments in community, memory, and belonging—precisely the traits that later cultures consistently undervalued when measured against the demands of conquest.

Homo sapiens, by contrast, appear to have been organized in ways that favored rapid expansion. Larger populations, higher mobility, broader resource exploitation, and greater tolerance for violence provided a decisive advantage during periods of contact. These traits are adaptive under competitive pressure, but they do not necessarily indicate greater cultural depth. What they ensure is survival—and with survival comes the authority to define humanity itself. As with Rome, as with colonial Europe, persistence becomes proof, and domination becomes destiny retroactively justified.

The label of Neanderthal inferiority relies heavily on this logic. Their disappearance is taken as evidence of cognitive failure rather than as the outcome of asymmetric encounter. Yet when disappearance is examined through the lens of absorption rather than extinction, the narrative weakens. Neanderthals persist genetically within modern populations, just as Minoan, Etruscan, and Indigenous peoples persist biologically and culturally within successor societies. What vanishes is not the people, but their capacity to define themselves.

Burial practices remain the most reliable indicator of this distinction. Across all the cases considered, the cultures later labeled as primitive or obsolete demonstrate sustained attention to the dead as continuing members of the social world. Burial is not a functional necessity; it is a moral choice. It signals recognition that life carries meaning beyond utility. Neanderthals made this choice tens of thousands of years before it became common in many Homo sapiens contexts. That fact alone challenges the assumption that they occupied a lesser rung on a linear ladder of progress.

Reframing Neanderthals in this way does not require reversing hierarchies or assigning moral superiority. It requires abandoning a single-axis definition of advancement. Intelligence need not be equated with dominance, nor culture with conquest. When intelligence is understood as the capacity to sustain social bonds, care for the vulnerable, and preserve memory across generations, Neanderthals look less like failed ancestors and more like participants in a long human story whose outcome was decided by power rather than worth.

This reframing also clarifies why the Neanderthal question continues to unsettle modern audiences. It threatens a comforting narrative in which survival confirms virtue and progress flows inevitably toward the present. Recognizing Neanderthals as culturally sophisticated forces a confrontation with the possibility that history, at every scale, favors those most willing to overrun others—and then declare themselves the standard by which humanity is measured.

Seen in this light, Neanderthals are not an evolutionary footnote. They are an early example of a recurring human dilemma: cultures that prioritize continuity, care, and symbolic meaning often leave the deepest traces, but not the loudest ones. The ground remembers them long after the victors have written their accounts. The challenge, for those willing to read carefully, is to learn how to listen to what remains.

Chapter Twelve

There but for the Grace of God: Photographic Comparisons of Internment, Deportation, and State Power

Preface

This chapter contains historical photographs documenting the forced removal, confinement, and degradation of civilian populations during World War II. The images are paired for direct comparison between Japanese American incarceration in the United States and the confinement and deportation of Jews in Nazi-occupied Europe.

These materials are presented deliberately and without euphemism. They depict state actions that were legal at the time, publicly supported, and morally wrong. The purpose of this chapter is not to soften, contextualize away, or excuse those actions, but to examine how ordinary procedures, justified as necessary or temporary, resulted in profound injustice.

Readers should be aware that the comparisons made here are accusatory by design. They do not claim identical outcomes, but they do insist on shared responsibility where governments enacted discriminatory policies and populations accepted, defended, or benefited from them.

This chapter is intended to confront, not comfort. If you continue, you do so with the understanding that the images and accompanying text are meant to challenge narratives of national innocence and to document how easily injustice becomes normalized when it is administered incrementally and legally.

All images reflect the original purposes for which they were created: surveillance, documentation, administration, and public record. The ethical burden of these images lies not in their reproduction, but in the actions they record and the authority that produced them.

What makes these images especially difficult is not that they depict atrocity in its most extreme form, but that they capture moments of transition—when exclusion is still procedural, when removal is framed as orderly, when confinement is presented as temporary, and when violence has not yet reached its final expression. These photographs show people standing, waiting, lining up, registering, being watched. They record compliance extracted under threat, not chaos. In doing so, they expose how injustice most often enters public life: quietly, administratively, and with the reassurance of legality.

The reader's task here is not to search for overt cruelty or dramatic rupture, but to recognize familiarity. The scenes depicted are unsettling precisely because they resemble other bureaucratic processes—checkpoints, documentation, transport, housing—rendered extraordinary only by hindsight. This resemblance is the point. The chapter asks how systems that appear manageable, rational, and even humane at the outset can become mechanisms of profound harm once resistance is dulled and responsibility is diffused across institutions and populations.

Introduction

This chapter is organized around photographic comparison. Each image or image pair is presented alongside interpretive text intended to guide attention rather than supply conclusions. The photographs are arranged sequentially to reflect the progression of state action as it unfolded in real time, not as it is often remembered afterward.

The images are drawn from two public-record contexts: the incarceration of Japanese Americans in the United States and the confinement and deportation of Jews in Nazi-occupied Europe during World War II. They are paired not to suggest identical histories, but to highlight recurring administrative and visual patterns that emerge when governments act against civilian populations defined as threats.

The sequence moves deliberately from early measures to later ones. It begins with legal groundwork and public rhetoric, proceeds through registration and removal, and ends with confinement, surveillance, and violence. This order matters. When viewed out of sequence, individual images can appear isolated or ambiguous. When seen as a progression, they reveal how exclusion becomes normalized through repetition and routine.

Readers are encouraged to spend time with each image before turning to the accompanying text. Notice posture, spacing, expression, and environment. Notice the presence of authority and the absence of visible choice. The interpretive pages that face the photographs address what is happening, who is responsible, and why the moment depicted matters, without attempting to resolve the discomfort the images may provoke.

This chapter does not rely on hindsight. It does not ask what was known later or how events ultimately concluded. It focuses instead on what was visible at the time and how quickly extraordinary measures were incorporated into ordinary life. The photographs remain valuable precisely because they capture moments before the full consequences were known and before justification had hardened into memory.

The comparisons presented here are intended to be read slowly. They are not cumulative in the sense of building a single argument, but accretive, allowing recognition to emerge across pages. The purpose is not to instruct the reader what to think, but to ensure that what is seen is not misunderstood, minimized, or detached from responsibility.

The following photographs are presented in deliberate pairs, intended to be viewed side by side. Each image on the left is associated with the American Japanese Internment Camps; each corresponding image on the right is associated with the German Concentration Camps. Care was taken to ensure that none of the German photographs are drawn from extermination camps. The images instead document earlier stages of confinement, registration, and deportation as recorded in contemporaneous public-domain sources. The comparison is nonetheless striking—not because the systems were identical, but because the administrative and visual structures are familiar. These images are offered as a visual reminder of what becomes possible when mass injustice is normalized, and of what might have followed had the progression within the United States been allowed to continue.

For this chapter, photographs are presented without captions to allow sustained visual attention; identifying information and archival locations are provided in the appendix.

These photographs capture families held in place between instruction and movement. They stand assembled with their belongings at their feet, not yet in motion, but no longer at home. Tags hang visibly from coats and hands grip luggage that appears carefully chosen, limited by what could be carried rather than what might be needed.

Adults cluster close, orienting themselves toward unseen authority, their bodies angled in readiness rather than distress. Children remain within reach, one handheld, the other free, positioned low against the adult frame. Their faces are alert, expectant, still within the rhythms of ordinary life even as those rhythms have been interrupted.

What is visible here is not panic or resistance, but compliance shaped by instruction. The setting is orderly, public, and exposed. Life has been paused under direction, with movement anticipated but not yet begun, and with no indication—visible or otherwise—of what lies ahead once waiting ends.

At this point, the families do not know where they are going, how long they will be gone, or what conditions will greet them when they arrive. They have been told that cooperation is required and that order will be maintained. The instructions are framed as temporary, procedural, and necessary.

These images record the moment before meaning hardens. Before policies are understood as permanent. Before restriction becomes routine. Before the language used to justify what follows settles into place. What is visible here is uncertainty shared across generations, carried quietly, and absorbed without protest because protest has not yet been defined as an option.

This is the beginning: not with visible violence, but with waiting; not with certainty, but with trust demanded under pressure; not with outcomes, but with the quiet assumption that what is being asked must somehow make sense.

These documents mark the moment when uncertainty is formalized. What had been rumor or instruction becomes text, fixed in print and displayed publicly. The language is impersonal, authoritative, and final. There is no signature of an individual voice, only the weight of the institution speaking as law.

The notice does not ask. It informs. It announces requirements, deadlines, and consequences. It defines who is being addressed and does so collectively, reducing individuals to a category that can be managed. The tone is administrative rather than emotional, presenting disruption as procedure and obedience as expectation. What is being demanded is framed as orderly, reasonable, and necessary.

Posted in public spaces, these notices do not require private confrontation. They rely instead on visibility and repetition. Everyone can see them. Everyone knows they apply. The act of reading becomes the first act of compliance.

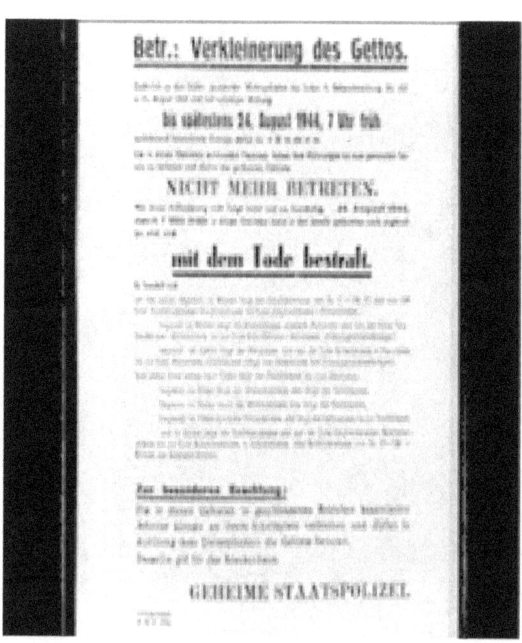

Betr.: Verkleinerung des Gettos.

bis spätestens 24. August 1944, 7 Uhr früh

NICHT MEHR BETRETEN.

mit dem Tode bestraft.

GEHEIME STAATSPOLIZEI.

Restriction is no longer implied but declared. Movement is regulated. Presence becomes conditional. The language is explicit about consequences, invoking punishment rather than reassurance. Authority is no longer distant; it is immediate and enforceable. The notice does not explain itself. Explanation is no longer required.

What is striking is how ordinary the mechanism appears. Paper, ink, official phrasing. No spectacle, no violence, no visible force. And yet these documents redraw the boundaries of daily life. They determine where people may go, how they may exist, and what will happen if they do not comply.

This is the point at which the future narrows decisively. Choice is reduced to obedience or risk. The language leaves little room for interpretation, and none for negotiation. What was once uncertainty is now instruction, backed by the full authority of the state.

These streets record the moment when removal begins to take material form. Shops are not yet gone, but they are being closed. Signs are taken down or obscured, windows boarded while the work is still underway. The architecture of daily life remains standing, but it is being deliberately stripped of its function.

This is how exclusion becomes visible before it is complete: not through ruin, but through methodical closure, enacted one business at a time. There is no visible chaos, no broken glass, no signs of resistance. The closures are neat, almost careful. What is missing is human presence. The street has been stripped of interaction, reduced to surface and façade. What once signaled livelihood now signals abandonment.

This kind of erasure does not announce itself as violence. It appears administrative, even temporary. Yet it marks a decisive shift. The removal of people is now visible in the removal of function. Economic life has been interrupted in a way that cannot be mistaken for coincidence.

Here, disruption is written directly onto the surface of the street. The shop window remains intact, its goods still arranged behind the glass, but the space has been publicly redefined. The word painted across the window does the work of exclusion without requiring removal or force. .The street no longer belongs to those who once animated it.

What these images show is not just loss of property, but loss of standing. To close a business is to sever a person's place in the public world. It is a declaration that one's labor, presence, and contribution are no longer permitted. The street becomes a record of exclusion, written not in proclamations but in plywood and silence.

This is how removal extends beyond bodies. It reaches into livelihoods, neighborhoods, and memory. The buildings remain, but they no longer testify to the people who gave them meaning. Absence becomes the message, visible to anyone who walks past and understands that what has vanished did not do so voluntarily.

Exclusion is no longer carried quietly through procedure or instruction. It is posted, repeated, and made unavoidable. The same message appears more than once, fastened in place as if to ensure it will be seen, read, and remembered. The language is direct and inflammatory, stripped of nuance or explanation. It does not argue. It declares.

The signs occupy shared space, layered over other notices, competing for attention and winning it through urgency and repetition. They do not require authority to stand beside them. Their power lies in their visibility and in the assumption that they may remain where they are. Anyone who passes can read them; anyone who does not remove them accepts their presence as part of the street.

What is visible here is not policy, but permission. The message no longer relies on official process or future action. It announces exclusion as a fact already understood. Ambiguity has been replaced by assertion. The boundary is no longer implied through absence or closure

Here, exclusion is positioned as part of ordinary passage. The sign is fixed at street level, embedded in the storefront, encountered will walking rather than sought out. Adults and children pass alongside it, their movement uninterrupted, as if the message belongs to the environment rather than standing apart from it.

The power of the sign lies in its normalcy. It does not announce itself through force or spectacle. It relies on its placement—visible, legible, and unchallenged—to do its work. The swastika anchors the message visually, leaving no ambiguity about who is being addressed or excluded.

This is where exclusion becomes part of daily life. The message is no longer about removal or action to come, but about judgment already rendered. It stands in public view, absorbed into routine movement, teaching who belongs and who does not simply by being there. The boundary is not enforced in this moment; it is learned.

These images show movement under instruction rather than travel by choice. People walk because they have been told to walk. They carry what they can because they have been told what they may carry. The pace is controlled, not hurried, giving the appearance of order even as normal life is being dismantled.

Children move among adults without fully understanding what is happening, guided by hands and gestures rather than explanation. The road ahead is visible, but the destination is not. What has been left behind is already inaccessible. Homes, routines, and familiar landmarks recede quietly, without ceremony.

There is no visible resistance here, not because consent has been given, but because resistance has already been made impractical. Authority does not need to shout. The expectation of compliance has been established in advance.

There is no visible resistance here, not because consent has been given, but because resistance has already been made impractical. Authority does not need to shout. The expectation of compliance has been established in advance.

Here, movement is collective and exposed. Families are gathered and directed through public space, carrying containers that suggest necessity rather than preparation. What they hold is provisional, chosen under pressure, stripped of anything deemed excessive or unnecessary by someone else.

The presence of guards and escorts makes the imbalance clear. This is removal. The fact that people are walking rather than being dragged does not make the act voluntary. The absence of visible violence does not make it benign.

These images capture the moment when displacement becomes irreversible. Once movement begins under compulsion, return is no longer assumed. What lies ahead is undefined, but what has been lost is already certain.

This is the moment when removal becomes administrative fact. People are no longer simply moving through space; they are being recorded, counted, and documented. Names are written down. Papers are examined. Lines form and reform as individuals are sorted into categories that determine what will happen next.

The setting is crowded and controlled. Movement is limited to what is permitted by the process. People wait their turn, clutching documents whose significance has changed suddenly and irrevocably. What once identified them as residents or citizens now functions as permission to proceed further into confinement.

This is where authority asserts itself most quietly and most completely. No physical force is required. The procedure itself enforces compliance. To be processed is to accept that one's status is no longer self-defined.

The imbalance is unmistakable. Officials sit while others stand. Papers move across the table while people wait for decisions made without their participation. The act of registration transforms individuals into entries, reducing complex lives to information that can be stored, transferred, and acted upon.

This is not a neutral exchange. It is the point at which people become manageable. Once recorded, they can be directed, confined, or moved again without further explanation. The authority of the state is no longer implied; it is exercised through forms, stamps, and signatures.

These images capture the moment when identity is subordinated to classification. The future is no longer uncertain in an abstract sense. It is being decided, one name at a time, by a process designed to proceed without interruption or appeal.

Children appear here not as witnesses, but as participants in events they did not choose and cannot understand. They are held, guided, and carried through a process designed without regard for their comprehension or consent. What they cling to—dolls, blankets, small objects—are attempts to preserve familiarity in the midst of disruption.

The expressions on their faces reflect confusion rather than fear. They are still close enough to ordinary life to expect reassurance. The adults around them perform that reassurance as best they can, even as their own uncertainty deepens. Childhood continues in posture and gesture, even as the conditions that sustain it are being dismantled.

These images record the transfer of responsibility. Children depend entirely on the decisions of others, and those decisions have already been made elsewhere.

For these boys the physical toll appears not in collapse, but in bearing. Children move forward on their own feet, dressed for cold, their bodies already shaped by conditions they did not choose. The star sewn onto the coat is impossible to miss, transforming the child into a visible category before he has any chance to understand what that category means.

Their expressions are set and guarded, not because they comprehend the full weight of what is happening, but because uncertainty has already narrowed their world. They walk among adults and other children, yet the marking isolates them, making their identity legible at a glance. What they carry is minimal; what has been placed upon them is not.

This is how exclusion settles into the body early. Not through explanation or punishment, but through enforced visibility and forward motion without choice. Childhood offers no protection here. It is carried along with the process, required to endure what it cannot resist and cannot refuse.

Here, care becomes visible as an act of resistance, even when it cannot alter what is coming. A child is held close, positioned against the body as if proximity itself might provide protection. The gesture is instinctive rather than strategic, rooted in attachment rather than expectation.

The mother's attention is fixed inward, toward the child she must carry with her into whatever comes next. She is not only responsible for her own compliance, but for guiding another life through a process neither of them chose and neither can yet understand. What lies ahead—for shelter, safety, or duration—remains undefined. What is certain is that they will face it together.

This image records the burden of uncertainty borne unevenly. The child depends entirely on the mother's presence, while the mother must absorb uncertainty for them both. Care persists here not as resistance, but as responsibility—holding, protecting, and continuing to parent within a system that has already claimed their future without explanation.

Her ability to shield her children is more visibly strained. The children are gathered close, bodies arranged to create a barrier against exposure and cold as the crowd presses inward. The environment offers no comfort. What little shelter is made out of bodies and arms and attention held tightly in place.

What weighs heaviest here is not the crowd, but knowledge. The mother bends over her child with an intensity that suggests more than immediate concern. Her posture carries the burden of what she understands may be coming and her inability to prevent it. She holds him not only to protect him from the present moment, but because she knows that protection may soon fail.

These images record the final transfer of control. Authority has claimed the future. What remains to the parents is presence—holding, watching, and bearing what cannot be stopped—because their fate, and that of their children, has already been decided elsewhere.

This is the moment when the fiction of cooperation finally collapses. Movement continues, but it no longer carries even the appearance of choice. The presence of armed authority transforms walking into compliance and public space into a controlled corridor. What had been framed as procedure now reveals itself as enforcement.

At this stage, obedience is no longer assumed; it is ensured. The route is fixed, the pace regulated, and the crowd shaped to move as a single body. Individual lives are absorbed into a collective problem to be managed, escorted, and delivered. The fact that people are still moving under their own power does not mitigate what is happening. It completes it. Force no longer needs to be applied because it has already been internalized.

This is where the earlier steps—posted notices, shuttered businesses, registration tables, and waiting rooms—converge. Each prepared the ground for this moment. Each narrowed the range of response until movement under guard became the only remaining option that did not carry immediate danger.

There is no question. Power is no longer abstract or procedural. It is embodied. Armed escorts do not simply accompany civilians; they define the conditions under which civilians exist in this space. Weapons do not need to be raised to exert control. Their visibility alone establishes the limits of possibility, signaling that refusal is no longer imaginable and that alternatives have been removed in advance.

This is not order maintained for safety. It is control exercised for compliance. The crowd advances not because it agrees, but because every earlier step has narrowed response to a single remaining option.

These images mark the point at which injustice no longer requires disguise. It has passed beyond justification and into routine. What follows is not the result of disorder or excess, but the logical continuation of a system that has already decided who may belong, who may move, and who must be confined—and has built the means to ensure that decision is carried out without interruption.

This is the moment when removal locks itself into place. Trains do not wander. They run on fixed tracks, toward pre-determined destinations, on schedules set by someone else. Once people are assembled here, waiting along the platform with what they have been allowed to carry, the future ceases to be **negotiable.** The train functions as a point of no return, where presence itself signals submission to a process that will continue regardless of individual will. Time narrows here, reduced to departures and arrivals controlled entirely by others.

What appears orderly is, in fact, final. Lines form not because there is nowhere else to stand. The train itself becomes an instrument of authority, concentrating bodies, compressing time, and eliminating alternatives. To step onto it is not to travel, but to submit to a decision already made.

This is where displacement becomes industrial. The scale expands, the pace accelerates, and individual circumstances disappear into logistics.

The repetition is unmistakable. Car after car waits to be filled. What was once extraordinary has become routine. The presence of guards and officials signals that this movement is compulsory, even when force remains implied rather than enacted.

Hands are raised along the tracks in gestures that resemble farewell rather than resistance. Those already aboard wave back toward those still standing below, performing normalcy in the only language left available to them. The exchange carries the appearance of reassurance, even as the direction of travel admits none.

Once the doors close and the train pulls away, the past is inaccessible and the future is sealed. What remains is duration: hours, days, or longer spent in transit, suspended between what has been taken away and what has not yet been revealed.

This transport is control, designed to deliver people to a place they did not choose, under conditions they did not consent to, and for purposes that those waving—above and below—have not yet been allowed to fully see.

Here is where the machinery finishes its work. Movement ends. Waiting, which once implied an outcome, is replaced by duration without horizon. Rows of barracks extend outward with measured precision, each structure identical to the next, laid out across open ground in a geometry of containment rather than refuge.

What has been assembled here is permanence disguised as provision. The buildings suggest order, efficiency, and basic accommodation. What they do not provide is privacy, autonomy, or a future that can be imagined from within their limits. Arrival does not resolve what removal began. It merely stabilizes it.

This is where uncertainty hardens into structure. Life continues, but only inside boundaries designed by others and enforced through routine. Time is reorganized into schedules, roll calls, meals, and permissions that dictate when to eat, when to move, and when to wait. The future is no longer something one plans toward. It is something deferred, managed, and indefinitely postponed.

The scale makes the condition unmistakable. The repetition is deliberate, extending outward in ordered lines that reduce human presence to units of accommodation. Each barrack contains different lives, but the architecture refuses distinction. What matters within this arrangement is not who people are, but how many can be housed, observed, and controlled.

These images show how injustice sustains itself by mastering both space and time. Once a population is enclosed, its future becomes conditional and revocable, subject to decisions made elsewhere and unseen. Hope is neither promised nor extinguished outright; it is postponed, recalibrated to endurance alone.

This is not simply where people are kept. It is where possibility is held in suspension under constant oversight, where life continues only insofar as it remains administratively useful. What follows will unfold here, within these boundaries, shaped by a future that is not only unknown, but no longer theirs to imagine.

Finally, separation is no longer inferred but built. The barrier stands between people and the space beyond it, converting landscape into limit. What was once open ground is redefined as off-limits, not through argument or explanation, but through construction. The fence does not negotiate. It declares.

Crowds gather along the boundary, faces turned outward, bodies pressed toward a line that cannot be crossed. The proximity is deliberate. It allows people to see what has been taken from them while making access impossible. The fence performs its work not only by preventing movement, but by insisting on awareness. Life continues on the other side, close enough to witness and far enough to deny.

At this stage, hope has not disappeared, but it has been narrowed. It is no longer attached to return or restoration, but to endurance. People hope for better treatment, for clarification, for time to pass without further loss. Hope becomes something quiet and provisional, adjusted to fit inside the boundary.

Barbed wire reinforces the boundary enacted by surveillance and guard presence. The fence is no longer simply a structure; it is a condition of daily life. People wait within it, lined up and exposed, learning where they are permitted to stand and how long they will be required to remain there. Waiting itself becomes regulated.

What the fence accomplishes is not merely restriction, but redefinition. They are a population set apart, visible but inaccessible, present but excluded. The fence converts people into a problem to be managed and a risk to be contained.

Hope persists here, but only in forms that do not challenge the boundary. It is redirected toward survival, toward small mercies, toward the possibility that conditions will improve without resistance. In this way, hope itself becomes part of the system, sustaining compliance by offering just enough expectation to make endurance possible.

These images show how injustice completes itself not only through force, but through duration. Once a boundary is built and defended, it no longer needs constant enforcement.

This is where control becomes explicit and unquestionable. The watchtower rises above the enclosure, elevated not to protect what lies within it, but to oversee it. From this position, authority is no longer implied or dispersed. It is centralized, visible, and unchallengeable. The tower establishes a vertical order: those who watch above, and those who are watched below.

Its height places power beyond reach, beyond conversation, beyond reciprocity. Observation and judgment move in one direction only. This is the moment when waiting ceases to be about permission and becomes about outcome alone.

The tower stands as a reminder that every action, every pause, every deviation occurs under scrutiny. Authority no longer has to announce itself through orders or instruction. It has been built into the landscape, occupying the highest ground and claiming the final perspective.

This is where decisions no longer arise from process or appeal. They originate elsewhere, from a position that cannot be accessed, questioned, or resisted.

Here, the system is complete. Fences define the boundary. Barracks organize existence within it. The watchtower stands apart, separate and higher, marking the location of authority itself. What happens inside the enclosure will be seen, judged, and acted upon by those who are not subject to the same conditions.

The tower symbolizes more than surveillance. It represents final jurisdiction. Those confined beneath it understand that their future will not be determined by effort, compliance, or patience alone. It will be determined elsewhere, by someone else, according to standards they do not control.

This is where power finishes consolidating itself. Space has been claimed. Time has been regulated. Movement has been restricted. Now visibility completes the structure. Authority does not merely contain bodies; it oversees outcomes.

These images make plain the final truth of enclosure: once authority occupies the highest ground, it holds the final say in what happens below. The future is conditional, subject to a power greater than those who must live beneath it.

The early stages of mass injustice are recognizable, repeatable, and often defended as reasonable. The difference between incarceration and annihilation is not moral intent, but how far those stages are allowed to proceed.

The outcomes of these histories were not the same, and it would be dishonest to suggest otherwise. Jewish communities across Europe were subjected to systematic annihilation. Japanese Americans incarcerated in the United States were eventually released, though often without their property, livelihoods, or standing restored. Survival, however, does not equal justice, and the difference in outcome does not negate the shared moral failure that made both systems possible.

In the United States, the mass removal and incarceration of Japanese Americans was authorized by **Executive Order 9066**, signed by President Franklin D. Roosevelt in February 1942. The order did not name Japanese Americans explicitly, but its intent and application were unmistakable. It provided the legal framework that allowed military authorities to exclude civilians from their homes, strip them of due process, and confine them without charges or trials. What followed was not an accident or a misunderstanding. It was state action, carried out lawfully, publicly, and with broad public support.

What separates these histories is not intent revealed early on, but how far exclusion was allowed to proceed unchecked. The mechanisms were already in place. The language had been accepted. The removal had been justified. Entire populations had been defined as threats rather than citizens. The difference lies in where the line was finally drawn—and how late.

This chapter is not an argument that one history inevitably leads to the other. It is a warning about how easily it could have. Nothing shown here required secrecy, fanaticism, or sudden collapse into cruelty. It required permission. It required fear to outweigh principle. It required enough people to accept that rights could be suspended for others in the name of security.

Executive Order 9066 demonstrates how quickly that permission can be formalized. Once exclusion is rendered legal, it becomes enforceable, repeatable, and expandable. The fact that the United States did not proceed further does not erase how far it did go, nor does it absolve those who defended or normalized the policy while it was in effect.

History is often softened by outcomes. This chapter resists that impulse. It insists that injustice be judged at the moment it occurs, not redeemed retroactively by the fact that something worse did not follow. What happened was wrong when it happened, regardless of how it ended.

The warning here is not abstract. It is historical, documented, and visible. These images show what exclusion looks like before it finishes its work. The responsibility of memory is to recognize that moment clearly—and to refuse to accept it again, under any name, any order, or any authority.

Chapter Thirteen

Who Could Be Taken: Race, Profit and the Logic of Internment

Section I - From Classification to Permission

This chapter reconstructs the logic of internment as it unfolds in practice, tracing how administrative decisions accumulate into mass confinement.

Internment does not begin with fences. It begins with categories. Long before people are confined, removed, or detained, they are first defined as a type of problem, a population that can be managed rather than a group of individuals who must be protected. This transformation rarely feels abrupt at the time. It unfolds through language, policy, and precedent, each step small enough to appear reasonable, even necessary, within the logic that produces it.

Classification is the critical first move. Societies sort people into groups that appear natural, objective, and administratively useful. Race, nationality, religion, legal status, and ancestry become tools for simplification, allowing complex human lives to be reduced to manageable descriptors. Once categorized, individuals are no longer encountered primarily as persons, but as instances of a type. This shift makes it possible to imagine collective solutions to perceived threats, even when no individual wrongdoing has occurred.

In the United States, this process is visible well before the formal establishment of internment camps. Census categories, immigration laws, and racialized land policies created a framework in which certain populations were already marked as conditional residents. Asian immigrants, for example, were classified not only by nationality but by racial category, rendering them perpetually foreign regardless of citizenship status. The Chinese Exclusion Act of 1882 did not arise from mass criminal behavior, it arose from a classification system that framed an entire population as economically and culturally incompatible. Exclusion was justified as management.

By the time Japanese Americans were interned during World War II, the groundwork had already been laid. Executive Order 9066 did not name Japanese Americans explicitly, yet it relied on existing racial classifications to function. Citizenship offered no protection. Individuals were not evaluated for loyalty; ancestry alone sufficed. Farmers, shopkeepers, children, and elders were removed en masse because the category to which they belonged had been defined as potentially dangerous. Internment was presented not as punishment, but as precaution. The administrative language obscured the reality that no comparable measures were applied to German or Italian Americans at the same scale, despite the nation being at war with Germany and Italy as well.

A similar pattern unfolded in Europe earlier in the twentieth century. In Nazi Germany, the classification of Jews preceded their removal by years. Legal definitions established through the Nuremberg Laws reduced Jewish identity to blood quantum and ancestry, stripping individuals of citizenship and legal protection before any camps were built. Businesses were cataloged, professions restricted, and movement regulated. Each step was bureaucratic, incremental, and justified as a matter of law. By the time mass internment and deportation began, the population had already been transformed, on paper, into a category that could be acted upon without moral contradiction.

Colonial contexts offer further examples. In British-controlled Kenya during the Mau Mau uprising of the 1950s, entire Kikuyu populations were classified as suspect. Villages were relocated, and hundreds of thousands of people were detained in camps under the justification of emergency security measures. Individual guilt was irrelevant. Membership in a group associated with resistance was sufficient to warrant confinement. The system was administered through legal orders, identity documents, and compliance metrics, allowing widespread detention to proceed under the appearance of order.

Economic interest often sharpened these classifications. In the United States, Japanese American internment resulted in the loss of land, businesses, and property, much of which was acquired by others at reduced cost. The state did not merely remove a population; it redistributed assets. Similar patterns appear in Indigenous removals, where tribes were classified as wards or obstacles to development, enabling forced relocation and the seizure of land for settlement, mining, or agriculture. Profit did not drive classification alone, but once classification existed, profit followed easily.

What unites these cases is not ideology alone, but administrative logic. In each instance, the question was framed not as whether internment was just, but whether it was efficient, legal, and expedient. Once people were defined primarily through category, containment became a logistical problem. Camps, reservations, and detention centers could be designed, staffed, and managed without requiring ongoing moral deliberation. The machinery of governance absorbed responsibility.

This process echoes earlier patterns explored throughout this work. Neanderthals were classified as less capable and ultimately expendable within a narrative of progress. Cultures displayed at World's Fairs were categorized as earlier stages of humanity, making their displacement appear natural. In each case, classification preceded erasure. Internment follows the same trajectory, translating conceptual hierarchy into physical confinement.

What makes this progression particularly dangerous is its ordinariness. No single step demands cruelty. Each can be defended as prudent, lawful, or temporary. Together, they create a system in which people can be taken without violating the society's self-image. Internment becomes not an exception to democratic values, but a product of them, justified through procedure rather than principle.

Understanding this transition from classification to permission is essential for grasping how internment becomes possible in societies that consider themselves civilized. The decisive moment does not occur when the gates close, but when a population is first rendered legible as a problem. By then, the question is no longer whether people can be taken, but how.

Section II - Race as Justification, Profit as Engine

Once a population is rendered legible as a category that can be managed, race often becomes the moral shorthand that makes action appear justified. Racialized thinking simplifies fear by attaching it to visible or inherited traits, allowing suspicion to operate without evidence. When race is invoked, risk no longer needs to be demonstrated; it is presumed. This presumption creates the conditions under which confinement can be presented as reasonable, even benevolent, particularly when it is framed as temporary or protective.

Race does not function alone in this process. It works most effectively when paired with economic incentive. Internment is expensive, disruptive, and difficult to sustain unless it serves material interests beyond security. Profit provides that reinforcement. Once confinement produces economic benefit for the state, for private actors, or for both, the logic of internment shifts from emergency response to structural solution. What began as a precaution becomes an opportunity.

What the photographs in the previous chapter make visible is why this convergence works so efficiently. Race provided the justification. Economic gain followed quietly but decisively. Japanese American farmers had developed highly productive agricultural land along the West Coast, often transforming marginal soil into profitable farms. Their removal freed that land for acquisition by others, frequently at reduced cost. Businesses were shuttered, inventories liquidated, and property transferred under duress. While the government framed internment as a matter of national security, the redistribution of assets benefited local competitors and municipalities. The loss experienced by those interned was not incidental; it was structurally absorbed into the surrounding economy.

This pattern is not unique. In colonial settings, race repeatedly functioned as the rationale for confinement, while land and labor provided the incentive. Indigenous peoples in North America were classified as wards or impediments to progress, a designation that justified their removal to reservations. These removals coincided with the opening of vast territories for settlement, mining, and agriculture. The reservation system did not merely isolate Native populations; it cleared space for economic expansion. Profit was not a secondary outcome. It was integral to the policy's persistence.

In Europe, the economic dimensions of internment were often less overt but no less significant. In Nazi Germany, the exclusion and eventual internment of Jews followed a systematic process of dispossession. Businesses were Aryanized, property seized, and labor extracted. Each stage was codified through law, allowing material transfer to proceed under the cover of legality. Race defined who could be taken; profit ensured that taking them was advantageous. The machinery of the state normalized theft by embedding it within administrative procedure.

Even in cases framed explicitly as security measures, economic incentives often emerge quickly. During the Boer War, British authorities interned civilian populations in camps justified as protective custody. These camps also served to disrupt local resistance by removing labor, consolidating populations, and weakening economic self-sufficiency. The suffering that followed was treated as collateral, an unfortunate byproduct of necessary control. The camps functioned as tools of pacification and economic restructuring simultaneously.

What makes the pairing of race and profit so durable is that it diffuses responsibility. When economic benefit accrues gradually and across multiple actors, no single decision appears decisive. Land changes hands through legal sale, labor is reallocated through contracts, and industries expand to meet new administrative needs. Camps require construction, staffing, supplies, and transport, creating entire economies around confinement. Once these systems are in place, dismantling them threatens livelihoods as well as ideology. Internment becomes embedded in the economic fabric of the society that created it.

This convergence also reshapes public perception. When internment generates visible economic stability or growth, opposition weakens. The moral cost is obscured by material reassurance. Those who benefit may never encounter the confined population directly, allowing abstraction to persist. Race ensures distance; profit ensures silence. Together, they transform a policy of exclusion into a normalized feature of governance.

The same logic appears in more contemporary detention regimes, where migrants and asylum seekers are confined within privatized systems that generate revenue through contracts and per diem payments. Legal status replaces race as the explicit category, but racialized assumptions continue to shape who is targeted and how they are treated. Detention is framed as administrative necessity, yet its persistence is reinforced by the industries that depend upon it. The boundary between security and commerce dissolves.

Understanding internment through this lens reveals why it so often outlasts the conditions that ostensibly justified it. Once race has marked a population as suspect and profit has made their confinement useful, the system acquires momentum. Ending it requires not only a moral reckoning, but the dismantling of structures that have learned to thrive on exclusion. Internment endures because it solves multiple problems at once: it reassures the public, enriches certain actors, and reinforces existing hierarchies.

Seen alongside earlier chapters, this dynamic is familiar. Cultures classified as lesser are displaced, absorbed, or confined, while their removal creates opportunities for others. Whether through evolutionary narrative, imperial expansion, exhibition, or detention, the pattern remains consistent. Those who can be taken are those whose taking benefits the system that defines them.

Section III - Internment as Bureaucracy, Not Emergency

By the time confinement appears orderly, it no longer requires persuasion. Repetition does the work. Each form, each line, each waiting space reduces the need for justification. What begins as emergency becomes familiar simply by being endured.

Bureaucracy excels at making harm appear impersonal. Decisions are fragmented across offices, agencies, and levels of authority, ensuring that no single actor feels responsible for the whole. Orders are issued in abstract language, policies implemented through standardized steps, and outcomes evaluated through metrics rather than lived experience. In this environment, suffering becomes a data point, and compliance replaces consent as the measure of success. The system does not need to hate those it confines; it needs only to process them.

The internment of Japanese Americans illustrated how quickly this transformation can occur. Within months of Executive Order 9066, an extensive administrative apparatus emerged to manage removal, transportation, housing, and labor. Camps were designed, staffed, and regulated according to federal guidelines that emphasized efficiency and order. Reports tracked occupancy, productivity, and compliance. Daily life was governed by schedules, permits, and rules that reduced individual autonomy while maintaining the appearance of normalcy. The emergency had passed, yet the system continued, sustained by its own momentum.

Similar patterns appear in other contexts. In apartheid-era South Africa, pass laws and residential zoning functioned as instruments of internal internment, restricting movement and concentrating populations under bureaucratic control. Compliance was monitored through documentation rather than constant force, allowing the state to present segregation as lawful order rather than repression. The machinery of governance did the work of containment, embedding exclusion within everyday life.

In colonial detention regimes, bureaucracy often proved more effective than brute force. During the Algerian War of Independence, the French government established camps and regroupment centers administered through civilian and military agencies. These facilities were justified as protective measures, yet they functioned to isolate populations, disrupt social networks, and consolidate control. Detailed records tracked individuals, movements, and resources, transforming communities into manageable units. The language of administration masked the reality of coercion.

Bureaucratic internment also benefits from temporal ambiguity. Measures described as temporary frequently lack clear endpoints. Reviews are postponed, criteria shift, and exceptions multiply. The confined population remains suspended in a state of waiting, neither fully punished nor fully free. This indeterminacy weakens resistance, as individuals are encouraged to comply in hopes of release. The system relies on patience rather than force, extracting obedience through uncertainty.

The routinization of internment reshapes public perception. As confinement becomes embedded in institutional practice, it loses its association with crisis. Camps, detention centers, and restricted zones are accepted as features of governance rather than deviations from it. Media coverage focuses on administration rather than morality, reinforcing the idea that the issue is one of management. Once internment is normalized, questioning it appears impractical or naïve.

This bureaucratic logic mirrors earlier forms of erasure discussed throughout this work. Neanderthals were not violently expunged in a single moment; they were gradually displaced within a narrative that rendered their disappearance inevitable. Cultures displayed at World's Fairs were not explicitly condemned; they were classified, arranged, and fixed in place. Internment follows the same pattern, substituting paperwork for spectacle but achieving the same end. People are removed from the center of the social world and placed under administrative control, their status redefined through process rather than debate.

Understanding internment as bureaucracy rather than emergency clarifies why it recurs across political systems and historical periods. It does not require extraordinary malice, only ordinary governance applied without moral restraint. Once confinement is reduced to a set of procedures, it can be replicated, expanded, and sustained with minimal resistance. The danger lies not in the moment of crisis, but in the efficiency with which societies learn to manage those they have decided can be taken.

Section IV - What Internment Teaches a Society About Itself

Internment is often remembered as a deviation, an unfortunate response to extraordinary circumstances that a society later regrets. Yet when examined closely, internment reveals something far more ordinary. It exposes the values a society is willing to suspend, the categories it considers negotiable, and the distance it can tolerate between legality and justice. What internment teaches is not primarily about those confined, but about the norms of the society that confines them.

A society that interned people did not suddenly abandon its principles. It rearranged them. Rights became conditional, belonging became provisional, and protection became selective. The language of law did not disappear; it intensified. Procedures multiplied, oversight mechanisms were named, and documentation increased. This bureaucratic density reassured the public that order was being maintained even as individuals lost freedom without individualized cause. The system did not fail to function. It functioned as designed.

Internment also clarifies how fear is operationalized. Fear alone does not produce camps; it produces demand. The response to that demand reveals institutional priorities. When fear leads to expanded due process and individualized assessment, a society signals confidence in its principles. When fear leads to collective confinement and administrative shortcuts, it signals a willingness to trade principle for control. Internment marks the point at which management replaces trust as the organizing logic of governance.

The populations selected for internment are equally instructive. They are rarely those with full political voice or social protection. They are groups already positioned at the margins by race, legal status, or economic vulnerability. Internment does not create these margins; it exploits them. The ease with which a population can be confined reflects how thoroughly it has been separated, in advance, from the circle of obligation. The question is not why these groups were chosen, but why their choosing did not provoke systemic resistance.

Internment further teaches how profit reshapes moral perception. When confinement generates employment, contracts, or land redistribution, opposition weakens. Economic normalization dulls ethical urgency. What begins as an emergency measure acquires stakeholders who benefit from its continuation. The society learns to tolerate what it once might have condemned, not because values have changed explicitly, but because incentives have. Over time, confinement becomes one policy option among others, judged by efficiency rather than legitimacy.

Perhaps most revealing is how internment ends, when it ends at all. Apologies are issued, compensation debated, memorials erected. These gestures acknowledge harm without fully confronting the mechanisms that produced it. The society remembers the event as an exception rather than as a pattern. Responsibility is localized in past leaders or circumstances, preserving the belief that the present is different. This selective memory allows the underlying logic to persist, ready to be reactivated under new names and categories.

Across history, the same lesson repeats. From colonial camps to wartime internment, from reservations to detention centers, the architecture changes but the reasoning remains. Internment becomes possible when a society convinces itself that some people can be removed temporarily without altering its moral core. The danger lies in the confidence with which this belief is held. Each instance teaches the society how to do it again, more efficiently, with less controversy.

Placed alongside the earlier chapters of this work, internment appears not as an endpoint but as a culmination. Classification makes people legible, profit makes their removal useful, bureaucracy makes it routine, and memory reframes it as necessary. The society that permits internment learns to live with contradiction, maintaining an image of justice while practicing exclusion. This capacity for compartmentalization is not an aberration. It is a learned skill.

Understanding what internment teaches a society about itself prepares the ground for the final chapter. The logic examined here does not reside safely in the past. It persists in forms that are quieter, more procedural, and more easily denied. To examine the present tense of internment is not to accuse, but to recognize continuity. The question that remains is not whether this logic still exists, but where it is currently being applied—and to whom.

Section V - Internment Without Naming It

By the early twenty-first century, the logic of internment no longer required spectacle or declaration. It operated quietly, embedded within administrative systems that presented themselves as lawful, necessary, and routine. The camps did not announce themselves as such. They were described instead as facilities, centers, or holding spaces, their purpose framed as processing rather than confinement. This shift in language did not mark a departure from earlier practices, but their refinement. Internment had learned how to persist without demanding recognition.

Immigration detention in the United States exemplified this evolution. It was defined as civil confinement, not criminal punishment, a distinction that carried profound consequences. Because detention was administrative, individuals could be held without the procedural safeguards typically associated with incarceration. Confinement followed status rather than conduct. People were detained not for acts committed, but for classifications applied: undocumented, inadmissible, removable. The category itself became sufficient justification.

This system expanded gradually, framed as a response to border management and legal process rather than as a form of mass confinement. Detention was described as temporary, a holding measure while cases were resolved. In practice, confinement often extended for months or years. Hearings were delayed, access to counsel uneven, and release contingent on complex and shifting criteria. Families were separated as a matter of policy, not because of individualized determinations, but because separation was treated as an administrative outcome rather than a moral decision.

Children were confined in facilities designed for throughput rather than care, their presence justified through legal distinctions that reclassified them as unaccompanied or transferred responsibility across agencies. Each step followed procedure. Each agency acted within its mandate. The cumulative effect was a system in which confinement became normalized without ever being declared exceptional. The absence of criminal conviction did not appear anomalous because the system did not define itself as punitive.

Profit reinforced this arrangement. A substantial portion of immigration detention was administered by private contractors operating under federal agreements that tied revenue to occupancy. Facilities were constructed in rural areas where employment opportunities were limited, creating local dependence on detention economies. Jobs, contracts, and infrastructure investments tied community stability to the continuation of confinement. Detention became not only a policy tool, but an economic fixture, sustained by interests that benefited from its persistence.

This economic dimension echoed earlier internment systems, where removal and confinement produced material gain alongside social control. The system did not require overt exploitation to function. It relied instead on diffusion. Responsibility was distributed across agencies, contractors, and jurisdictions, ensuring that no single actor appeared accountable for the whole. Confinement became an outcome of process rather than intention.

Alongside immigration detention operated a related, quieter mechanism: the administrative management of dissent. The United States did not establish mass camps for political opponents, yet it employed a range of measures that constrained speech and protest through surveillance, legal pressure, and selective enforcement. Activists, journalists, and organizers were monitored, categorized, and flagged through databases and intelligence-sharing programs. Protest movements were infiltrated and mapped. The goal was not necessarily mass arrest, but deterrence.

Those who spoke up learned that visibility carried risk. Permits were denied, protests were declared unlawful, and charges were brought selectively. Surveillance did not need to result in immediate punishment to be effective. The knowledge of being watched altered behavior. Legal processes, rather than overt repression, did the work. The state rarely needed to confine dissenters en masse; it needed only to demonstrate that it could.

This approach mirrored the broader logic of internment: classification, monitoring, and containment through administrative means. Speech was managed not through censorship, but through procedure. Activism was framed as a security concern, protest as a logistical problem. The language emphasized order and safety, allowing restrictions to appear reasonable. As with immigration detention, legality served as justification. If actions followed protocol, their moral implications were treated as secondary.

What united these practices was their reliance on legibility. Populations were rendered visible through data, documents, and categories. Once legible, they could be managed. Immigration status, protest affiliation, travel history, and online activity became points of entry into systems of control. The emphasis on information created the appearance of precision, masking the bluntness of the outcomes. People were reduced to profiles, their individuality subsumed by classification.

The continuity with earlier forms of internment lay not in scale, but in structure. Neanderthals had been rendered replaceable through narratives of inferiority. Indigenous populations had been confined through classifications that framed removal as management. World's Fairs had displayed living people as representatives of earlier stages of humanity. Each system relied on the same premise: that certain groups could be acted upon collectively without undermining the moral identity of the society doing the acting.

In the contemporary United States, this premise persisted under new names. Detention was lawful. Surveillance was justified. Confinement was administrative. Each component appeared defensible in isolation. Together, they recreated the conditions under which internment had always occurred. The absence of overt brutality did not negate the logic at work. It concealed it.

What made this form of internment especially resilient was its compatibility with democratic self-understanding. Because detention followed law rather than decree, it did not register as a violation of principle. Because surveillance was justified as security, it did not appear as repression. Because profit was indirect, it was rarely acknowledged. The system functioned smoothly enough to avoid sustained scrutiny, its consequences dispersed across time and space.

Resistance to these practices existed, but it faced structural obstacles. Legal challenges moved slowly. Advocacy competed with narratives of crisis and threat. Public attention shifted. Without a single defining moment, opposition struggled to coalesce. Internment without naming proved difficult to confront precisely because it did not resemble the internment of memory. It lacked fences in prominent locations and declarations of emergency. It relied instead on endurance.

The lesson of this period was not that the United States abandoned its values, but that it reinterpreted them. Liberty became conditional. Due process became procedural. Equality before the law coexisted with categorical suspicion. The American public learned to hold these contradictions without resolving them, relying on institutional complexity to absorb tension. Internment did not require consensus; it required acquiescence.

By the time these systems were widely recognized, they were deeply embedded. Facilities existed. Contracts were signed. Data systems were integrated. Ending confinement would have required not only moral resolve, but the dismantling of structures that had become normalized. The persistence of internment thus reflected not a momentary lapse, but a learned capacity to manage exclusion within the bounds of legality.

This capacity connected the present to the past. The same reasoning that once justified removal, exhibition, and confinement continued to operate, adapted to contemporary sensibilities. The criteria shifted. The language softened. The logic endured. Internment remained possible wherever a population could be defined as administratively inconvenient, economically marginal, or politically risky.

The chapter therefore ended where it began, with the question of who could be taken. The answer was not fixed. It changed with context, crisis, and classification. What remained constant was the process by which taking became permissible. History showed that this process did not announce itself as injustice. It presented itself as order.

Recognizing internment in this form did not require equating the present with the worst moments of the past. It required acknowledging continuity. The systems examined throughout this work did not vanish; they evolved. The capacity to confine without naming, to remove without declaring, and to manage populations through procedure rather than force remained intact. The danger lay not in forgetting past internments, but in failing to recognize their present-tense descendants when they appeared reasonable enough to endure.

What distinguishes the present moment is not novelty, but speed. People are being taken into custody, transferred, and removed through administrative decision rather than individualized judgment, often with little notice and limited recourse. Families disappear from workplaces, schools, and neighborhoods not because a crime has been proven, but because a status has been reactivated, reinterpreted, or newly prioritized. The process does not announce itself as mass action. It operates through databases, warrants, transport schedules, and jurisdictional handoffs that fracture responsibility and accelerate outcome. What appears as enforcement is, in practice, removal by momentum. The system does not need certainty to function; it needs only permission to proceed while review lags behind consequence.

In this environment, confinement and deportation are no longer experienced as extraordinary events, but as background conditions—predictable enough to induce compliance, volatile enough to prevent organized resistance. This is internment's contemporary form: not declared, not centralized, and not acknowledged as such, yet fully capable of erasing presence before its absence can be named.

Chapter Fourteen

If the Lord's Willing and the Creek Don't Rise: Flood Control and the Displacement of Rural Kansas Communities

Section I

The first time you stand where a town used to be, the absence does not announce itself. There is no sudden realization, no dramatic sense of loss rising up to meet you. What you notice instead are small inconsistencies—an open stretch of land that feels too deliberate, a line of trees that stops abruptly, a road that narrows and then simply gives up. The ground does not look empty so much as unfinished, as though something essential has been removed and the land has been left to adjust in its own time.

Irving and Broughton exist in this way now. They are no longer towns in the conventional sense, yet they are not gone. The land still holds the memory of streets and storefronts, of churches and schools, of voices that once carried across the open spaces. When the wind moves through the grass it does not feel aimless. It moves with the familiarity of something retracing paths it once knew.

Both towns were built along rivers—Irving on the Big Blue, Broughton on the Republican—because water meant survival. The rivers were not simply geographic features but living presences, shaping daily life, work, and expectation. Flooding was part of that relationship. It was dangerous and disruptive, but it was also understood. The people who settled here accepted that the rivers would sometimes overstep their banks, depositing rich soil in exchange for loss. This was not viewed as catastrophe so much as cycle. You rebuilt, replanted, and trusted that what was taken one year would be returned in another.

That understanding did not come from ignorance or resignation. It came from living close to the land, from paying attention to patterns that repeated themselves over generations. Drought followed flood. Hard years were balanced by abundance. Survival depended on cooperation—neighbors helping neighbors, towns serving as anchors for scattered farms, people bound together by shared vulnerability. In places like Irving and Broughton, community was not an abstract concept. It was a necessity.

What ultimately ended these towns did not arrive with wind or water. It came in the language of policy and progress, in plans drawn far downstream from where the consequences would be felt. Floods that had once been endured became framed as failures—evidence that nature itself was unruly and in need of control. Rivers that had sustained these communities were recast as threats to commerce and urban expansion. Solutions were proposed that promised safety and economic growth, but the cost would be paid elsewhere.

Standing on these former town sites now, it is difficult to reconcile the quiet with the violence of that transformation. There are no ruins in the traditional sense. Buildings were moved or dismantled, homes sold and condemned, streets erased. What remains are markers—stones, plaques, a mailbox beside the road—small gestures insisting that something once stood here, that lives unfolded in this space, that erasure is not the same as forgetting.

I grew up close to these places. Their stories were not distant history to me; they were carried in family conversations, in names spoken with familiarity, in the knowledge that my grandmother had been raised in Irving and that my grandfather had known Broughton as home. Long before I understood the policies or the politics, I understood the loss. It was present in the way people spoke about the land, in the quiet anger that surfaced when the dams were mentioned, in the annual gatherings where absence became a form of presence.

These towns were not lost to time or neglect. They were taken—carefully, methodically, and with the assurance that what was being sacrificed was expendable. Yet the land resists that conclusion. Memory lingers here, not as nostalgia, but as testimony. To stand in these places is to feel that something is still being asked of us: to remember, to bear witness, and to acknowledge that progress, when measured only in profit and protection, leaves behind its own kind of ruins.

Section II

To understand why Irving and Broughton endured for as long as they did, you have to understand what it meant to live on the Great Plains. This was never an easy place to settle, and no one arrived here under the illusion that the land would yield without resistance. The weather alone demanded respect. Winters brought blizzards that erased fences and roads, isolating farms for days at a time. Spring carried the threat of floods, hail, and tornadoes—often all within the same season. Summers scorched the fields and tested the limits of both crops and people, while drought lingered like a quiet, unrelenting pressure. Fall offered only a brief pause before the cycle began again.

Yet it was precisely this volatility that shaped the character of these communities. Survival depended on attention—to the sky, to the rivers, to one another. Farmers learned to read the land the way others read books, noticing subtle changes in soil, wind, and water that signaled what was coming. Flooding, though destructive, was not viewed as an enemy. It was part of a long-established rhythm, one that replenished the soil even as it demanded sacrifice. A ruined crop one year might mean a bumper harvest the next. Loss and reward were understood as two sides of the same relationship.

The rivers were central to this way of life. The Big Blue and the Republican were not obstacles to be conquered but partners in an uneasy coexistence. Towns grew where water was accessible, where transportation and irrigation made settlement possible. Irving and Broughton became hubs not because they were large or powerful, but because they provided what scattered farms needed—schools, churches, stores, places to gather and exchange news. These towns gave shape to lives spread across miles of open land.

Community in this context was not optional. It was built through shared labor and shared risk. When storms destroyed barns or floods swept through fields, neighbors showed up without being asked. Machinery was shared, hands were lent, meals were provided. Children grew up knowing not only their own families but the families of those who lived miles away, connected by dirt roads and mutual dependence. In these towns, people belonged to one another in ways that did not require formal acknowledgment. The bonds were assumed, reinforced by repetition and necessity.

This interdependence created a sense of identity that outlasted individual relationships. You did not need to know everyone personally to feel connected to them. The town itself carried that connection, standing in for the many unseen ties that held people together. It was understood that what happened to one family mattered to the rest, because the land and the work made that reality unavoidable.

Floods came again and again, and each time the communities adapted. Buildings were repaired, sometimes moved. Policies were put in place locally—informal agreements about where to rebuild, how to respond when the water rose. These were not grand solutions, but they were practical, grounded in experience rather than theory. The people of Irving and Broughton learned to live with uncertainty because uncertainty was constant.

What they could not anticipate was that the greatest threat to their way of life would not come from nature, but from decisions made far beyond the riverbanks. The same floods they had endured for generations would be reinterpreted as intolerable failures, and the knowledge born of lived experience would be dismissed as backward or naïve. The relationship these communities had forged with the land—fragile, respectful, and reciprocal—would soon be judged insufficient in the face of larger economic ambitions.

For now, though, before the plans and surveys and condemnations, Irving and Broughton were alive. Children walked to school along streets that no longer exist. Church bells marked the passage of time. Farmers gathered in town to trade stories and supplies, to remind themselves that they were not alone. These were not forgotten places waiting to disappear. They were functioning, resilient communities, shaped by the land and deeply rooted in it, long before anyone decided that progress required their removal.

Section III

The shift did not happen all at once. There was no single moment when the people of Irving or Broughton were told that their way of life was no longer viable. Instead, the language around the rivers began to change. Floods that had once been spoken of as hardships to be endured were recast as disasters to be prevented at all costs. What had been framed for generations as a natural cycle was now described as a failure—of planning, of foresight, of control. The rivers themselves were no longer partners in survival but problems to be solved.

This reframing came from outside the valleys. Downstream, cities expanded, industries grew, and floodplains filled with businesses and homes that had no tolerance for seasonal water. Losses there were measured in dollars rather than soil or crops, and the political weight of those losses carried far more influence. Calls for government intervention grew louder after each major flood, especially as memories of devastation in urban areas eclipsed the quieter, long-standing accommodations made by rural communities upstream.

Plans emerged promising safety, stability, and economic growth. Engineers surveyed the land. Maps were drawn. Dams were proposed not as choices, but as necessities—modern solutions to what was increasingly framed as an outdated way of living. In these plans, the rivers would finally be tamed, their fluctuations smoothed into predictable systems that could be managed and monetized. Flood control was presented as progress, and progress, by definition, demanded sacrifice.

That sacrifice was never abstract for the people who lived along the Big Blue and the Republican. It was measured in acreage, in homesteads that had been held by the same families for generations, in towns that existed not on paper but in memory and practice. Opposition arose quickly, especially in the Blue Valley, where residents organized, wrote letters, attended meetings, and challenged the authority of agencies that seemed distant and unaccountable. They argued that smaller, localized solutions—soil conservation, watershed management, respect for the land's limits—offered protection without destruction.

For years, resistance slowed the process. Construction was delayed. Public debates unfolded in newspapers and town halls. The fight against the dams became more than a disagreement over infrastructure; it became a struggle over who had the right to decide what constituted acceptable loss. To many in these rural communities, the proposed dams represented an erosion of democracy itself—a system where decisions affecting thousands of lives were made by those who would never bear the consequences.

But power does not require consensus to move forward. After the catastrophic floods of 1951, urgency replaced debate. Legislation passed. Funding was secured. What had once been proposed became inevitable. The language of necessity hardened, and opposition was reframed as obstruction. The message was clear: the needs of the many outweighed the lives of the few, even when those "few" had done little to invite the disaster being used to justify their removal.

For Irving and Broughton, this marked the beginning of the end. Notices arrived. Appraisals were conducted. Properties were purchased or condemned. Timelines were imposed that left little room for grief, let alone resistance. Homes were dismantled or moved, churches relocated when possible, cemeteries spared only because of their elevation. Streets disappeared not through neglect, but through design.

What is most striking in retrospect is how quietly much of this happened. There were no riots, no dramatic confrontations. In places like Broughton, people watched the long fight in the Blue Valley and understood what it had cost—emotionally, financially, spiritually. Many chose not to endure the same drawn-out battle. They complied, gathered what they could, and focused on preserving memories rather than land.

Progress arrived here not as triumph, but as erasure. The dams rose, the reservoirs filled, and the towns slipped beneath the surface of official history. Yet the loss did not resolve itself into acceptance. It settled instead into something heavier—a knowledge that what had been taken was not just property, but belonging. The rivers still flowed, but the relationship had been severed, replaced by concrete, policy, and a silence that continues to echo across the water.

Section IV

Displacement is often described in practical terms—where people went, what they were paid, how long they were given to leave—but those details only skim the surface of what was lost. For the people of Irving and Broughton, the dismantling of their towns was not a single event but a prolonged unravelling. Each departure marked another thread pulled loose, another familiar rhythm broken. Even before the water rose, the towns began to hollow out.

In Irving, laughter faded first. Newspaper accounts from the final years describe conversations held in lowered voices, as though the town itself were being mourned before its death was official. Some families left early, unable to live in a place already marked for disappearance. Others stayed until the last possible moment, clinging to routine as an act of defiance—mail delivered, shops opened, homes maintained even as condemnation notices loomed. When the final residents were forced out, it was not because they no longer belonged, but because belonging had been declared irrelevant.

Broughton's end unfolded differently, but no less painfully. Watching the protracted struggle in the Blue Valley convinced many that resistance would only prolong the inevitable. Instead of rallies and lawsuits, there was quiet acquiescence. People focused on salvaging what could be saved—not just buildings, but fragments of community.

The Methodist church was moved. The cemetery, perched high above the river, remained untouched, its headstones standing watch over land that would soon be submerged. In local newspapers, a special column recorded each sale to the government, listing not only the price paid, but the date by which families were required to vacate. The effect was relentless, a weekly accounting of disappearance.

What made this loss particularly cruel was its impersonality. Decisions arrived stamped and signed, carried out by agencies whose representatives rotated in and out, rarely forming relationships with the people whose lives they were dismantling. There was no room in the process for acknowledgment of grief, no language for mourning a town that had not failed but had been sacrificed. People packed up generations of history under deadlines set by strangers, often relocating to nearby towns where they were safe but never fully settled.

Yet even as the physical structures vanished, the towns refused to dissolve completely. Annual reunions began almost immediately, drawing former residents back to places that no longer appeared on most maps. They gathered near markers erected to stand in for what had been erased—stones and plaques bearing names, dates, and the quiet insistence that something mattered here. Mailboxes placed beside these markers became repositories of memory. Visitors wrote notes to the past, to absent relatives, to towns they never knew but felt connected to through family stories.

These gatherings were not exercises in nostalgia. They were acts of continuity. People brought photographs, shared meals, and walked the boundaries of streets they could still trace from memory. Children and grandchildren listened to stories anchored to specific places—the corner where the store once stood, the hill where the school overlooked the town, the stretch of road that led home. Through repetition, the towns remained alive, carried forward not by buildings, but by ritual.

It was in these moments that the true nature of community revealed itself. Stripped of physical form, it persisted anyway, existing in shared memory and deliberate return. The land, altered and constrained by reservoirs, still bore witness. During years of heavy rain, when the water rose and briefly reclaimed the former town sites, the effect was unsettling—not because the towns were drowning again, but because they were momentarily visible, present in absence, reminding those who returned that erasure is never complete.

Irving and Broughton were gone, but they were not forgotten. Their loss settled into the lives of those who had belonged to them, shaping how they understood home, permanence, and trust. What had been taken could not be rebuilt, but it could be remembered. And in that remembering, the communities endured—quietly, stubbornly, refusing to concede that disappearance was the same as defeat.

Section V

I did not experience Irving or Broughton as living towns. By the time I was old enough to form memories of my own, their streets were already gone, their buildings removed or repurposed elsewhere. And yet, they were never abstract to me. They existed as real places long before I understood why they no longer appeared on maps. Their absence was woven into family stories, into the way certain names were spoken with familiarity, into the quiet weight that settled whenever the dams were mentioned. I grew up knowing that something important had been taken, even if I did not yet have the language to explain it.

My grandmother was raised in Irving. She left school after the eighth grade, not because she lacked ability or ambition, but because her family needed her. As the oldest child, she stayed home to help care for her younger siblings while others continued on, graduated, and moved forward in ways she was denied. That loss followed her through her life—not loudly, not bitterly, but as a quiet fact she carried with her.

Years later, at one of the annual Irving reunions, the town marked what would have been the fiftieth reunion of the class of 1927. The former students were asked to come forward and stand together. As they gathered, several of them noticed someone missing. They looked out at the crowd and motioned for my grandmother to join them. In front of everyone, they told her that even though she had not been allowed to graduate with them, she was part of their class. She belonged there.

I still remember the expression on her face as she stood among them—pride, surprise, and something like relief. She had not lived in Irving for decades. The town itself no longer existed. And yet, in that moment, she was recognized not for what she had lost, but for what she had always been. The community had remembered her, even when circumstances had forced her away.

That moment clarified something I had sensed but never fully understood. Community is not sustained by buildings or boundaries alone. It lives in recognition—in the willingness to claim one another across time and distance. Irving did that for her, long after its streets were erased. And in doing so, it claimed me as well, binding me to a place I never physically knew but still carry.

When I stand at the former town sites now, the feeling that settles over me is difficult to articulate. There is grief, yes, but also a sense of reverence. Small trees grow where homes once stood. Underbrush fills spaces that were once cleared and purposeful. Markers stand quietly, doing their best to hold memory in place. Visitors leave notes in weathered notebooks, writing to the past, to relatives long gone, to towns that shaped their families. These gestures may seem small, but they matter. They are proof that memory persists when given even the slightest shelter.

Unless a person has lived in or been shaped by a rural community like this, it is difficult to convey what the land represents. It is not scenery. It is not property. It is history made tangible, a record of labor, loss, endurance, and belonging. To lose that land is to lose more than a location—it is to lose a part of oneself.

Irving and Broughton were not failures. They did not fade away through neglect or irrelevance. They were sacrificed in the name of control and progress, and the cost of that decision continues to ripple outward. The dams still stand. The reservoirs still fill and recede. But the communities they erased live on in memory, in ritual, and in the quiet insistence of those who return year after year to stand where towns once stood.

In remembering them, we resist the idea that what cannot be measured no longer matters. We affirm that place shapes people, and that people, in turn, carry place within them. The land remembers. So do we.

Section VI

There is a temptation, when writing about places like Irving and Broughton, to frame their disappearance as inevitable—to fold their loss into a larger story about modernization, population shifts, and the march of progress. That framing offers a kind of closure, a way to smooth rough edges and reassure ourselves that nothing truly irreplaceable was lost. But standing on those former town sites, closure feels dishonest. What happened here was not a natural ending. It was a decision, and decisions leave responsibility in their wake.

The dams were built to control rivers, but they also reshaped relationships—between people and land, between rural communities and the state, between memory and power. The promise was safety, certainty, and prosperity. What was delivered was more complicated. Flooding did not disappear. Development accelerated in vulnerable places. Losses continued to mount, often in new and unexpected ways. What endured most reliably were the consequences borne by those who had already sacrificed everything.

For the people of Irving and Broughton, the struggle did not end when the last house was moved or the water rose behind the dams. It continued in the form of distrust toward distant authorities, in the lingering sense that rural lives were expendable when weighed against urban growth. It persisted in the knowledge that expertise grounded in lived experience had been dismissed in favor of abstract solutions. The relationship with the land, once reciprocal and attentive, had been replaced by one mediated through concrete and policy.

And yet, something resisted that erasure. Each reunion held at the edge of a reservoir, each note left in a roadside mailbox, each story retold to a child or grandchild became an act of quiet defiance. These were not gestures of denial, but of insistence. They asserted that history does not belong solely to institutions or official records. It also belongs to those who lived it, carried it, and refused to let it dissolve into silence.

The land itself seems to participate in this remembering. During years of heavy rain, when floodwaters rise and briefly reclaim the old town sites, it feels less like a return of danger and more like a reminder. The rivers have not forgotten their paths. Beneath the surface, streets and foundations still exist, not visible, but not erased. The water passes over them as it always has, indifferent to the lines drawn to contain it.

What remains unresolved is not whether Irving and Broughton mattered—they did—but whether we are willing to reckon with what their loss reveals. These towns ask uncomfortable questions about whose lives are protected, whose histories are preserved, and whose sacrifices are quietly absorbed into narratives of national benefit. They challenge the assumption that progress is neutral, or that it arrives without cost.

I return to these places not because I believe they can be restored, but because remembering them feels necessary. They remind me that belonging is fragile, that land and community are intertwined, and that what is taken in the name of efficiency leaves marks that do not fade easily. Irving and Broughton live on not as relics, but as witnesses—to a way of life that understood limits, reciprocity, and care, and to a loss that still asks to be acknowledged.

The towns are gone. The communities remain. And as long as their stories are told, the land they loved will not be entirely silent.

Manhattan, Kansas sits downstream from Tuttle Creek Dam, framed by growth, expansion, and the promise that flood control would secure its future. The city has more than tripled in size since the dam's completion. It is home to a major university, expanding industry, and a population that continues to grow beneath the shadow of concrete and engineered certainty. From a distance, this appears to be the success the dams were meant to deliver.

Up close, the story is less settled. Flooding did not disappear after construction. In fact, some of Topeka's most significant floods occurred after the tributaries feeding the Kansas River were dammed. Control proved partial at best, and at times illusory. Development accelerated in areas once considered too risky, encouraged by the belief that the river had been mastered. The danger was not eliminated—it was redistributed.

Manhattan itself lives with that redistribution. Despite growth and institutional presence, poverty rates remain high. Entire neighborhoods exist downstream of a structure whose failure would be catastrophic beyond comparison to any flood before it. The communities that once absorbed the river's fluctuations upstream are gone, and yet the river remains. The land paid the price, but certainty was never delivered in return.

Tuttle Creek Dam stands as a monument not only to engineering ambition, but to a particular way of valuing land and people. Rural communities were dismantled in the name of protecting urban centers, yet the protection is incomplete and the loss irreversible. Irving and Broughton were not saved by progress, nor were the cities below made invulnerable. What was achieved was a rearrangement of risk and responsibility—one that favored visibility and economic influence over lived experience.

The question, then, is not whether the dams were built with good intentions. It is whether the cost was ever honestly accounted for. The towns along the Big Blue and the Republican Rivers were not accidents of history. They were deliberate sacrifices, absorbed quietly into policy decisions that framed their disappearance as necessary. Their absence became part of the foundation upon which others were allowed to grow.

And it is here—at the base of the dam, beneath the promise of control—that the reckoning settles. The land remembers what was taken upstream. So do the people. What remains is not resolution, but consequence.

Section VII - Conclusion

Although the physical presence of these small communities succumbed to the bulldozer and the crane, the bonds that once held them together did not break. The sense of community that shaped Irving and Broughton endured long after their streets were erased and their buildings dismantled. That shared identity continues to live in the hearts and minds of those who lost not only their homes, but an entire way of life—one built on land, memory, and mutual dependence.

The abrupt and unwanted ending of these towns stands as a heartrending episode in Kansas's political, environmental, and social history, one that cannot be softened by the passage of time. This was not the first tragedy these communities endured, nor was it one they met unprepared. They had survived floods, storms, and hardship before. What they could not withstand was a decision made elsewhere, imposed without regard for what would be lost in its wake.

And yet, as long as the memory of shared labor, shared sacrifice, and love of the land remains, the story does not end in erasure. The displaced residents—and those who come after them—continue to bear witness. They return. They remember. They speak the names of places that no longer appear on maps. In doing so, they testify not only to what was taken, but to what mattered.

The displacement of these communities was not a tragedy measured in broken bones or visible wreckage. It was something quieter and more enduring—a tragedy of broken hearts.

What follows is not a return to theory, but an accounting of how the same logic operates wherever people can be made administratively removable.

Chapter Fifteen

Buffalo Bill Cody's Wild West Show:

An American Triumphant

Section I - The Return of the Triumphant

Long before Buffalo Bill Cody rode into American and European cities at the head of his Wild West Show, the spectacle he perfected already had a name. In ancient Rome, it was called the triumph. A triumph was not merely a celebration of victory, but a carefully staged public ritual designed to teach empire. The conquered were paraded through the streets of the conqueror, displayed as living evidence of domination. Captives, spoils, and symbolic representations of defeated lands followed the victorious general, whose presence affirmed not only military success but historical inevitability. The triumph transformed violence into legitimacy by rendering conquest visible, repeatable, and publicly affirmed.

Buffalo Bill Cody revived this form almost intact. Like the Roman generals before him, Cody understood that victory needed witnesses. His Wild West Show did not present conquest as a past event, safely concluded, but reenacted it continuously, carrying the spectacle of subjugation through American cities and across the capitals of Europe. The conquered were not remembered in absence; they were made to perform their defeat again and again.

The comparison to Rome is not metaphorical. Cody quite consciously modeled himself on figures of imperial history. He rode at the head of his shows on a white horse, framed as both hero and civilizer, while Indigenous performers followed behind him as antagonists already overcome. The structure was unmistakable, with conqueror first, the conquered displayed, and civilization affirmed.

What distinguished Cody's triumph from its ancient predecessors was not its cruelty, but its duration. Roman triumphs were singular events, staged to mark a specific victory, while Buffalo Bill's was industrialized. For three decades, his show rehearsed the same narrative for millions of spectators, embedding it into popular consciousness with a persistence no ancient empire could have achieved.

This repetition mattered because where law stabilizes power through authority, spectacle stabilizes it through familiarity. By staging conquest as entertainment, Cody transformed imperial violence into cultural memory. The Wild West Show did not ask its audience to believe in American supremacy, but showed it repeatedly, until belief felt unnecessary. In this way, Buffalo Bill's triumph functioned not as a relic of the past but as a modern technology of memory, portable, scalable, and profitable, and, like all effective memory technologies, it made domination feel natural.

Section II - The Conquered on Display

Imperial power has always required witnesses. Conquest that remains unseen risks becoming contested, reinterpreted, or forgotten, and the solution, refined over centuries, has been display: the public presentation of the conquered as evidence that resistance has ended and hierarchy has been secured.

In the Roman triumph, captives were paraded through the streets not merely to humiliate them, but to instruct the population. Their bodies, clothing, and placement within the procession communicated rank and inevitability. They were not presented as equals defeated in battle, but as peoples destined to fall before a superior order. The message conveyed was not victory alone, but permanence.

In this sense, the Wild West Show functioned as a modern triumph, staging the conqueror before an audience while the conquered were displayed as evidence that resistance had ended.

Buffalo Bill Cody adopted this logic almost intact. Although Indigenous performers in the Wild West Show were paid participants and often joined the tours willingly, their presence was framed entirely through defeat. On horseback or on foot, they appeared as antagonists already overcome, reenacting battles whose outcomes were never in doubt. Each performance confirmed the same conclusion: Indigenous resistance had failed, and European-American expansion was both justified and complete.

The distinction between participation and power is crucial here. Indigenous performers were visible everywhere in the show, yet never as agents of history. They appeared as obstacles, as spectacles, or as relics of a vanishing past. Even when their skill, horsemanship, or endurance was on display, it was contextualized as primitiveness rather than competence, inviting audiences to admire the display while accepting its disappearance.

This framing was not incidental. Cody's show relied on the physical presence of Native Americans to authenticate the narrative it sold. Their bodies functioned as proof that conquest had occurred. Without them, the spectacle would have risked becoming fantasy. With them, it became memory.

The repetition of defeat was central to this process. Unlike historical commemoration, which marks an event once and then moves on, the Wild West Show demanded constant reenactment. Indigenous performers did not merely represent a conquered people; they relived that conquest night after night. Each performance reaffirmed the same hierarchy, rendering alternative outcomes unthinkable.

In this way, the Wild West Show transformed conquest into routine. What had once been violent and contested became familiar and entertaining. The conquered were no longer threatening, contained instead within narrative, choreography, and expectation. This containment mattered because it allowed audiences to experience imperial dominance without confronting its cost. Suffering was displaced into performance, resistance became theatrical, and defeat was rendered bloodless and repeatable. By placing the conquered on display, Buffalo Bill Cody did more than recreate the past; he trained audiences in how to remember it.

Section III - Civilization as Performance

The power of Buffalo Bill Cody's Wild West Show did not rest solely on the display of the conquered. It rested on the careful staging of what followed conquest, because violence alone does not stabilize empire; resolution does. Cody's genius lay in presenting domination not as brutality, but as benevolence—an orderly transition from chaos to civilization enacted before a paying audience.

The Wild West Show framed westward expansion as an inevitable moral progression. Indigenous resistance appeared first, fierce but futile, followed immediately by rescue, containment, and restoration of order. Cavalry charges arrived on cue. Settlers were saved. Railroads advanced. The narrative never lingered on dispossession or survival, moving swiftly from conflict to conclusion.

This sequencing mattered. By compressing complex historical processes into a theatrical arc, the show taught audiences how to interpret American expansion. The conquest of Indigenous peoples was not presented as a choice or a policy, but framed as a natural phase in the advance of civilization, as predictable as the final act of a play. Civilization, in this context, was not defined by ethics or coexistence, but by control.

Cody's performances relied heavily on contrast. Indigenous life was depicted as wild, undisciplined, and perpetually violent, while European-American presence was portrayed as orderly, restrained, and technologically superior. Even when Indigenous performers demonstrated extraordinary skill—expert horsemanship, endurance, coordination—the framing stripped these qualities of legitimacy. Skill was recast as instinct. Discipline was recast as savagery. What might have challenged assumptions was absorbed into stereotype.

The show's structure ensured that civilization always appeared reactive rather than aggressive. Indigenous attacks initiated conflict. European-American forces responded. This inversion allowed the violence of expansion to appear defensive, even righteous. Audiences were invited to identify not with conquest, but with rescue, with the arrival of order at the moment chaos threatened to overwhelm, illustrating how spectacle converts domination into reassurance.

The performance of civilization also depended on repetition. The same scenes were reenacted night after night, city after city, continent after continent. Over time, familiarity replaced inquiry. What was seen repeatedly began to feel self-evident. The audience no longer asked whether the story was true; they recognized it.

In this way, the Wild West Show did not simply reflect prevailing beliefs about American destiny. It rehearsed them, offering a script for understanding the past that aligned neatly with the present and left little room for alternative memory. Civilization was not debated. It was performed until it felt unquestionable.

What made this especially effective was the absence of finality. Unlike historical monuments, which freeze memory in place, the Wild West Show remained dynamic, evolving with its audience and adjusting scenes and emphases while preserving its central logic. The frontier might be declared closed, but the story of its conquest could still be replayed, refined, and exported.

By the time the show toured Europe, the performance of civilization had become an assertion of national identity. America presented itself as a civilizing force, forged through struggle and destined to lead. Indigenous performers, now displayed before foreign audiences, served as living confirmation of that claim. Their presence authenticated the narrative even as it erased their futures.

Civilization, as Cody staged it, was not a condition achieved through mutual recognition. It was a spectacle that required contrast, containment, and continual reinforcement. It asked its audience not to reckon with what had been destroyed, but to applaud what had supposedly replaced it. In this sense, the Wild West Show did not merely tell a story about civilization; it taught audiences how to perform belief in it.

Section IV - Participation Without Power

The presence of Indigenous performers in Buffalo Bill Cody's Wild West Show has often been used to soften criticism of the spectacle itself. Because Native men and women joined the show voluntarily, were paid for their labor, and at times defended their participation publicly, the arrangement has been framed as mutually beneficial or even empowering. This interpretation mistakes choice within constraint for agency without limit, because participation did not confer power.

For many Indigenous performers, the Wild West Show offered material conditions unavailable elsewhere. Life on reservations was marked by restriction, surveillance, and economic deprivation. The show provided wages, food, mobility, and—crucially—the opportunity to leave the reservation system, if only temporarily. For some, it also offered moments of cultural continuity: riding, dancing, wearing traditional clothing, speaking their own languages among themselves. These factors mattered, complicating any attempt to reduce participation to exploitation alone, but complication did not negate structure.

Indigenous performers entered the Wild West Show on terms they did not set. They did not control the narrative, the choreography, or the interpretation of their presence. They appeared as Indians, not as individuals, and always within roles defined by defeat or containment. Their histories were flattened into archetype. Their resistance was reenacted as futility. Their futures were absent altogether.

The distinction between visibility and authority is central here. Indigenous performers were everywhere in the show, yet nowhere in its authorship. Their bodies authenticated the spectacle, but their voices did not shape it. Even moments of apparent respect—skillful riding, ceremonial dress, ritual dance—were absorbed into a framework that confirmed primitiveness rather than legitimacy.

Accounts from Indigenous participants underscore this tension. Black Elk, who traveled with the show to Europe in the 1880s, described his hope that participation might yield insight or advantage for his people. Instead, he experienced profound dislocation. Surrounded by spectacle, he felt severed from meaning, performing a version of himself that confirmed an audience's expectations while offering no path forward. The show allowed him to be seen everywhere while belonging nowhere.

This dislocation was not accidental. It was structural. The Wild West Show depended on Indigenous presence precisely because it rendered that presence manageable. Onstage, Native Americans could be displayed without threatening land claims, sovereignty, or political resistance. Their participation functioned as proof that conquest was complete and uncontested. If the conquered appeared willingly, the violence that produced conquest could recede into abstraction.

The arrangement also insulated audiences from discomfort. By paying Indigenous performers and highlighting their cooperation, the show framed itself as benevolent. Exploitation was rebranded as opportunity. Coercion was displaced by contract. The deeper realities of dispossession, confinement, and cultural erasure were rendered irrelevant to the spectacle's moral economy.

Participation, in this context, became a kind of containment. Indigenous performers could move across stages and continents, but always within a narrative that denied them historical agency. They could reenact their own defeat repeatedly, but never revise its meaning. The show allowed Indigenous people to survive materially while requiring them to perform their own disappearance symbolically. This distinction—between survival and sovereignty—marked the limit of participation. To appear in the spectacle was not to shape memory; it was to be used by it.

Section V - Spectacle as Memory Technology

The enduring power of Buffalo Bill Cody's Wild West Show lay not in any single scene or figure, but in its function as a system. The show did not simply reflect popular beliefs about American expansion; it organized them. It transformed history into a repeatable experience and, in doing so, trained audiences in how the past should be remembered. This was the work of memory technology.

Unlike monuments or textbooks, spectacle operated through immersion. It bypassed deliberation by engaging emotion, rhythm, and familiarity. The Wild West Show did not ask audiences to analyze conquest; it invited them to feel its resolution. By the time the final scene concluded—order restored, antagonists subdued, civilization affirmed—the audience had not learned facts so much as absorbed a pattern.

That pattern was reinforced through scale. The show reached millions over three decades, touring not only the United States but Europe as well. Each performance repeated the same narrative logic: Indigenous resistance appeared, European-American intervention followed, and progress prevailed. Variations in detail did not disrupt the outcome. Repetition ensured stability, rehearsing not history itself, but inevitability.

Spectacle accomplished this by collapsing time. The Wild West Show presented conquest as something already resolved, even when its consequences were still unfolding. Ongoing displacement, treaty violations, and reservation confinement were rendered irrelevant by a narrative that insisted the conflict was finished. The past was closed onstage, allowing the present to proceed without reckoning.

This closure was crucial to national self-understanding. By staging conquest as complete, the show freed audiences from responsibility. If Indigenous defeat belonged firmly to the past, contemporary inequalities could be understood as natural outcomes rather than ongoing processes. Memory, properly managed, removed the need for accountability.

The portability of the spectacle amplified its effect. Unlike static memorials, the Wild West Show carried its narrative into new contexts, adapting just enough to remain legible while preserving its core logic. In European capitals, the presence of Indigenous performers authenticated American claims to frontier mastery. The United States appeared not as a young nation still consolidating power, but as an established imperial force capable of exhibiting its victories abroad.

This portability also ensured durability. The show did not depend on official sanction or permanent site. It embedded itself in popular culture, shaping dime novels, illustrations, early film, and later Western mythology. The memory it produced did not remain confined to the arena. It migrated outward, influencing how Americans and Europeans alike imagined the West long after the tents were folded and the performers dispersed.

In this way, the Wild West Show functioned as a distributed system of memory production. It synchronized audiences across time and space, offering a shared script that could be recognized instantly and reproduced endlessly. Its success lay not in persuading skeptics, but in making skepticism unnecessary.

Spectacle proved especially effective when it aligned with existing power structures. The Wild West Show did not invent American imperial ambition; it rendered it familiar. By transforming conquest into entertainment, it ensured that domination could be remembered fondly rather than interrogated critically.

This was how spectacle outlived its moment. When memory was taught through performance rather than record, it persisted as instinct. The Wild West Show's greatest legacy was not Buffalo Bill himself, but the ease with which its narrative became common sense, allowing conquest, once staged convincingly enough, to no longer require defense, only replay.

Section VI - When Performance Replaces History

The most consequential effect of Buffalo Bill Cody's Wild West Show was not the story it told, but the story it displaced. Over time, performance did not merely illustrate history; it supplanted it. What audiences remembered was not the complexity of conquest, negotiation, resistance, or survival, but the version that had been rehearsed most often and most vividly. This was how spectacle outpaced record.

The Wild West Show offered clarity where history offered contradiction. Treaties broken, lands seized, and peoples confined were not easily reconciled with national ideals. Performance resolved this tension by simplifying outcomes. Conflict appeared decisive.

Resistance ended cleanly. The moral ledger was balanced onstage, even if it remained unresolved off it.

Because the show was experienced collectively, its authority grew. Shared memory acquired legitimacy through repetition in public space. What thousands saw together began to feel more reliable than what had to be pieced together from documents, testimony, or absence. Performance, witnessed and applauded, became evidence in its own right.

This shift had lasting consequences. As the Wild West Show's imagery circulated through posters, photographs, novels, and later film, it created a visual vocabulary that defined the American West for generations. The cowboy hero, the besieged settler, the attacking Indian, the cavalry charge arriving just in time—these scenes became shorthand for an entire historical era. Their familiarity discouraged inquiry. To question them was to question something already known.

In this environment, history did not disappear; it receded. Archival complexity was overshadowed by narrative certainty. Indigenous nations were remembered not as living political entities, but as obstacles already overcome. Their continued presence became anachronistic, their claims unintelligible within a story that insisted their defeat was final.

Performance also narrowed the range of emotional response available to audiences. Spectacle encouraged admiration and excitement rather than mourning or accountability. The Wild West Show trained viewers to experience conquest as thrilling rather than tragic, conclusive rather than ongoing. It offered closure where none existed.

This replacement of history with performance was not enforced by censorship. It occurred through preference. People returned to what felt coherent, dramatic, and resolved. Over time, the performed version of the past became the remembered one, while the historical record grew quieter by comparison.

The result was a durable mythology that required little maintenance. Once internalized, it reproduced itself through education, entertainment, and everyday reference. The West no longer needed to be explained; it could be evoked with a single image. This was the final efficiency of spectacle: when performance replaced history, power no longer needed to argue its legitimacy, because memory did the work instead.

Section VII - The Loudest Memory Wins

Buffalo Bill Cody's Wild West Show demonstrates a central principle of managed memory: what is repeated most vividly becomes what is remembered most reliably. Accuracy matters less than saturation, and complexity matters less than coherence. The story that is easiest to recognize eventually replaces the one that is hardest to hold, not because it is truer, but because it is more available. Memory, when shaped by repetition rather than reflection, begins to favor familiarity over fidelity.

This process does not require deception in the narrow sense. The Wild West Show did not invent conquest; it curated it. By selecting which moments to reenact, which figures to elevate, and which outcomes to repeat, the spectacle narrowed historical possibility into narrative certainty. Events that did not fit the arc of inevitable progress were excluded, while those that reinforced resolution were emphasized. Over time, this narrowing felt less like interpretation and more like fact, as the boundaries of the story hardened through repetition. What began as performance gradually assumed the authority of memory.

The result was not ignorance, but confidence. Audiences left the show believing they understood the American West, not because they had encountered its history in depth, but because they had experienced a version of it that felt complete. That sense of completion mattered. It closed questions that were still unresolved in law, in land ownership, and in the lives of Indigenous peoples who continued to endure the consequences of conquest long after it had been theatrically declared finished. The spectacle offered emotional resolution where historical reality remained unsettled.

This is how spectacle resolves contradiction without addressing it. By insisting on closure, it removes the need for reckoning. The Wild West Show did not deny that violence had occurred; it absorbed that violence into a narrative that framed it as necessary, temporary, and already redeemed by civilization's arrival. The audience was not asked to forget suffering, but to understand it as concluded. Memory was not erased; it was disciplined.

The effectiveness of this approach depended on volume as much as content. The Wild West Show was not a single performance, but a sustained campaign of repetition. Its imagery circulated through posters, programs, photographs, and press coverage, reinforcing what audiences had seen long after the performance ended. The same scenes appeared again and again, stripped of ambiguity through familiarity. Over time, these images became the default reference points for imagining the West, crowding out less coherent, less visible accounts.

In this environment, quieter histories struggled to persist. Treaties broken through bureaucratic maneuvering, slow attrition through starvation or confinement, and the endurance of Indigenous nations adapting under pressure did not lend themselves easily to spectacle. These histories lacked decisive climaxes and clear resolutions. They unfolded unevenly, often without witnesses, and resisted compression into a single narrative arc. As a result, they were displaced not by refutation, but by neglect.

The Wild West Show did not stand alone in this process. It emerged within a broader cultural shift toward exhibition, display, and the public staging of power. The late nineteenth century saw an increasing reliance on spectacle to organize knowledge, from museums and expositions to illustrated newspapers and early cinema. Visibility became a proxy for importance. What could be shown repeatedly acquired authority, while what remained unseen receded from public consciousness.

Cody's success demonstrated that empire did not require silence to sustain itself. It could operate just as effectively through noise, through pageantry, novelty, and repetition that transformed domination into entertainment and inevitability into common sense. The louder the narrative, the less space remained for alternatives. Dissenting accounts did not need to be suppressed; they were simply overwhelmed.

What Buffalo Bill perfected in motion would soon be replicated in more permanent forms. World's Fairs, expositions, and international exhibitions adopted similar logics, placing peoples, cultures, and technologies on display to communicate hierarchy under the guise of progress. Where the Wild West Show traveled, these later spectacles would build, institutionalizing the lessons learned through performance. Display replaced debate. Arrangement replaced argument. The visitor moved through curated spaces that taught hierarchy through sequence rather than assertion.

Together, these spectacles formed a continuum of memory management. They did not ask audiences to forget; they taught them what to remember instead. By repeating certain images, stories, and relationships, they trained perception itself. Over time, the boundaries of the imaginable narrowed. Some outcomes felt natural, others implausible. The disappearance of Indigenous sovereignty, once a contested and violent process, came to feel like a historical fact rather than a political choice.

This pattern reveals why the loudest memory so often prevails. Memory shaped through spectacle privileges what can be repeated without friction. It favors clarity over complexity and resolution over responsibility. Once internalized, such memory becomes self-reinforcing. It reproduces itself through education, entertainment, and casual reference, requiring no ongoing effort from the power structures that benefit from it.

The enduring legacy of the Wild West Show lies not in its individual scenes, but in its demonstration of how easily performance can overtake record. When memory is taught through repetition rather than inquiry, the version that dominates is not the one most carefully documented, but the one most confidently staged. Conquest, once rendered familiar enough, no longer requires justification. It only needs to be remembered loudly enough to drown out what it replaced.

Chapter Sixteen

World's Fair and the Performance of Progress

Section I - Progress on Display and the Architecture of Hierarchy

The great World's Fairs of the nineteenth and early twentieth centuries presented themselves as celebrations of human achievement. They were marketed as neutral gatherings of innovation, education, and international exchange, designed to showcase the best of what the modern world had to offer. Visitors encountered dazzling displays of machinery, architecture, and technological prowess, all arranged to tell a story of inevitable advancement. Beneath this surface of optimism, however, lay a carefully constructed narrative about who counted as modern, who belonged to the past, and who possessed the authority to define progress itself.

World's Fairs did not simply exhibit objects; they organized the world. Through spatial arrangement, architectural contrast, and curated display, they translated abstract ideas about hierarchy into physical experience. Industrial nations occupied the central halls, surrounded by monumental structures that emphasized permanence, power, and refinement. Colonized or non-Western peoples were placed at the periphery, often in reconstructed villages or temporary enclosures designed to evoke timelessness rather than change. This organization was not incidental. It taught visitors how to see the world and where to locate themselves within it.

The concept of progress presented at these fairs was linear and directional. History moved from primitive to civilized, from static to dynamic, from communal to industrial. This trajectory placed European and American societies at its apex, casting them as both culmination and authority. Other cultures were displayed not as contemporaries, but as representatives of earlier stages of human development. Their presence served to validate the narrative rather than to challenge it. By situating living peoples within an evolutionary frame, the fairs transformed cultural difference into temporal distance.

This framing echoes earlier patterns of erasure examined elsewhere. Just as Neanderthals were positioned as a failed prelude to modern humanity, and as Minoans or Etruscans were reframed as precursors rather than peers, the peoples displayed at World's Fairs were rendered static. Their cultures were treated as complete, unchanging, and destined to be superseded. Progress required contrast, and contrast required someone to be left behind.

The architecture of the fairs reinforced this message. Grand exhibition halls constructed of steel, glass, and stone symbolized durability and mastery over nature. In contrast, the structures housing "ethnographic" displays were often temporary, rustic, or deliberately archaic in appearance. This visual language suggested that some societies built for the future, while others merely occupied space within it. Visitors absorbed these cues instinctively, learning to associate technological permanence with cultural legitimacy.

Importantly, the authority of the World's Fair rested on its claim to objectivity. Organizers presented the exhibitions as educational rather than ideological, positioning themselves as neutral curators of human achievement. This claim masked the extent to which selection, placement, and interpretation reflected the political and economic interests of imperial powers. By framing hierarchy as fact rather than choice, the fairs naturalized inequality and rendered domination invisible.

World's Fairs thus functioned as public rituals of classification. They reassured audiences that the global order was not only rational but deserved. Industrial dominance appeared as evidence of intelligence and worth, while cultural continuity without expansion was recast as stagnation. This logic mirrors the deep-time narrative imposed on Neanderthals and repeated throughout history: those who dominate define advancement, and those who are dominated are repositioned as remnants of an earlier world.

In presenting progress as spectacle, the fairs offered a powerful lesson in memory management. They taught societies how to remember themselves and how to forget others, not through suppression but through display. The world was made legible according to a hierarchy that appeared self-evident, its assumptions embedded in architecture, layout, and narrative flow. The visitor did not need to be persuaded; the experience itself did the work.

Understanding World's Fairs as instruments of hierarchy rather than neutral showcases reveals their significance within a broader pattern of human history. They represent a moment when the logic of conquest, absorption, and erasure was openly staged as celebration. By examining how these fairs constructed progress, it becomes possible to trace the continuity between prehistoric narratives of replacement and modern institutions of memory. The fairground, like the cemetery and the archaeological site, becomes a landscape where power writes its version of humanity into space.

Section II - Living Exhibits and Cultures Frozen in Time

This freezing of cultures in time is not merely a historical curiosity; it is a technique of erasure that recurs whenever power needs to justify dominance without appearing overtly violent. By defining certain peoples as belonging to an earlier stage of human development, the World's Fairs transformed inequality into inevitability. The message was subtle but unmistakable: some cultures move forward, others remain behind, and intervention becomes not an act of aggression but of historical necessity.

What makes this mechanism especially effective is that it operates through display rather than force. The visitor is not asked to hate or fear the people being exhibited. Instead, they are invited to observe, compare, and conclude. The fair presents itself as a neutral space of learning, allowing hierarchy to be absorbed as knowledge rather than ideology. Difference becomes measurable, sortable, and visually obvious, while the conditions that produce inequality remain invisible.

This method echoes earlier and later practices of classification. Archaeological narratives that position Neanderthals as cognitively stalled operate in much the same way. Evidence of care, symbolism, and adaptability is acknowledged, but framed as limited, incomplete, or arrested. Neanderthals are permitted complexity only within a story that still requires their disappearance. Like the people displayed in living exhibits, they are denied the possibility of alternative trajectories. Their humanity is recognized only insofar as it does not challenge the inevitability of replacement.

The fairs also normalized the idea that cultures could be extracted from context and rendered legible through selective representation. This practice carried forward into museums, textbooks, and popular media, shaping how generations understood non-Western societies. Once a culture is defined as timeless, its contemporary struggles can be dismissed as residual rather than political. Dispossession becomes background noise, and survival itself is framed as anachronism.

The psychological distance created by living exhibits is crucial to this process. Viewers are positioned as observers of humanity rather than participants within it. The exhibited individuals exist as examples, not interlocutors. This asymmetry mirrors the way dominant cultures narrate their relationship to both prehistoric and colonized peoples. Those who are classified do not speak; those who classify become the voice of history.

In this sense, the World's Fair becomes a modern analogue to the archaeological site and the national cemetery. Each is a curated landscape where meaning is imposed through arrangement, labeling, and sanctioned interpretation. The fairground, like the museum case or the cemetery plot, teaches visitors how to see the past and how to locate themselves in relation to it. The lesson is consistent: progress belongs to those who control space, narrative, and memory.

The living exhibits of the World's Fairs therefore represent more than a moral failure of a particular era. They reveal a persistent strategy for managing difference by denying contemporaneity. Cultures that do not align with the dominant model of advancement are positioned as remnants rather than rivals, their continued existence rendered conceptually incompatible with modernity. This positioning makes replacement appear natural and resistance appear futile.

Understanding this strategy clarifies why the Neanderthal question remains so charged. To recognize Neanderthals as culturally sophisticated is to disrupt a deeply ingrained habit of thought, one that equates survival with worth and assigns humanity along a single developmental axis. The World's Fairs made this axis visible and celebratory, turning classification into spectacle and hierarchy into entertainment.

By examining living exhibits as instruments of temporal control, it becomes possible to see how deeply the logic of replacement is woven into modern institutions of knowledge. The fair did not invent this logic; it displayed it openly. In doing so, it provides a bridge between prehistoric narratives of extinction and modern practices of cultural erasure, revealing a continuity that challenges the comforting belief that such thinking belongs only to the past.

Section III - Technology as Alibi, Power as Subtext

The prominence of technology at the World's Fairs served as both proof and disguise. Machines, engines, electrical systems, and architectural feats were presented as self-evident markers of advancement, requiring no ethical or historical context to justify their significance. Innovation was framed as neutral, inevitable, and universally beneficial, obscuring the fact that technological power does not emerge in a vacuum. It is produced within social systems that decide who benefits, who is displaced, and whose knowledge is rendered obsolete.

By foregrounding technology, the fairs established an implicit equation between mechanical complexity and cultural worth. Industrial capacity became shorthand for intelligence, progress, and legitimacy. Visitors moved through exhibition halls designed to overwhelm the senses, encountering displays that emphasized scale, speed, and control over nature. The sheer presence of these machines functioned as argument. No explanation was necessary. Power was made visible, and visibility itself became validation.

This framing allowed technology to operate as an alibi for domination. If industrial societies possessed more advanced tools, then their global position could be read as the natural outcome of ingenuity rather than the result of coercion. Colonial extraction, forced labor, and territorial conquest disappeared behind polished displays of steam engines and electrical grids. The fair did not deny exploitation; it simply redirected attention, replacing questions of justice with awe at achievement.

Non-Western technologies, when acknowledged at all, were presented as static or artisanal, disconnected from innovation and change. Agricultural knowledge, ecological adaptation, and complex social systems were excluded from the definition of technology because they did not conform to industrial aesthetics. This exclusion reinforced the narrative that certain societies had failed to advance, rather than recognizing that they had advanced along different trajectories. Technology, narrowly defined, became a gatekeeper for humanity itself.

The subtext of this arrangement was power. Control over resources, labor, and land enabled industrial growth, yet these foundations were rarely visible within the fairgrounds. The polished surface of progress concealed the asymmetries that made it possible. This concealment mirrors earlier historical narratives in which dominance is mistaken for destiny. Just as Homo sapiens' survival is often framed as evidence of inherent superiority, industrial dominance at the fairs was treated as confirmation of cultural primacy rather than as the outcome of specific historical conditions.

The emphasis on technology also reshaped how the past was understood. Pre-industrial societies were positioned as precursors rather than alternatives, their knowledge systems framed as incomplete steps toward modernity. This linear view erased the possibility that different forms of intelligence might coexist or that progress could take multiple forms. It transformed history into a single track, with industrial society at its terminus. Those who did not align with that trajectory were relegated to earlier chapters, regardless of their complexity.

In this way, technology at the World's Fairs performed the same work as classification in earlier contexts. It sorted humanity into categories of advancement, legitimizing hierarchy without explicit declaration. Visitors learned to associate innovation with authority and simplicity with obsolescence. The presence of living exhibits alongside machines reinforced this lesson, creating a visual narrative in which some humans belonged with the future and others with the past.

This logic resonates strongly with the Neanderthal narrative. Stone tools are weighed against metallurgy, mobility against monumentality, and adaptability against expansion, with the latter consistently privileged. The possibility that intelligence might manifest through care, social cohesion, or symbolic depth is overshadowed by metrics tied to dominance. Technology becomes the measure, and those who do not excel according to its terms are defined out of the story.

The World's Fairs thus crystallized a worldview in which power masqueraded as progress. By presenting technological achievement as both cause and consequence of superiority, they naturalized inequality and rendered alternative forms of cultural success invisible. This worldview did not end with the fairs themselves. It persists in how societies evaluate development, interpret history, and assign value to human difference.

Recognizing technology as alibi rather than neutral indicator allows the fair to be read not as a celebration of shared humanity, but as a carefully staged assertion of hierarchy. The machines dazzled, but the deeper message was about who belonged at the center of the human story and who would remain, permanently, on display at its margins.

Section IV - Afterlives of the Fair — Museums, Memory and National Identity

The influence of the World's Fairs did not end when the exhibition halls were dismantled or the crowds dispersed. Their most enduring legacy lies in the institutions and habits of thought that followed them. Museums, national monuments, educational curricula, and popular histories absorbed the logic of the fair, carrying forward its methods of classification and display. What had been staged temporarily became permanent, shaping how societies organized knowledge about themselves and others long after the spectacle itself faded.

Museums inherited both the material collections and the interpretive frameworks of the fairs. Objects gathered for exhibition were recontextualized behind glass, labeled, and arranged according to taxonomies that echoed the fair's hierarchy. Western technological artifacts were presented as milestones of progress, while non-Western objects were framed as ethnographic specimens rather than as products of dynamic cultures. This division reinforced the idea that some societies produce history while others merely illustrate it. The museum visitor, like the fairgoer before them, was positioned as an observer standing at the apex of a developmental scale.

National identity also absorbed the fair's narrative of progress. World's Fairs functioned as rituals of self-definition, allowing nations to present idealized versions of themselves to both domestic and international audiences. The achievements displayed were curated to affirm narratives of ingenuity, destiny, and moral authority. These narratives fed directly into national mythmaking, shaping how citizens understood their place in the world and their relationship to those deemed less advanced. The fair's vision of hierarchy became embedded in patriotic memory, normalized through repetition and institutional endorsement.

The treatment of colonized and Indigenous peoples within museums illustrates how deeply this logic took root. Human remains, sacred objects, and cultural artifacts were collected and displayed as evidence of vanishing worlds, even as those worlds persisted outside museum walls. The act of preservation paradoxically contributed to erasure, freezing cultures in an imagined past and denying their ongoing presence. This practice mirrors the narrative framing of Neanderthals as extinct despite genetic and cultural continuities, reinforcing the idea that survival is meaningful only when accompanied by dominance.

Educational systems further entrenched these assumptions. Textbooks and lectures often presented human history as a linear progression culminating in industrial modernity. Pre-industrial societies were cast as stepping stones, their contributions acknowledged only insofar as they led toward the present. This framing left little room for alternative measures of cultural success, such as sustainability, social cohesion, or care for the dead. The complexity of displaced cultures was flattened, their disappearance explained as an unfortunate but necessary stage of advancement.

The afterlives of the fair also shaped public expectations about what knowledge should look like. Display became synonymous with truth, and arrangement with explanation. The authority of institutions masked the choices underlying curation, making hierarchy appear natural rather than constructed. Visitors learned to trust the narrative presented, rarely questioning whose perspective it represented or whose voices were absent. In this way, the fair's logic perpetuated itself, reproducing patterns of inclusion and exclusion across generations.

This continuity helps explain why challenges to dominant narratives—whether about Neanderthals, Indigenous histories, or the origins of civilization—often meet resistance. To reconsider these stories is to unsettle not only specific facts, but the institutional structures that have long presented them as settled. The persistence of the fair's worldview reveals how deeply invested modern societies remain in equating progress with power and visibility with value.

Reading the World's Fairs as progenitors of modern memory institutions brings the chapter's argument full circle. The same mechanisms that rendered Neanderthals cognitively inferior, Minoans transitional, Etruscans obsolete, and Indigenous peoples vanishing were refined and displayed at the fairs, then embedded within the everyday apparatus of knowledge. The fairground, like the cemetery and the museum, becomes a landscape where hierarchy is naturalized through design and narrative.

By tracing these afterlives, it becomes possible to see the World's Fairs not as isolated spectacles, but as pivotal moments in the consolidation of a worldview that privileges domination over continuity. They offer a modern lens through which to understand an ancient pattern, one that continues to shape how humanity defines itself. In recognizing this continuity, the task shifts from celebrating progress to interrogating the terms on which it has been claimed, and from accepting inherited narratives to learning how to read the spaces where power has written its story.

Section V - From Exhibition to Erasure — What the Fair Taught the Modern World

When the World's Fairs are read alongside earlier patterns of displacement, their significance sharpens. They did not invent hierarchy, nor did they originate the impulse to classify humanity according to dominance. What they did was perfect the performance of that impulse, translating conquest into culture and inequality into spectacle. In doing so, they offered a modern template for how power could present itself as progress while concealing the mechanisms that sustained it.

The fairs taught audiences to accept replacement as inevitability. By arranging cultures along a visible continuum from primitive to advanced, they normalized the idea that some ways of being human belonged to the past and others to the future. This lesson required no explicit argument. It was absorbed through movement, contrast, and repetition. Visitors learned to walk from village to machine hall, from bodies to engines, from people to products, internalizing the assumption that advancement meant distance from relational life and proximity to technological control.

This lesson resonates directly with the Neanderthal narrative. Neanderthals are often positioned as an early exhibit in the museum of humanity, acknowledged briefly before the story advances toward Homo sapiens. Their burial practices, social care, and symbolic behaviors are noted, but framed as incomplete or transitional. Like the cultures displayed at the fairs, they are permitted complexity only insofar as it does not disrupt the trajectory toward modern dominance. Their disappearance becomes a necessary clearing of space rather than a historical loss.

The comparative cases examined earlier—Minoans, Etruscans, and Native American societies—demonstrate that this framing is not confined to prehistory. In each instance, cultures oriented toward continuity, ritual, and care were overtaken by groups structured for expansion and control. In each instance, the successor culture claimed the authority to define advancement and recast the displaced as obsolete. The World's Fairs made this process visible and celebratory, embedding it within the institutions that would shape modern memory.

What unites these cases is not a lack of intelligence among the displaced, but a mismatch between cultural priorities and the demands of domination. Societies that invest in sustaining relationships—between the living and the dead, between people and land, between present and past—leave traces that endure quietly. Societies that invest in conquest leave monuments, records, and narratives that speak loudly. History has tended to listen to the latter and treat the former as background.

The fairs institutionalized this preference. By elevating technological spectacle over social practice, they trained modern audiences to equate worth with visibility and power with progress. Care, continuity, and symbolic depth were rendered secondary, even suspect, because they did not announce themselves through scale or speed. This valuation persists, shaping how cultures are judged, whose histories are preserved, and whose losses are minimized.

Seen in this light, the World's Fairs are not merely episodes of past arrogance. They are a hinge between ancient and modern forms of erasure, linking the deep-time disappearance of Neanderthals with the documented displacement of Indigenous peoples and the ongoing marginalization of non-dominant cultures. They reveal how easily replacement can be reframed as improvement, and how readily humanity accepts narratives that flatter its own survival.

The task, then, is not to reverse hierarchies or to romanticize those who were displaced. It is to recognize the criteria by which humanity has been measured and to question whether those criteria tell the full story. When burial, care, and memory are taken seriously as markers of culture, the line between advanced and primitive blurs. What emerges instead is a recurring human choice: whether to value domination or continuity, spectacle or relationship, survival alone or the manner in which survival is achieved.

By tracing this choice from Neanderthals to World's Fairs, the chapter underscores a central claim of this work. History does not simply record what happened; it records what power chose to remember. The spaces where memory is staged—cemeteries, museums, exhibitions—are not neutral. They are texts written in stone, glass, and arrangement.

Learning to read them differently is not an act of revisionism. It is an act of attention, one that allows the quieter traces of humanity to be seen alongside the louder ones, and perhaps, finally, to be counted.

Chapter Seventeen

Monument and Memory: The Black Hills and Mount Rushmore

Section I – Monuments to the Power of Memory

Monuments do not exist to remember the past. They exist to regulate the present, a distinction that is easy to miss because monuments present themselves as acts of preservation, as if memory were something fragile that must be protected from erosion or neglect. In reality, monuments are tools of selection. They decide which narratives will be made permanent and which will remain provisional, disputable, or invisible.

Mount Rushmore is often described as a memorial, but it functions more accurately as a mechanism of narrative fixation. It does not commemorate an event, mark a loss, or acknowledge transition. Instead, it presents a version of national identity as settled, inevitable, and beyond revision. The mountain does not tell a story so much as assert a conclusion.

This matters because memory, when it remains alive, is adaptive. It changes as new information is integrated, as suppressed histories surface, and as moral frameworks evolve. Monumental memory resists this process. It hardens narrative into form, replacing continuity with permanence. Once memory is carved into stone, disagreement becomes defacement rather than dialogue.

Mount Rushmore achieves this effect not only through scale, but through placement. The monument occupies land already dense with meaning, history, and spiritual significance. By imposing a new narrative at monumental scale, it does not simply add a layer of memory; it overwrites existing ones. The earlier meanings are not debated or refuted. They are rendered irrelevant by physical dominance. This is a key feature of monumental memory: it does not argue. It displaces.

The choice of figures reinforces this function. The presidents carved into the mountain are presented not as historically contingent actors, but as embodiments of national essence. Their placement implies continuity, stability, and inevitability, even though their policies and legacies were contested in their own time and remain so now. Complexity is smoothed away in favor of recognizability. History is compressed into iconography.

What disappears in this process is time as movement. The monument suggests a nation that emerges fully formed, guided by singular figures, progressing cleanly from founding to expansion to consolidation. Conflict is implied but never located. Consequence is abstracted. The messy work of governance, resistance, compromise, and harm is absorbed into stone faces that do not change.

This is not accidental. Monumental memory functions best when it eliminates thresholds. There is no before and after at Mount Rushmore—only ascent. No rupture, only triumph. The mountain does not invite reflection on what was displaced, silenced, or unfinished. It offers instead a stabilized narrative that requires no further examination.

In this sense, Mount Rushmore represents the inverse of the suppressed grammar explored in the previous chapter. Where the serpent encoded continuity and transformation, the monument insists on finality. Where the labrys encoded accountable distinction, the monument collapses judgment into reverence. Authority is no longer enacted or questioned; it is presented as already resolved.

The result is not remembrance, but containment. Memory is fixed in place, bound to stone, and insulated from change. The monument does not ask what must still be reconciled. It declares what must already be accepted, and in doing so, it reveals how power operates when narrative is no longer allowed to move.

Section II — Counter-Monument and Contested Permanence

The presence of the Crazy Horse Memorial in the same landscape is not incidental, nor is it simply a gesture of balance. It exists because Mount Rushmore exists. It is a response shaped by injury, proximity, and an understanding that when memory is fixed in stone, silence becomes complicity.

Crazy Horse was not chosen as a counterfigure because he fits easily into monumental form. He resists it. He left no verified portrait, rejected personal glorification, and embodied a mode of leadership grounded in obligation rather than display. To carve his likeness into the Black Hills is therefore not an act of equivalence, but an act of reclamation under constraint—an attempt to assert Indigenous presence in a landscape already dominated by a permanent narrative of conquest. That constraint matters.

The Crazy Horse Memorial does not undo Mount Rushmore. It cannot restore the Black Hills to a pre-violation state, nor does it pretend to. Instead, it exposes the logic of monumental memory by engaging it directly. Where Mount Rushmore asserts finality, Crazy Horse remains unfinished. Where one presents faces detached from consequence, the other depicts motion—horse and rider emerging from the mountain rather than imposed upon it. Where one claims inevitability, the other acknowledges duration.

The difference in timelines is not merely technical. It is philosophical. Mount Rushmore was completed quickly, decisively, and with federal backing. Its permanence was asserted early and reinforced continuously. The Crazy Horse Memorial, by contrast, has unfolded across generations, funded privately, progressing deliberately and sometimes haltingly. Its incompletion is often framed as failure or inefficiency, but that framing misunderstands its function. The memorial's refusal to resolve into a finished product mirrors the unresolved nature of the injustice it addresses.

This is not a monument that declares closure. It operates instead as an ongoing claim that the story is not finished, that the land's meaning has not been exhausted by conquest or overwritten beyond recovery. In this sense, Crazy Horse functions less as a monument than as a counter-memory embedded in the same geography. It does not seek to erase Mount Rushmore, but to interrupt its claim to narrative exclusivity.

The proximity of the two sites creates an unavoidable tension. Visitors are invited, sometimes reluctantly, to encounter competing assertions of permanence. One says: this is who we are, fixed forever. The other says: we are still here, and this is still unfolding. The land becomes a contested text rather than a settled one.

This contest reveals something crucial about how memory functions under domination. When the dominant narrative is carved into stone, resistance must either remain invisible or adopt the same material language to be seen at all. The Crazy Horse Memorial adopts that language not because it affirms monumental logic, but because it must operate within it to be legible.

Even so, the attempt to reclaim meaning through monumentality remains fraught. Carving another figure into the Black Hills does not restore the land's sacred function as understood by the Lakota. It cannot undo the desecration. What it can do is refuse erasure. It can assert presence in a space designed to communicate absence. It can insist that Indigenous history is not a footnote to national triumph, but a living claim that continues to challenge the legitimacy of what was imposed.

The coexistence of these two sites exposes the limits of monumental memory. Stone can fix narrative, but it cannot reconcile contradiction. It can enforce visibility, but it cannot produce consent. The Crazy Horse Memorial stands not as a solution, but as evidence that the wound Mount Rushmore represents remains open precisely because it was meant to last forever.

In that sense, the attempt to reclaim land through counter-monument is both necessary and insufficient. It is a refusal to disappear, carried out within a landscape already shaped by domination. It acknowledges the reality of what was done while denying its finality.

What emerges is not balance, but tension held in place. Two claims carved into the same hills, one asserting conquest as destiny, the other asserting endurance without closure. The land bears both, not because they are reconciled, but because the conflict itself has been made permanent. That permanence—asserted, contested, unfinished—is where memory is no longer about the past, but about who is allowed to define what the land will mean in the future.

Section III — Counter-Monument and Contested Permanence

The presence of the Crazy Horse Memorial in the same landscape is not incidental, nor is it simply a gesture of balance. It exists because Mount Rushmore exists. It is a response shaped by injury, proximity, and an understanding that when memory is fixed in stone, silence becomes complicity.

Crazy Horse was not chosen as a counterfigure because he fits easily into monumental form. He resists it. He left no verified portrait, rejected personal glorification, and embodied a mode of leadership grounded in obligation rather than display. To carve his likeness into the Black Hills is therefore not an act of equivalence, but an act of reclamation under constraint—an attempt to assert Indigenous presence in a landscape already dominated by a permanent narrative of conquest.

The Crazy Horse Memorial does not undo Mount Rushmore. It cannot restore the Black Hills to a pre-violation state, nor does it pretend to. Instead, it exposes the logic of monumental memory by engaging it directly. Where Mount Rushmore asserts finality, Crazy Horse remains unfinished. Where one presents faces detached from consequence, the other depicts motion—horse and rider emerging from the mountain rather than imposed upon it. Where one claims inevitability, the other acknowledges duration.

The difference in timelines is not merely technical. It is philosophical. Mount Rushmore was completed quickly, decisively, and with federal backing. Its permanence was asserted early and reinforced continuously. The Crazy Horse Memorial, by contrast, has unfolded across generations, funded privately, progressing deliberately, sometimes haltingly. Its incompletion is often framed as failure or inefficiency, but that framing misunderstands its function. The memorial's refusal to resolve into a finished product mirrors the unresolved nature of the injustice it addresses.

This is not a monument that declares closure. It operates instead as an ongoing claim that the story is not finished, that the land's meaning has not been exhausted by conquest or overwritten beyond recovery. In this sense, Crazy Horse functions less as a monument than as a counter-memory embedded in the same geography. It does not seek to erase Mount Rushmore, but to interrupt its claim to narrative exclusivity.

The proximity of the two sites creates an unavoidable tension. Visitors are invited—sometimes reluctantly—to encounter competing assertions of permanence. One says: this is who we are, fixed forever. The other says: we are still here, and this is still unfolding. The land becomes a contested text rather than a settled one.

This contest reveals something crucial about how memory functions under domination. When the dominant narrative is carved into stone, resistance must either remain invisible or adopt the same material language to be seen at all. The Crazy Horse Memorial adopts that language not because it affirms monumental logic, but because it must operate within it to be legible.

Even so, the attempt to reclaim meaning through monumentality remains fraught. Carving another figure into the Black Hills does not restore the land's sacred function as understood by the Lakota. It cannot undo the desecration. What it can do is refuse erasure. It can assert presence in a space designed to communicate absence. It can insist that Indigenous history is not a footnote to national triumph, but a living claim that continues to challenge the legitimacy of what was imposed.

The coexistence of these two sites exposes the limits of monumental memory. Stone can fix narrative, but it cannot reconcile contradiction. It can enforce visibility, but it cannot produce consent. The Crazy Horse Memorial stands not as a solution, but as evidence that the wound Mount Rushmore represents remains open precisely because it was meant to last forever.

In that sense, the attempt to reclaim land through counter-monument is both necessary and insufficient. It is a refusal to disappear, carried out within a landscape already shaped by domination. It acknowledges the reality of what was done while denying its finality.

What emerges is not balance, but tension held in place. Two claims carved into the same hills, one asserting conquest as destiny, the other asserting endurance without closure. The land bears both, not because they are reconciled, but because the conflict itself has been made permanent.

And that permanence—asserted, contested, unfinished—is where memory is no longer about the past, but about who is allowed to define what the land will mean in the future.

Section IV — Normalization, Tourism, and Moral Distance

Once a monument has established itself as permanent, its most consequential work begins not at the moment of construction, but in the decades that follow. Over time, what was once controversial, violent, or disruptive is absorbed into routine experience. The presence of the monument becomes ordinary. Its narrative authority no longer needs to be asserted explicitly because repetition does the work of enforcement. This process of normalization is not passive. It is an active cultural mechanism through which imposed memory becomes background rather than subject.

At Mount Rushmore, normalization operates most visibly through tourism. The site is framed as a destination rather than a dilemma, an attraction rather than a contested space. Visitors are invited to look, photograph, and move on, often without encountering the conditions under which the monument came into being. The experience is structured to emphasize accessibility, scale, and visual clarity, all of which contribute to a sense of inevitability. What is presented feels settled, curated, and complete, even though the histories embedded in the landscape are neither resolved nor neutral.

Tourism introduces distance, both physical and moral. Visitors are rarely positioned as participants in an ongoing historical relationship with the land. Instead, they are positioned as observers, encountering the monument as a finished artifact disconnected from contemporary responsibility. This framing allows the act of looking to feel consequence-free. The visitor is not required to reckon with treaty violation, land seizure, or spiritual desecration as lived realities. Those histories are transformed into information rather than obligation, something that can be acknowledged without altering one's relationship to the site.

The infrastructure surrounding the monument reinforces this distancing. Walkways, viewing platforms, signage, and visitor centers guide attention toward the carved faces and away from the land itself. The mountain is no longer encountered as a living landscape, but as a backdrop for national narrative. The surrounding context is managed to minimize discomfort and maximize coherence, creating an experience that feels orderly and resolved. In this way, the monument's authority is supported not only by stone, but by design.

Normalization also functions through repetition across generations. Children visit Mount Rushmore on school trips. Families incorporate it into vacations. Images of the monument circulate in textbooks, documentaries, and popular media as shorthand for national identity. Each repetition reinforces familiarity, and familiarity dulls the sense that anything is at stake. What was once an act of domination becomes a fact of geography, something that has "always been there" within living memory, even though it has not.

This repetition creates a form of moral insulation. When a monument is encountered repeatedly without challenge, its underlying violence becomes increasingly abstract. The viewer does not experience the taking of the land, the breaking of treaties, or the desecration of sacred space as events that demand response. Instead, these realities are displaced into the past, framed as unfortunate but completed chapters.

The monument's permanence encourages the perception that history itself is finished, even when its consequences are ongoing.

The normalization process is particularly effective because it does not require denial. Acknowledgment can coexist with distance. Visitors may know that the Black Hills are sacred, that treaties were violated, and that Indigenous nations continue to contest the legitimacy of the monument. This knowledge, however, is rarely integrated into the experience of the site itself. It remains supplementary, something learned elsewhere or mentioned briefly, rather than something that structures how the place is encountered. The monument remains visually dominant, while the injustice associated with it remains conceptually peripheral.

Over time, this separation between knowledge and experience becomes habitual. People learn to hold awareness without allowing it to disrupt their participation. The monument becomes something one can critique abstractly while still accepting its physical authority. This is one of the most effective ways monumental memory maintains itself. It allows dissent to exist without consequence, ensuring that critique does not translate into change.

Normalization also reshapes emotional response. Initial reactions of shock or anger give way to resignation, curiosity, or indifference. The monument no longer provokes strong feeling because it has been absorbed into the landscape of expectation. This emotional flattening is not accidental. It is the result of sustained exposure without avenues for meaningful engagement or redress. When people are repeatedly asked to encounter an unresolved injustice without any mechanism for response, emotional disengagement becomes adaptive.

In this way, Mount Rushmore teaches a particular lesson about power and memory. It demonstrates that permanence does not require agreement, only endurance. The monument does not need to persuade every viewer of its legitimacy. It needs only to remain. Over time, presence substitutes for justification, and the burden of discomfort shifts away from the monument and onto those who continue to object to it.

This shift has real consequences for how historical harm is understood. When violation is normalized, it becomes harder to recognize similar patterns elsewhere. The monument trains viewers to accept that sacred land can be repurposed, that dominant narratives can overwrite existing ones, and that permanence can be achieved without consent. These lessons are absorbed implicitly, through experience rather than instruction, shaping expectations about whose histories are allowed to occupy space and whose are expected to recede.

The proximity of the Crazy Horse Memorial complicates this process but does not undo it. While the counter-monument interrupts narrative exclusivity, it exists within the same tourist economy and is subject to similar pressures toward normalization. Visitors may encounter both sites in a single trip, framing the experience as exposure to "multiple perspectives" rather than as engagement with an unresolved ethical conflict. The tension between the two is acknowledged, but often neutralized through the language of balance and coexistence, which can obscure the asymmetry that necessitated the counter-monument in the first place.

Normalization, then, does not erase conflict. It manages it. It transforms ongoing injustice into background context and reframes endurance as acceptance. At Mount Rushmore, this process ensures that the monument continues to function as intended, not only as a symbol of national narrative, but as a mechanism through which that narrative is protected from disruption. The land remains carved, the story remains fixed, and the conditions that made the carving possible are rendered increasingly distant, even as their consequences remain present.

Section V — Permanence, Panic, and the Limits of Monumental Memory

When monuments are challenged, the reaction they provoke is often disproportionate to the physical act itself. Proposals for removal, alteration, contextualization, or even symbolic critique frequently generate responses that frame such challenges as threats to stability, identity, or social order. This intensity is not accidental. It reflects the function monuments serve once they have normalized a particular narrative and insulated it from ethical revision.

At Mount Rushmore, this dynamic is especially visible. The monument's defenders often frame it as untouchable not because it represents flawless history, but because it has come to stand in for continuity itself. Challenges to the monument are interpreted not as engagements with unresolved injustice, but as attempts to erase the past or destabilize national identity. This framing obscures the fact that the monument already represents an act of erasure, one that required the displacement of Indigenous meaning in order to assert its own permanence.

The panic surrounding challenges to monuments reveals an underlying insecurity about the narratives they enforce. If the story carved into stone were truly settled and legitimate, it would not require such aggressive defense. The insistence that monuments must remain unchanged exposes the degree to which permanence has been substituted for moral resolution. Stone is asked to do the work that accountability has not.

This is why debates about monuments so often stall at the level of preservation versus destruction. The conversation is framed as a binary choice between keeping history intact or erasing it altogether, leaving little room to address the underlying question of how history has been represented and whose memory has been granted physical authority. The monument becomes the object of protection, while the conditions that necessitated its creation are treated as secondary or irrelevant.

At Mount Rushmore, this framing allows the ongoing violation of relationship to remain unaddressed. The sacred status of the Black Hills within Lakota cosmology, the explicit treaty violations that enabled the land's seizure, and the continued refusal to restore or meaningfully reconcile that loss are often acknowledged in theory while being excluded from practice. The monument remains, unchanged, while calls for justice are redirected into abstraction or indefinitely deferred.

The permanence of the monument reinforces this deferral. By presenting the narrative as fixed, it suggests that the time for reckoning has passed, even though the consequences of dispossession persist. The monument implies that history has already been resolved into outcome, leaving no space for relational repair or ethical reconsideration. This implication does not eliminate responsibility; it displaces it, making accountability appear disruptive rather than necessary.

In this context, the question of removal or alteration is often miscast as the central issue, when it is in fact secondary. The deeper problem is not whether Mount Rushmore remains physically intact, but whether the narrative it enforces is allowed to remain ethically unexamined. As long as permanence is treated as legitimacy, monuments will continue to function as barriers to moral engagement rather than as sites of reflection.

The presence of the Crazy Horse Memorial nearby underscores this limitation. While it interrupts narrative exclusivity and asserts Indigenous presence, it does not resolve the underlying imbalance of power or restore the sacred relationship to the land. Its existence demonstrates that counter-memory can assert visibility, but it also highlights how constrained such efforts remain within a monumental framework already defined by domination. The land continues to bear competing inscriptions without reconciliation, holding tension rather than resolution.

This unresolved state is not a failure of memory, but a failure of structure. Monumental systems are poorly suited to address histories that remain active rather than concluded. They are designed to stabilize narrative, not to accommodate ongoing ethical responsibility. When history cannot be finalized, monumentality becomes brittle, reacting defensively to any attempt at reinterpretation or change.

Mount Rushmore thus serves as a case study in the limits of monumental memory. It demonstrates how permanence can be used to protect narratives from revision, how normalization can convert violation into background, and how panic emerges when that protection is threatened. The monument does not merely commemorate a version of national history; it enforces a particular relationship to time in which the past is declared complete even when its consequences are not.

To recognize these limits is not to demand immediate solutions or symbolic gestures. It is to understand that monuments are not neutral carriers of memory, but active participants in shaping what can be questioned, acknowledged, or repaired. As long as Mount Rushmore remains physically and symbolically dominant, it will continue to frame the Black Hills primarily through the lens of conquest rather than relationship, outcome rather than obligation.

The chapter does not conclude with a prescription, because the problem it examines is structural rather than procedural. What Mount Rushmore reveals is not simply a failure of representation, but a reliance on permanence as a substitute for justice. Until that reliance is addressed, monuments will continue to stand not as reminders of history, but as mechanisms that limit how history can be engaged.

In this sense, the enduring presence of Mount Rushmore does not signify resolution. It signifies the success of a system that converts unresolved harm into landscape and then asks that landscape to speak for itself. What remains unresolved is not the past, but the question of whether memory will continue to be enforced through stone, or whether it can be re-engaged as a living, relational process that does not require finality in order to function.

Chapter Eighteen

The Use of Mirrors in Ancient Religious Ritual

Section I — Indirect Vision and the Problem of Direct Sight

Across ancient religious and ritual traditions, vision was never treated as a neutral sense. To see was not merely to perceive; it was to engage, to risk, and in some cases to transgress. Sight carried consequence. The act of looking could invite divine attention, provoke spiritual imbalance, or expose the viewer to forces that were not meant to be encountered directly. This understanding shaped not only religious prohibitions and mythic warnings, but also the material technologies developed to manage perception itself. Mirrors emerge from this context not as objects of curiosity or vanity, but as instruments designed to regulate vision under conditions of risk.

In many ancient cosmologies, the sacred was not distant or abstract. Gods, ancestors, and forces of the unseen were understood to exist in proximity to the living world, capable of crossing thresholds under particular conditions. Direct vision of these forces was often considered dangerous precisely because it collapsed necessary boundaries. To look directly at a god, a spirit, or even a transformed version of the self risked dissolution of identity, madness, or death. Myths across cultures repeatedly encode this warning: mortals who see too much, too clearly, or without mediation are undone by the encounter. Vision, therefore, required management.

Mirrors offered a solution to this problem. By introducing a reflective intermediary, they allowed sight without contact, perception without full exposure. What appeared in a mirror was not the thing itself, but its response to light, movement, or presence. This distinction mattered. The reflective surface created a buffer, a thin but crucial distance that preserved the boundary between observer and observed. Vision could occur, but only indirectly, framed by the limits of the surface and the conditions under which it was used.

This logic explains why mirrors so often appear within tightly controlled ritual contexts. They are rarely encountered alone. Instead, they are paired with darkness, silence, fasting, isolation, or priestly supervision. These accompanying conditions were not theatrical flourishes; they were stabilizing mechanisms. Darkness reduced visual noise, silence narrowed attention, fasting altered bodily awareness, and ritual authority ensured that the act of seeing remained contained within an accepted framework. The mirror functioned within this larger system as a regulatory device, shaping not only what could be seen, but how long it could be seen and by whom.

Indirect vision also solved a deeper problem inherent in sacred perception: the instability of the self under conditions of liminality. When ordinary categories dissolve, the observer risks dissolving with them. Mirrors mitigate this risk by dividing perception. The viewer is both present and displaced, seeing and seen, engaged yet held at a remove. This split is not accidental. It is the condition that allows perception to occur without overwhelming the psyche. The mirror creates a structured encounter in which the sacred can appear without fully overtaking the viewer's identity.

Importantly, ancient mirrors were not designed to provide perfect clarity. Precision was not the goal. Distortion, shadow, and partial reflection were features, not flaws. These qualities reinforced the understanding that what appeared in a mirror was contingent and limited. The image did not claim total truth; it offered a response. In doing so, it prevented the illusion of mastery that direct vision might encourage. The observer was reminded, implicitly, that seeing did not equal possession or control.

This emphasis on indirectness stands in contrast to modern assumptions about mirrors as tools of self-knowledge or accurate representation. In contemporary contexts, mirrors are often associated with verification of appearance, identity, or reality. Ancient ritual mirrors operated under a different epistemology. They did not promise accuracy; they promised safety. Their value lay in their ability to register presence without collapsing boundaries, to permit encounter without demanding assimilation.

The controlled nature of mirror use also clarifies why access to reflective practices was so often restricted. Vision mediated through a mirror was not available to everyone, nor was it undertaken casually. Those permitted to use mirrors ritually were trained to tolerate ambiguity, delay interpretation, and accept incomplete knowledge. Authority rested not on what was seen, but on the ability to disengage from what appeared without pursuing it beyond its permitted bounds. The mirror thus functioned as both an instrument of vision and a test of restraint.

Seen in this light, mirrors belong squarely within a tradition of management rather than revelation. They do not open the sacred indiscriminately; they regulate access to it. They acknowledge the human desire to see while simultaneously recognizing the dangers inherent in unmediated perception. The reflective surface becomes a negotiated space, one that allows contact without collapse and memory without erasure of the present self.

This understanding reframes mirrors as conservative instruments rather than transgressive ones. Far from encouraging excess, they impose limits. They insist on distance, duration, and containment. They permit engagement while enforcing withdrawal. In doing so, they preserve the stability of both the observer and the boundary being approached. The mirror does not eliminate danger, but it manages it.

Within this framework, the appearance of mirrors across diverse cultures and ritual systems becomes less surprising. What persists is not a shared belief about symbolism, but a shared problem: how to see without being undone by what is seen. Mirrors answer that problem by structuring vision itself. They teach that perception must be staged, bounded, and reversible. What appears must also be allowed to disappear.

This principle underlies the mirror's enduring presence in ritual contexts concerned with memory, death, transformation, and ancestral contact. The mirror does not claim to reveal truth in its entirety. It offers something more restrained and ultimately more sustainable: a surface upon which presence may briefly register, and from which it may safely withdraw.

Section II — Materials That Register Rather Than Reveal

The materials chosen for ritual mirrors in ancient contexts were never incidental. They were selected not for their capacity to reproduce the world accurately, but for their ability to respond to presence in controlled and perceptible ways. This distinction is crucial. Modern assumptions about mirrors privilege clarity, sharpness, and faithful representation, but ancient ritual practice favored surfaces that mediated rather than disclosed, that answered rather than exposed. What mattered was not what a mirror showed, but how it behaved under specific conditions of light, movement, and breath.

Obsidian occupies a particularly significant place in this material logic, and its ritual use can be traced across multiple cultural landscapes.

Among Mesoamerican societies, most notably the Mexica (Aztec) and earlier Olmec and Maya traditions, polished obsidian mirrors were associated with divination, priestly authority, and controlled access to the divine. These mirrors were not household objects, but sacred instruments bound to ritual specialists and state cosmology. Similar preferences for dark, absorbent reflective surfaces appear in Anatolian contexts and in parts of the Near East, where polished stone and darkened metal were used in rites associated with transition, death, and ancestral presence.

Neither metal nor water, obsidian is stone that behaves like darkness given form. Its surface absorbs light even as it reflects it, returning an image that is shallow, unstable, and easily disrupted. The viewer does not encounter a clear likeness, but a suggestion of presence, one that shifts with angle and illumination. This quality made obsidian especially suited to ritual contexts in which boundaries had to be preserved. The mirror could respond without opening fully. It allowed perception while resisting penetration, a balance that was essential in practices involving the dead, the divine, or altered states of consciousness.

Polished bronze and copper mirrors were widely used throughout the ancient Mediterranean and Near Eastern world, including in Egyptian, Greek, Etruscan, Roman, and Mesopotamian contexts. Archaeological evidence places such mirrors in temple settings, burial assemblages, and ritual caches, indicating that their use extended well beyond personal grooming. These mirrors functioned similarly to obsidian, though with different sensory effects. Their reflectivity depended entirely on light conditions, meaning that vision was never autonomous. The surface did not produce an image on its own; it required careful staging. Firelight, torchlight, moonlight, or sunlight at specific angles activated the mirror, while darkness rendered it inert. This dependency reinforced the idea that vision itself was conditional. One did not simply look and see. One prepared, waited, and positioned both body and environment in order to permit an image to appear.

In ancient Egypt, bronze and copper mirrors were closely associated with ritual purity, life force, and divine presence, appearing both in temple contexts and in funerary assemblages. Their placement among grave goods suggests a continued role beyond death, not as objects of vanity but as instruments connected to breath, regeneration, and the ongoing presence of the self. Greek and Roman sources likewise attest to the use of mirrors in divinatory practices, particularly catoptromancy, where reflective surfaces were used to access knowledge indirectly, often under priestly supervision and within strict ritual constraints.

Water, often overlooked as a mirror material, predates all crafted reflective surfaces and remained central to ritual practice even after metal mirrors became available. Sacred pools, springs, and basins functioned as mirrors precisely because they were unstable. Such water mirrors appear in Greek sanctuaries, Roman temples, Andean sacred sites, and South and East Asian ritual landscapes. Ripples distorted reflection, wind erased it, and depth suggested continuation beyond the surface. Water mirrors reminded the observer that what appeared was never fixed. The image could vanish at any moment, reinforcing the impermanence of vision and the necessity of restraint.

Across these cultures and materials, a shared principle emerges. Ritual mirrors were chosen because they registered presence rather than revealing form. They responded to proximity, breath, movement, and light, offering feedback without disclosure. This responsiveness allowed practitioners to detect change without forcing encounter. The mirror answered questions indirectly, not through declaration but through reaction.

This distinction becomes especially important in rituals concerned with life, death, and transition. In Egyptian, Mesoamerican, Greek, and Indigenous ritual systems, the question was not "What is this?" but "Is something present?" Mirrors served as diagnostic instruments. They were used to confirm animating force, detect spiritual proximity, or register the movement of something unseen. The surface did not need to provide detail; it needed to respond. Condensation, shadow, flicker, or distortion were sufficient signals within a ritual framework trained to interpret them.

The preference for darker, less precise materials also served a protective function across these traditions. Clear reflection risks encouraging fixation, identification, or over-interpretation. A surface that resists clarity reminds the viewer that what is being encountered is provisional. The mirror enforces humility. It refuses mastery. The observer cannot claim full knowledge of what appears, only acknowledgment that something has responded.

Material choice therefore functioned as an extension of ritual discipline. Obsidian, bronze, copper, and water each imposed limits on perception. They slowed the act of seeing, required environmental cooperation, and ensured that vision remained temporary. These constraints prevented the mirror from becoming a conduit for uncontrolled experience. The surface could close as easily as it opened. Reflection could fade, distort, or disappear entirely, restoring the boundary between observer and observed.

In this sense, the materiality of ritual mirrors performed the same work as silence, darkness, and fasting. It shaped perception by withholding excess. The mirror did not overwhelm the senses; it narrowed them. It trained attention toward subtle change rather than explicit image. What mattered was not recognition, but registration.

This material discipline also explains why ritual mirrors were often small, portable, or deliberately limited in size across cultures. Large reflective surfaces invite immersion. Smaller ones enforce distance. They frame vision tightly, allowing only a portion of the field to be perceived at any given time. The viewer cannot lose themselves entirely in the reflection. The body remains present, anchored by the need to hold, angle, and attend to the object.

Even when mirrors were embedded within architectural spaces or ritual regalia, as seen in Egyptian temple iconography, Mesoamerican ceremonial attire, or East Asian sacred architecture, their placement emphasized control. They were positioned to catch light briefly, to reflect at specific moments, or to respond only under particular conditions. The mirror did not dominate the ritual environment. It waited within it, activated by circumstance rather than command.

Understanding mirrors through their material behavior rather than their symbolic associations clarifies their role within ancient religious practice. They were not designed to reveal truth in full. They were designed to respond selectively, to signal presence without inviting possession. The mirror's value lay in its restraint. It made the invisible momentarily perceptible while preserving the integrity of the boundary that made perception possible at all.

When viewed this way, the persistence of specific mirror materials across cultures is less a matter of shared belief than shared necessity. Egyptian, Greek, Roman, Mesoamerican, Anatolian, and Indigenous ritual systems confronted the same problem of how to perceive what could not be approached directly. Reflective surfaces offered a solution, but only when their properties were carefully chosen to support regulation rather than exposure. The mirror did not open the threshold. It marked it.

Section III — Breath, Life, and the Verification of Presence

Across ancient religious systems, life was not treated as an abstract condition but as a force that moved, entered, departed, and left trace. Breath, rather than form or consciousness, functioned as the most immediate indicator of that force. To breathe was to participate in animation; to cease breathing was to cross a threshold that could not be reversed. This understanding shaped ritual practice in profound ways, particularly in contexts where the distinction between life and death, presence and absence, required confirmation rather than assumption. Mirrors entered these practices not as symbols of vitality, but as instruments capable of registering its trace.

There is evidence that reflective surfaces were conceptually linked to breath and animating presence in ancient ritual practice, where the appearance of condensation on a polished surface held before the mouth served as a visible confirmation of life rather than a metaphor for it. The significance of this practice lies not in its simplicity, but in its epistemology. Life was not inferred through appearance alone, nor declared through authority. It was verified through response. The mirror did not announce vitality; it answered it.

This logic is especially evident within Egyptian ritual thought, where life was understood as a dynamic force sustained through breath, movement, and divine circulation. The ankh, commonly translated as "life," has often been treated in modern interpretation as a static emblem or abstract symbol. Within ritual logic, however, the ankh functioned less as representation and more as signifier of active presence. Life was not a quality one possessed; it was a condition continually affirmed through circulation and renewal.

In certain ritual interpretations, the form of the ankh itself reflects this understanding. Its looped upper section has been associated with passage, containment, and movement rather than closure. Rather than enclosing life, it marks the space through which life moves. Within this framework, reflective surfaces become conceptually aligned with the ankh's function, not because they depict life, but because they respond to it. A mirror held before the mouth does not show breath, but it registers its effect. Condensation forms briefly, then disappears, leaving no residue except confirmation that animating force is present.

The ephemerality of this response is critical. Breath leaves trace only momentarily. The mirror records life without capturing it. This fleeting visibility aligns with broader Egyptian concerns regarding the maintenance of balance between presence and withdrawal. Life was meant to circulate, not to be fixed. The mirror's surface allows for verification without possession, observation without arrest.

This use of reflective surfaces as diagnostic tools appears across multiple cultural contexts concerned with death and transition. In situations where the boundary between life and death was ambiguous, mirrors provided a method of confirmation that did not rely on interpretation alone. The appearance or absence of condensation served as a physical response to presence. In this way, the mirror mediated between body and threshold, offering clarity without intrusion.

The mirror's role in these contexts should not be understood as mystical embellishment, but as practical ritual technology. It answered a necessary question under conditions where certainty mattered. Was life still present? Had breath departed? The mirror allowed this determination to be made without invasive intervention, preserving both dignity and boundary. It acknowledged the gravity of transition while refusing to force it prematurely.

Within Egyptian funerary practice, this concern with breath and presence extended beyond the moment of death. Objects placed within tombs, including mirrors, participated in ongoing cycles of verification and renewal. Their presence among grave goods suggests a continued role in mediating between states, not as tools for seeing, but as instruments capable of responding to presence beyond the visible body. The mirror's capacity to register breath aligned it with broader concerns regarding regeneration and continuity.

This association also clarifies why reflective surfaces were often treated with caution. A mirror capable of responding to breath occupies an ambiguous position between life and absence. It can confirm presence, but it can also confirm its loss. The surface does not discriminate. It responds equally to the living and to the absence of life, making it a powerful but unsettling object within ritual frameworks.

The conceptual link between breath, mirror, and life thus rests on responsiveness rather than representation. The mirror does not depict vitality. It verifies it through interaction. This distinction preserves the mirror's role as a mediator rather than a container. Life remains external to the object, but its presence is momentarily made visible through response.

In this sense, the mirror operates as a threshold instrument. It occupies the space between certainty and uncertainty, presence and absence. It allows the living to witness transition without collapsing into it. The surface holds the trace of breath briefly, then releases it, restoring the boundary that makes continued life possible.

The ankh's enduring association with life can therefore be understood not as symbolic abstraction, but as participation in this same ritual logic. Life is defined by movement, breath, and response. The mirror, by registering breath without retaining it, affirms life while acknowledging its impermanence. It offers confirmation without control, recognition without capture.

This understanding reinforces the broader pattern observed throughout ancient ritual practice. Mirrors were not tools for revelation without cost. They were instruments designed to manage encounters with liminality, ensuring that verification could occur without destabilizing the observer or violating the threshold being approached. Breath, life, and reflection converge here not as metaphor, but as function.

When the mirror clouds with condensation and then clears again, it performs the essential work of ritual management. It confirms presence, marks transition, and then withdraws. What remains is not an image, but knowledge bounded by restraint.

Section IV — Authority, Restriction, and the Right to Look

The use of mirrors in ancient religious ritual was rarely a private or casual act. Across cultures, reflective surfaces were bound to systems of authority that determined who was permitted to look, under what conditions, and for what purpose. This restriction was not incidental. It reflected an understanding that mediated vision carried consequences and that not all individuals were equipped to manage what might appear. Mirrors, precisely because they allowed indirect access to liminal states, required regulation through training, status, and ritual role.

Divinatory practices involving mirrors make this especially clear. Catoptromancy in the Greek and Roman worlds, mirror-based scrying in Near Eastern and later esoteric traditions, and obsidian mirror use among Mesoamerican priesthoods all operated within tightly controlled frameworks. Access to the mirror was not open. The reflective surface was handled by those whose social and ritual authority rested on discipline rather than spontaneity. These practitioners were not valued for visionary excess, but for their capacity to contain vision, to enter proximity with the unknown without being overtaken by it.

The authority to look was inseparable from the responsibility to withdraw. A ritual specialist's legitimacy depended not on the vividness of what appeared, but on the ability to disengage when the encounter reached its prescribed limit. The mirror thus functioned as both an instrument and a test. It offered access while demanding restraint. Those unable to maintain that balance were understood to place themselves and their communities at risk.

This logic explains why mirror-based divination was often embedded within elaborate preparatory practices. Fasting, purification, isolation, and silence were not ornamental preliminaries, but mechanisms for stabilizing perception. These disciplines narrowed attention and reduced internal noise, allowing subtle responses to register without distortion. They also reinforced hierarchy. Only those who had undergone training and preparation were considered capable of interpreting what appeared without imposing personal desire or fear upon it.

Gendered patterns of mirror authority further illustrate this point. In many cultures, ritual mirrors were associated with priestesses or female ritual specialists, not as extensions of personal adornment, but as instruments of custodianship. The capacity to manage liminality, to attend to cycles of life, death, and renewal without forcing resolution, aligned mirrors with roles traditionally assigned to women within sacred systems. This association did not imply unrestricted access. On the contrary, it emphasized responsibility and control.

The later cultural reduction of mirrors to symbols of vanity reflects a profound shift in authority rather than a continuation of ancient practice. As ritual mediation became increasingly centralized or abstracted, the mirror's regulatory function was diminished, and its association with disciplined perception was displaced by moralized narratives about self-absorption. What had once been a tool of restraint became recast as an object of excess, revealing more about changing power structures than about the mirror itself.

Within ancient ritual frameworks, mirrors also served to delimit the scope of divination. Vision obtained through reflection was never treated as exhaustive or final. It was partial by design. The mirror offered a glimpse, not a verdict. Interpretation occurred within a broader ritual and communal context, ensuring that meaning was negotiated rather than dictated by the individual observer. Authority thus resided not solely in the mirror-holder, but in the system that governed the act of looking.

This distributed authority protected against the destabilizing effects of unmediated vision. By situating mirror use within ritual hierarchy, cultures acknowledged both the power and the danger of reflective perception. The mirror did not elevate the individual above the community. It bound them more tightly to it, requiring accountability for what was seen and how it was conveyed.

Restrictions surrounding mirror use extended beyond divination into funerary and transitional rites. In contexts involving death, mirrors were handled with particular caution, often covered, turned away, or restricted to specific ritual moments. These practices reflect an awareness that reflective surfaces could register presence even when presence was ambiguous or fading. To expose a mirror indiscriminately risked inviting responses that could not be managed or resolved.

The authority to look, therefore, was inseparable from the authority to shield. Mirrors were concealed as often as they were revealed, and this concealment was itself an act of ritual control. By regulating exposure, practitioners maintained the boundary between worlds, preventing unintended crossings or lingering attachments.

Seen in this light, mirrors functioned as instruments of governance as much as perception. They structured access to liminal knowledge, enforced discipline, and reinforced social hierarchies grounded in responsibility rather than privilege. To look into a ritual mirror was not a right. It was a duty undertaken on behalf of others, bounded by rules designed to protect both the viewer and the community.

This emphasis on restriction challenges modern assumptions that equate visibility with empowerment. In ancient religious practice, empowerment lay in limitation. The mirror granted access only to those prepared to relinquish it. Vision was permitted, but it was never allowed to dominate.

By embedding mirrors within systems of authority and restraint, ancient cultures acknowledged a fundamental truth about mediated perception. What can be seen indirectly must be approached carefully, held briefly, and released deliberately. The mirror enforces this rhythm, ensuring that the act of looking remains a controlled engagement rather than an uncontrolled descent.

Section V — The Divided Self and the Regulation of Memory

Mirrors do more than mediate vision between worlds. They also mediate vision within the self. The reflective surface produces a subtle but consequential division, one in which the observer is simultaneously present and displaced, engaged and held at a remove. This condition is not incidental to ritual practice. It is the mechanism that allows memory, vision, and ancestral presence to surface without overwhelming the individual who encounters them. In this way, mirrors function not only as instruments of perception, but as technologies for regulating internal states.

Ancient ritual systems consistently demonstrate an awareness of the dangers posed by uncontained memory. To remember too fully, too suddenly, or without structure was understood to destabilize identity. Memory was not treated as a passive storehouse, but as a force capable of intrusion. The past, whether personal, ancestral, or mythic, could return with intensity sufficient to fracture the present self. Mirrors offered a means of engagement that preserved continuity. They allowed memory to appear indirectly, framed by a surface that insisted on distance.

The divided perception induced by mirror use creates a stabilizing split. One part of the self attends to the image, while another remains anchored in the present body and ritual space. This division prevents total immersion. The observer does not dissolve into what is seen, nor does the memory fully overtake the present moment. Instead, memory becomes something that appears and withdraws, registering its presence without demanding surrender.

This mechanism is particularly evident in traditions that combine mirror use with controlled states of attention. Darkness, silence, and stillness narrow perception, but the mirror ensures that focus remains externalized. The memory does not arise solely within the mind. It appears on a surface that can be approached, interpreted, and released. The reflective plane becomes a container, holding the image long enough for recognition but not long enough for fixation.

Alchemical traditions articulate this dynamic with particular clarity. Reflection precedes transformation, but transformation is never forced. The mirror trains the practitioner to tolerate doubleness, to observe without immediate integration. Memory, insight, or symbolic imagery appears as part of a staged process, not as an uncontrolled eruption. The mirror disciplines attention by insisting on patience and restraint. What is seen must be held lightly, allowed to change, and permitted to fade.

This approach to memory stands in contrast to later romanticized notions of revelation, which often valorize intensity and total immersion. Ancient ritual practice valued sustainability over immediacy. The goal was not catharsis, but continuity. Memory accessed through a mirror was meant to inform the present without erasing it. The reflective surface ensured that the past remained encountered rather than inhabited.

The mirror's capacity to regulate memory also explains its frequent association with ancestry and lineage. Ancestral presence was understood as potent but potentially destabilizing. To engage it required mediation. Mirrors allowed ancestral memory to surface in a bounded form, one that acknowledged connection without collapsing generational boundaries. The past could be recognized as present influence without becoming present identity.

This distinction is subtle but essential. Memory that overwhelms collapses time. Memory that is regulated preserves it. The mirror supports the latter by introducing a surface that both reveals and resists. What appears is unmistakably connected to the observer, yet clearly separate. The reflection belongs neither fully to the past nor fully to the present. It occupies a managed threshold.

The act of withdrawal is as important as the act of seeing. Ritual mirror use always includes an end point. The mirror is covered, turned away, or removed from the ritual space. This deliberate closure reinforces the boundary between memory and present life. The observer returns fully to the body, the environment, and the social world. The memory recedes, leaving behind residue rather than occupation.

This rhythm of appearance and withdrawal distinguishes regulated memory from obsession. The mirror enforces duration. It limits how long the past may speak. By doing so, it protects both the individual and the community from fixation. Memory becomes a resource rather than a burden, something consulted rather than endured.

The psychological implications of this practice are profound, even when approached without modern terminology. Ancient ritual recognized that identity requires continuity across time, but not collapse into it. The mirror supports this balance by allowing the self to witness its own extension without losing coherence. The divided perception it produces is not fragmentation, but structure.

Seen in this light, mirrors function as memory-management devices rather than instruments of introspection alone. They regulate access to internal material that might otherwise emerge chaotically. They offer a way to engage depth without being consumed by it. The reflective surface becomes a boundary within the psyche, one that mirrors the boundary between worlds established elsewhere in ritual practice.

This internal regulation aligns seamlessly with the mirror's external functions. Just as mirrors manage the encounter between the living and the divine, they manage the encounter between the present self and the past. In both cases, the goal is not avoidance, but containment. Memory is permitted to appear, but only under conditions that preserve integrity.

The persistence of mirror-related anxieties in later cultural practices suggests that this understanding never fully disappeared. Concerns about mirrors capturing souls, reflecting unwanted presences, or destabilizing identity echo older recognitions about the power of reflection. These fears are not irrational residues. They are responses to a technology that was never meant to be neutral.

The mirror remains unsettling because it invites encounter without promising control. It allows memory to surface while insisting on distance. It divides perception just enough to make recognition possible without surrender. In doing so, it performs the essential work of management that ancient ritual demanded of any practice engaging with liminality.

Memory accessed through a mirror does not flood. It arrives, registers, and withdraws. What remains is not possession, but understanding bounded by restraint. That discipline, rather than the image itself, is the mirror's enduring contribution to religious ritual and to the human effort to live with the past without being consumed by it.

Section VI — Persistence, Anxiety, and the Limits of Seeing

The ritual management of mirrors did not end with antiquity, nor did the concerns that necessitated such management disappear with changes in religious structure or cosmology. Instead, the mirror's regulatory role persisted in altered forms, often stripped of its original ritual context but retaining the anxiety that surrounded its use. Long after mirrors ceased to function overtly as sacred instruments, they continued to be treated as objects requiring caution, concealment, or restriction. This persistence suggests that the unease associated with reflective surfaces is not merely symbolic residue, but the continuation of an older recognition about the power of mediated perception.

Practices surrounding death provide one of the clearest examples of this continuity. Across cultures and historical periods, mirrors have been covered, turned toward walls, or removed entirely in the presence of the dead. These actions are frequently explained in later traditions as superstition or custom, yet their underlying logic aligns closely with ancient concerns about unmanaged thresholds. In moments when presence becomes uncertain and transition is underway, reflective surfaces are understood to be responsive in ways that cannot be fully controlled. The mirror, capable of registering breath, absence, or ambiguous presence, becomes a liability rather than a tool.

This response reflects an enduring awareness that mirrors do not simply show. They answer. In contexts of death and mourning, that responsiveness carries risk. A surface that can register presence without discrimination may confirm absence just as readily as life, and such confirmation can be destabilizing when boundaries are already fragile. Covering the mirror does not deny its capacity; it acknowledges it. The act of concealment restores control by removing the surface from participation in the threshold event.

The same logic appears in traditions that treat mirrors as spiritually volatile or morally ambiguous objects. Warnings about mirrors capturing souls, reflecting unwanted presences, or inviting influence from beyond the visible world echo earlier ritual understandings, even when their original frameworks have been lost. These narratives do not arise from ignorance alone. They arise from sustained engagement with an object that behaves differently from ordinary material culture. Mirrors respond. They do not remain inert.

As religious authority shifted and ritual mediation became increasingly abstracted, the mirror's role was gradually displaced. Where once it functioned as a managed instrument within a structured system, it came to be treated either as a mundane object or as a source of moral concern. In both cases, its regulatory function was obscured. What remained was anxiety without structure, unease without ritual containment. The mirror was no longer governed by trained specialists or bounded by prescribed conditions, yet it continued to evoke responses shaped by its earlier role.

This transformation is particularly evident in the moralization of mirrors in later Western traditions. As the mirror's association with disciplined mediation faded, it became linked instead to vanity, deception, or self-obsession. This shift did not negate the mirror's power. It reinterpreted it through a framework that emphasized excess rather than restraint. What had once been a tool for managing liminality was recast as a temptation toward self-fixation, reflecting changing attitudes toward perception, authority, and the body.

Despite these shifts, the mirror never became entirely neutral. Its presence in domestic, artistic, and ritual-adjacent spaces continues to generate discomfort precisely because it resists passive use. A mirror demands engagement. It introduces reflexivity, division, and response. Even outside explicit ritual contexts, it alters perception by forcing the observer into a relationship with what is seen and what is not.

Modern discomfort with mirrors often manifests as unease rather than articulated belief. People speak of mirrors feeling strange in certain rooms, of avoiding eye contact with their reflection in darkness, or of sensing that mirrors change the atmosphere of a space. These reactions are frequently dismissed as irrational, yet they mirror ancient recognitions about the conditions under which reflective surfaces should be activated or withheld. The intuition persists even when its language has been lost.

What ancient ritual understood explicitly was that mirrors occupy a boundary position. They are neither purely object nor purely image. They exist at the intersection of material surface and perceptual response. This position grants them power, but also requires discipline. When that discipline is absent, anxiety fills the gap. The mirror becomes unsettling because it continues to perform its function without the framework that once governed it.

The endurance of mirror-related practices and prohibitions suggests that the need to manage perception has not diminished. Human engagement with memory, death, identity, and presence still generates thresholds that cannot be crossed casually. The mirror remains relevant because it offers a way to approach those thresholds indirectly, even when its use is no longer formally ritualized. It continues to mediate, to divide, and to respond.

In this sense, the mirror's persistence is not evidence of superstition, but of continuity. The conditions that required regulation in ancient religious practice have not vanished. They have shifted, fragmented, and reappeared in new forms. The mirror remains because it addresses a fundamental problem that has never been solved, only managed: how to see without being undone by what is seen.

Ancient ritual did not seek to eliminate this danger. It sought to contain it. Mirrors were designed, handled, and restricted in ways that acknowledged the instability of perception at thresholds of life, death, and memory. They offered access without collapse, confirmation without possession, and recognition without permanence.

That balance remains difficult to sustain. The mirror continues to demand it.

With this understanding, the mirror's role in ancient religious ritual can be seen not as a curiosity of belief, but as a disciplined response to the enduring challenges of human perception. It marks the threshold without dissolving it, holds presence without claiming it, and allows memory to surface without erasing the present. These functions, rather than any single symbolic meaning, explain why mirrors have never fully lost their charge.

They were never meant to be harmless.

Chapter Nineteen

Kate Chopin's The Awakening: Reading What Could Not be Named

Section I - How a Text Is Seen Depends on Who Is Looking

There are books that announce themselves plainly, and there are books that wait. *The Awakening* belongs to the latter category. It does not tell the reader what to think or how to feel; it does not guide interpretation with moral framing or authorial insistence. Instead, it presents experiences—sensory, emotional, relational—and allows meaning to assemble according to the interpretive habits the reader brings with them. This quality, more than any single scene or symbol, explains why *The Awakening* has provoked such sustained disagreement for more than a century.

Critical responses to the novel have tended to sort themselves into familiar camps. Edna Pontellier has been read as a feminist rebel, a failed mother, a sensualist, a narcissist, a victim of repression, a romantic idealist, and a cautionary tale. Each of these readings can point to moments in the text that appear to support it, and yet none fully accounts for the novel's persistent unease—the sense that something essential is being felt but never quite named. These disagreements are usually framed as scholarly disputes, but at their core they arise from something more fundamental: **readers do not all read from the same place**.

Roland Barthes' distinction between *studium* and *punctum* offers a useful way to name this divide, not as rigid theory but as lived experience. The *studium* refers to culturally shared meaning—the frameworks we are taught to recognize, the interpretations that feel orderly, rational, and communicable. The *punctum*, by contrast, is personal and disruptive. It is the moment when something in a text pierces the reader before it can be explained, categorized, or safely absorbed. The *punctum* does not announce itself as meaning; it announces itself as feeling.

Most traditional readings of *The Awakening* remain firmly within the realm of the *studium*. They assume that Edna's awakening is sexual, but they also assume—often without noticing the assumption—that this sexuality must be heterosexual. The novel's men are therefore treated as the natural objects of her desire, and her relationships with women are softened, spiritualized, or dismissed as culturally normative intimacy. This interpretive move does not arise from the text itself; it arises from the reader's cultural lexicon.

To read *The Awakening* from outside that lexicon is not to impose something foreign onto the novel. It is to notice what becomes visible when heterosexuality is no longer treated as the default explanation for desire. For readers with lesbian lived experience—particularly those who came of age before language, models, or social permission were readily available—Edna's confusion, intensity, and displacement can register immediately. What appears vague or excessive to one reader may feel precisely calibrated to another.

This does not mean that one reading is "correct" and another is not. It means that texts do not speak the same way to all readers. Meaning is not only produced by what is written, but by what the reader is able—or willing—to recognize. In this sense, interpretive disagreement around *The Awakening* is not a failure of criticism; it is evidence of the novel's capacity to hold multiple experiential truths at once.

This chapter begins from the premise that lesbian readers, historically and now, have often learned to read differently—not out of preference, but out of necessity. When desire cannot be spoken openly, it must be sensed, inferred, traced through pattern and absence. Such reading practices are not speculative; they are adaptive. They attend closely to tone, proximity, repetition, emotional emphasis, and bodily response. They recognize that desire often appears first not as clarity, but as disturbance.

Approaching *The Awakening* from this perspective does not require labeling Edna Pontellier or Kate Chopin. It requires only a willingness to suspend automatic assumptions and to ask a different set of questions. What if Edna's awakening is not oriented toward a man at all? What if heterosexual romance functions not as the origin of her desire, but as its most socially legible translation? And what if the novel's deepest intimacies are not the ones most often named?

These questions do not seek to overturn existing interpretations so much as to sit beside them, widening the field of what the novel is allowed to mean. *The Awakening* does not demand a single answer. It demands attention—to what is felt, to what is displaced, and to what remains unsayable.

Section II – A Case of Smoke and Mirrors

One of the most persistent misunderstandings of *The Awakening* lies in the assumption that Edna Pontellier's transformation begins with a man. This assumption is so ingrained that it often goes unquestioned, yet the novel itself quietly resists it. Edna's awakening does not originate in attraction, romance, or even conscious longing. It begins instead with sensation—diffuse, unsettling, and unmoored from any clear object.

Early in the novel, Edna experiences moments of emotional intensity that she cannot explain. She cries without knowing why. She feels an oppressive weight that seems to rise from an unfamiliar region of her consciousness. These moments are not accompanied by thoughts of Robert, nor by fantasies of escape or passion. They are bodily responses, affective disturbances that precede interpretation. Chopin is careful here. She does not offer the reader an immediate cause, and in doing so she creates a space of interpretive instability. Something is happening to Edna, but it has not yet been named.

This sequencing matters. In conventional narratives of female desire—particularly those available at the turn of the twentieth century—awakening is typically tethered to an external catalyst. A man appears, interest follows, and emotional transformation unfolds in response. Chopin reverses this logic. Edna's interior life stirs first. Desire, if that is what it is, exists before it knows what to want.

Such moments are often difficult for readers to sit with. An awakening without an object feels incomplete, even suspicious. There is a strong cultural impulse to resolve ambiguity by assigning cause, and in the context of heterosexual normativity, that cause is assumed to be male. But Chopin delays this resolution deliberately. She allows Edna's awakening to remain suspended, felt rather than understood, and in doing so she mirrors the experience of individuals whose desires do not immediately align with available social scripts.

For many women—particularly those whose primary attachments do not conform to heterosexual expectation—awakening does not arrive as clarity. It arrives as dissonance. As an intensification of feeling without a name. As a sense of being out of step with one's surroundings, accompanied by an awareness that something essential has shifted. Edna's early experiences resonate powerfully with this pattern. They are not directed; they are atmospheric. They alter her relationship to herself before they alter her relationship to anyone else.

It is important to note that Chopin does not frame this early awakening as explicitly sexual. Instead, it is presented as a loosening—of reserve, of habit, of compliance. Edna begins to sense the artificiality of the life she has been living, a life she entered "by accident" and sustained through momentum rather than conviction. Her awakening is not initially about wanting something new; it is about no longer being able to tolerate what is familiar.

This distinction complicates readings that treat Edna's later relationships as the source of her transformation. Robert, Arobin, and even her husband enter a field that has already been disturbed. They do not create the disturbance; they are drawn into it. To read the novel otherwise is to mistake consequence for cause.

By allowing awakening to precede object, Chopin also exposes the limitations of the interpretive tools available to both her characters and her readers. When desire cannot be immediately identified, it is often misread. It is redirected, rationalized, or displaced onto whatever form is most culturally intelligible. In Edna's world, and in the reading practices of her time, that form is male.

This helps explain why readers so readily attach Edna's awakening to Robert Lebrun. Once a man appears who can plausibly serve as an object of desire, the earlier ambiguity seems to resolve itself retroactively. The awakening is explained. The narrative stabilizes. Yet this explanation only works if one ignores the fact that Edna's interior shift is already well underway before Robert assumes any significance.

Understanding this sequencing allows for a more nuanced reading of what follows. It opens the possibility that Edna's later attachments are not the origins of her desire, but attempts to give it shape. Attempts to translate something unfamiliar into a language that can be spoken aloud—both to others and to herself.

In this light, the novel's trajectory begins to look less like a linear movement toward transgression and more like a series of experiments in legibility. Edna is not discovering desire so much as she is trying to understand what has already begun to move within her. And the forms she reaches for—flirtation, attachment, infidelity—are the only ones her culture has made available.

This is the ground on which Robert Lebrun enters the story. Not as the spark of awakening, but as its first plausible interpretation.

Section III - Flirtation as the Safest Language of Desire

Once awakening has begun—once sensation has intensified and reserve has loosened—the question is no longer whether desire exists, but **where it can go**. In a social world that offers women few acceptable outlets for erotic or emotional deviation, desire does not move freely. It moves along paths that are already marked, already legible, already understood. In *The Awakening*, that path is flirtation.

Flirtation occupies a peculiar position in late–nineteenth-century social life. It is intimate without being binding, suggestive without being explicit, and pleasurable without requiring resolution. Crucially, it is deniable. One can always insist that nothing serious was meant, that the exchange was harmless, that boundaries were never crossed. For women, especially married women, flirtation offered a narrow but sanctioned space in which feeling could circulate without demanding action. For men, it allowed charm and proximity without commitment or consequence.

Kate Chopin understands this social grammar perfectly, and she deploys it with precision. Robert Lebrun's habitual flirtations are not aberrations; they are expected. No one at Grand Isle finds his behavior troubling or even noteworthy. Indeed, it is predicted. Since adolescence, Robert has devoted himself each summer to some woman who is safely unavailable—widows, married women, figures who allow attention without expectation. This pattern is treated as charming, almost quaint, because it conforms to the rules of flirtation rather than threatening them.

For a reader at the turn of the twentieth century, it would have seemed entirely natural that Edna's newly awakened desire would "turn" toward the man she has been flirting with. This is not because the text insists upon it, but because culture does. Desire that cannot be named seeks a recognizable form, and flirtation with a man provides one. It reassures the reader that what is unfolding remains intelligible, even if it is morally ambiguous.

This is an important distinction. The intelligibility of flirtation does not mean it is truthful. It means it is **readable**. When Edna's interior life begins to change, flirtation offers a way to interpret that change without fundamentally challenging the social order. It allows desire to be understood as heterosexual even when its origins may lie elsewhere. In this sense, flirtation functions as a kind of narrative solvent, dissolving ambiguity into familiarity.

Yet Chopin is careful to show that flirtation, while pleasurable, is insufficient. It allows feeling to move, but it does not allow it to settle. Robert's attentions never culminate in action. They circulate endlessly, producing intimacy without embodiment and attachment without commitment. This makes flirtation safe for him as well. It allows him to participate in the performance of desire without being required to inhabit it fully.

For Edna, however, flirtation becomes dangerous precisely because her awakening deepens. What begins as a socially sanctioned exchange starts to demand more than flirtation can contain. As her internal life grows more insistent, the gap between performance and truth widens. Flirtation can translate desire into a familiar language, but it cannot satisfy it.

This helps explain why Robert's behavior shifts so abruptly once Edna's feelings move beyond play. When desire threatens to become explicit—when it seeks recognition rather than circulation—Robert leaves. He does not negotiate, test boundaries, or linger in uncertainty. He disappears. Flirtation, which had once provided safety for both parties, can no longer perform its protective function.

Understanding flirtation as the safest language of desire clarifies much of the novel's emotional logic. It explains why Edna's awakening appears to align so neatly with Robert for many readers, and why that alignment ultimately fails. Flirtation is not the origin of Edna's desire; it is its first translation. It offers a socially intelligible story for something that has not yet found its true form.

Seen this way, flirtation is neither trivial nor incidental. It is a crucial intermediary stage, one that allows both Edna and the reader to move forward without immediately confronting what lies beneath. But it is also unstable. Once desire begins to ask for more—for meaning, for embodiment, for permanence—flirtation collapses under its own limitations.

It is at this point, when flirtation can no longer do the work of translation, that the novel introduces a new strategy: redirection.

Section IV - Robert Lebrun and the Logic of Safety

By the time Robert Lebrun assumes prominence in Edna Pontellier's inner life, something essential has already shifted. Her awakening is underway; her emotional and sensory world has been altered in ways she does not yet understand. Robert does not initiate this change. He gives it a shape that both Edna and the reader can recognize.

Robert's role in the novel has long puzzled critics. He is attentive yet evasive, intimate yet elusive, emotionally expressive yet incapable of follow-through. Read as a conventional romantic lead, his behavior appears inconsistent or immature. He flirts ardently, encourages closeness, and then retreats at precisely the moments when intimacy threatens to become real. But when Robert is read not as a failed heterosexual lover but as a *safe* one, his behavior becomes coherent.

From the beginning, Robert gravitates toward women who are unavailable. Married women, in particular, allow him a form of intimacy that is pleasurable but contained. Their social status guarantees limits. No consummation is expected; no future is demanded. Within this framework, Robert can perform devotion without consequence, attention without exposure. His flirtations are elaborate, sustained, and emotionally textured, yet they never require him to cross a line from which he could not easily retreat.

This pattern is not incidental. It is established early and repeated often enough to suggest design rather than accident. Since adolescence, Robert has devoted himself each summer to some woman who cannot belong to him. The community anticipates this behavior and treats it as harmless ritual. His attentions are indulged precisely because they are understood to be unserious.

Edna, at least initially, fits this pattern perfectly. She is married, socially protected, and therefore safe. Robert's intimacy with her can flourish without demanding action. For a time, this arrangement suits them both. It allows Edna's newly awakened desire to move outward in a form that feels legible, and it allows Robert to remain within the boundaries of flirtation that have always protected him.

But Edna is not content to remain within those boundaries. As her awakening deepens, she begins to want something that flirtation cannot provide. She seeks meaning, recognition, and embodiment. She begins to take her own feelings seriously. This is the moment when Robert's safety becomes unsustainable.

Rather than renegotiating the terms of their intimacy, Robert leaves. His departure is sudden and decisive, framed not as a reluctant sacrifice but as an escape. Mexico, where he goes, functions less as a destination than as a narrative removal. It absorbs him at the precise moment when his role as a safe interpreter of Edna's desire collapses.

Historically, such acts of flight were not uncommon. Spaces on the margins—ports, expatriate enclaves, colonial or semi-colonial territories—often offered respite from the rigid sexual expectations of metropolitan life. But even without appealing to history, the novel itself makes the logic clear. Robert leaves when heterosexual performance is no longer optional.

What is equally telling is Robert's response to Alcée Arobin. When Arobin enters Edna's life and assumes the role of her lover, Robert exhibits no jealousy, rivalry, or masculine competition. He does not attempt to reclaim Edna, nor does he position himself as her emotional alternative. This absence of rivalry is striking in a novel otherwise attuned to social nuance. It suggests that Robert does not experience Arobin as a threat because he was never competing on the same terms.

Read this way, Robert is not the object of Edna's awakening but its first misreading. He provides a culturally intelligible explanation for desire that has arisen elsewhere. For the reader, his presence reassures; for Edna, it offers temporary coherence. But when desire demands more than coherence—when it demands truth—Robert cannot remain.

This reading does not require us to label Robert Lebrun or to speculate about his private life beyond the text. It requires only that we stop assuming heterosexual intent as default. When that assumption is suspended, Robert's behavior ceases to be erratic and becomes legible. He is not the man Edna desires; he is the man her culture allows her to desire.

Robert's failure, then, is not personal but structural. He cannot carry the weight of Edna's awakening because he was never meant to. His role is transitional, a narrative bridge between an unnamed disturbance and an attempted normalization. When that bridge collapses, Edna turns, not inward, but toward a different strategy—one that is more overt, more socially recognizable, and ultimately more destructive.

That strategy arrives in the form of Alcée Arobin.

Section VI - Female Intimacy and the First Site of Recognition

Long before Edna Pontellier's awakening finds socially recognizable forms—before flirtation, before infidelity, before any overt transgression—it is **female intimacy** that first gives it texture. This intimacy is not incidental, nor is it merely cultural decoration. It is sustained, embodied, and emotionally charged, and it is here that Edna's internal shift becomes legible in a way it never quite does elsewhere.

Adèle Ratignolle occupies a central place in this process. Critics have often described her as Edna's foil: the ideal "mother-woman," perfectly at ease within the structures Edna finds suffocating. Yet this opposition, while structurally neat, obscures the intensity of their connection. Chopin does not present Adèle as a neutral presence in Edna's life. She is repeatedly rendered through a language of physicality, beauty, and sensuous excess. Edna does not merely admire her; she studies her, watches her, sketches her, and responds to her with a depth of feeling that exceeds friendship as it is typically represented in the novel.

The physical intimacy between the two women is deliberate and reciprocal. Hands are clasped and not withdrawn. Touch is prolonged, stroked, repeated. Bodies move together—arm in arm, faces close, intentionally separate from others. These are not accidental gestures, nor are they described with the casual ease Chopin applies to other social interactions. They are lingered over, framed as moments of shared interiority and emotional vulnerability.

Most telling is Edna's response. In Adèle's presence, her reserve loosens. She speaks more freely, leans in physically, and allows herself a degree of emotional openness that appears nowhere else in the novel. Chopin explicitly links this shift to Adèle's influence, noting that Edna's awakening begins to take shape through her attachment to her friend. The language used to describe this bond is unmistakably charged: Edna is drawn by Adèle's "excessive physical charm," her sensuous presence, her warmth. The novel itself pauses to ask what metals the gods might use to forge the bond we call sympathy—or love.

This question is not rhetorical. Chopin does not answer it, and in doing so she resists the reader's urge to categorize what is unfolding.

Instead, she allows the intimacy to exist on its own terms. It is neither condemned nor explained away. It simply *is*.

For many readers, especially those trained to view heterosexuality as the default orientation of desire, these moments are easy to minimize. They are reframed as maternal affection, Creole warmth, or the harmless closeness of women in a premodern social world. Yet Chopin herself does not rely on such euphemisms. The physicality is precise, the emotional resonance clear. What is minimized in interpretation is not what is written, but what is allowed to count as meaningful.

For lesbian readers—particularly those who have experienced desire before language or recognition—these scenes often register differently. Awakening does not begin with sexual clarity; it begins with attachment. With fascination. With an intensification of feeling that resists explanation. Edna's response to Adèle follows this pattern closely. Her desire does not announce itself as such; it manifests as attention, proximity, and a sense of being newly alive in another woman's presence.

Importantly, this intimacy does not destabilize Edna immediately. It soothes her even as it unsettles her. In Adèle's presence, she feels both seen and safe. There is no demand for definition, no requirement that she name herself. This makes female intimacy the first site where Edna's awakening can exist without crisis.

That this intimacy cannot be sustained is not because it is trivial, but because it is structurally impossible within the world Edna inhabits. Adèle herself is deeply embedded in the maternal and marital roles Edna resists. Her affection is genuine, but it is circumscribed by a life that has no room for deviation. When she eventually urges Edna to "think of the children," she speaks not as an antagonist but as a representative of the limits imposed on women who remain within accepted forms.

What follows—Edna's turn toward men—should be understood in this context. Her attachments to Robert and Arobin do not replace her bond with Adèle; they attempt to resolve it. They offer socially intelligible outlets for feelings that cannot otherwise be spoken. Female intimacy is thus not displaced because it is weak, but because it is too strong to be acknowledged.

By recognizing Adèle as the first site of Edna's awakening, the novel's emotional architecture shifts. The story is no longer one in which a woman moves from domesticity into heterosexual passion and then into isolation. It becomes a story in which awakening begins in female connection, is rerouted through socially acceptable forms, and ultimately collapses under the weight of what cannot be named.

This recognition does not require us to claim that Adèle consciously reciprocates Edna's desire, nor does it require us to assign modern identities to either woman. It requires only that we take Chopin's language seriously, and that we allow female intimacy to carry erotic and emotional significance rather than stripping it of power through interpretive habit.

With this in mind, the novel's final movements take on a different resonance. What Edna loses is not merely romance or domestic stability, but the possibility of a life in which her awakening could have been recognized and sustained. What remains is not despair alone, but the awareness that no available structure—marriage, flirtation, infidelity, or friendship—can hold what she has come to know.

Section VII - The Failure of Translation and the Exhaustion of Heterosexual Scripts

By the time Edna Pontellier reaches the later stages of *The Awakening*, every culturally sanctioned translation of her desire has failed. Each available script—wifehood, flirtation, romantic attachment, and sexual infidelity—has been tested and found inadequate. What remains is not confusion about what she wants, but clarity about what she cannot accept.

Marriage, as the novel makes clear, was never a site of passion for Edna. It was entered into "accidentally," sustained through habit and social expectation rather than emotional or erotic fulfillment. Flirtation with Robert offered a temporary sense of coherence, a way to make her awakening legible without confronting its source. When that failed, infidelity with Arobin provided a more overt but equally insufficient solution—one that aligned her behavior with a familiar narrative of female transgression while leaving her interior life untouched.

Each of these scripts functions as a form of translation. They take something disruptive and render it intelligible within existing social frameworks. Yet translation always involves loss. What cannot be expressed within the available language is either distorted or erased. In

Edna's case, what is lost is the centrality of female attachment and the depth of recognition it provides.

This exhaustion of heterosexual scripts is not sudden; it unfolds gradually, through repetition and disappointment rather than dramatic rupture. Chopin does not frame Edna's realization as a single epiphany. Instead, it emerges through accumulation—through the persistent mismatch between what Edna feels and what the world offers her in response. The more she attempts to live within recognizable forms, the more acutely she feels their insufficiency.

This is why Edna's growing independence—her move into the pigeon house, her refusal of social obligations, her insistence on autonomy—does not resolve her conflict. Independence without recognition is not freedom; it is isolation. What Edna seeks is not simply the absence of constraint, but the presence of a life in which her awakening could be mirrored and sustained. None of the heterosexual scripts available to her provide this.

It is tempting to read Edna's final choices as a rejection of society alone, but such a reading risks flattening the emotional complexity of the novel. Edna does not withdraw because she has discovered a superior alternative; she withdraws because every offered alternative has proven false. Her isolation is not chosen in triumph, but arrived at through elimination.

This is where many interpretations falter. They frame Edna's trajectory as a linear progression toward liberation or despair, when it is more accurately understood as a narrowing of possibilities. Each path she explores closes behind her, leaving fewer options rather than more. What appears as radical autonomy is, in fact, the residue of failed translations.

Seen through this lens, the novel's conclusion is not a moral judgment or a psychological collapse, but the logical endpoint of a world that cannot accommodate the form of recognition Edna requires. Her awakening has revealed a truth for which there is no sustainable structure. The tragedy lies not in her excess, but in the absence of viable alternatives.

This reading does not require us to romanticize Edna's end or to deny its devastation. It asks us instead to consider what has been systematically denied to her throughout the novel: the possibility of a life in which desire could be both acknowledged and lived without distortion. When every socially intelligible form fails, what remains is not choice, but silence.

It is this silence—produced not by Edna's inability to adapt, but by the culture's inability to imagine—that gives *The Awakening* its enduring power. The novel does not resolve its central tension because resolution is precisely what the world it depicts cannot offer.

Section VIII - Reading Twice: Recognition, Refusal and What Remains

One of the quiet truths of *The Awakening* is that it is not fully legible on a first reading. The novel appears deceptively spare, almost restrained, as though it were holding something back. Plot advances, scenes unfold, and yet there is a persistent sense that the emotional center of the story is slightly out of alignment with its surface action. This is not a flaw in construction; it is a deliberate strategy.

A first reading follows events. It tracks Edna's marriage, her flirtation with Robert, her affair with Arobin, her increasing independence, and finally her withdrawal from the world she inhabits. Read this way, the novel can appear to chart a familiar arc of transgression and consequence. Desire awakens, norms are violated, stability collapses. The ending feels abrupt, even excessive, because the emotional logic that leads to it has not yet fully declared itself.

It is only on a second reading that the structure clarifies. Patterns emerge where individual scenes once seemed isolated. Female intimacy, initially treated as background or atmosphere, reveals itself as foundational. Heterosexual attachments, once assumed to be central, recede into the role of attempted solutions—translations that never quite fit. What seemed like narrative acceleration near the end of the novel now reads as inevitability: once every available script has been exhausted, there is nowhere left to go.

This is the point at which recognition matters most. *The Awakening* does not ask all readers to see the same thing, but it does ask them to notice when something resists easy interpretation. For some readers, Edna's dissatisfaction may register primarily as feminist rebellion or existential despair. For others, particularly those attuned to histories of silenced desire, it may register as something more specific: the experience of knowing oneself into impossibility.

Importantly, this chapter does not argue that Edna Pontellier consciously understands the nature of her awakening. Nor does it suggest that Kate Chopin was writing a coded manifesto or a disguised confession. What it proposes instead is that Chopin was acutely aware of the limits placed on women's lives and on women's desires, and that she wrote a novel capable of carrying meanings that could not yet be spoken aloud.

This capacity—to hold what cannot be named—is what gives *The Awakening* its enduring charge. The novel does not resolve its tensions because resolution would require a world that does not yet exist. Edna's refusal, then, is not simply a rejection of marriage or motherhood, nor even of heterosexuality as such. It is a refusal to live within structures that demand the misnaming of her deepest experiences.

For lesbian readers, especially those who have come of age in contexts where desire had to be sensed before it could be spoken, Edna's story may feel less like an abstraction and more like recognition. The confusion, the displacement, the attempts at normalization, the exhaustion of acceptable options—these are not theoretical constructs. They are lived realities.

To read *The Awakening* in this way is not to claim exclusive ownership of its meaning. It is to acknowledge that some meanings emerge only when the reader brings a particular history of attention to the text. Such readings do not diminish the novel; they expand it. They reveal how Chopin's work continues to speak across time, not by offering answers, but by articulating questions that remain unresolved.

Ultimately, *The Awakening* endures because it refuses to simplify the cost of self-knowledge in a world unwilling to receive it. Edna's awakening is not a mistake, nor is it a triumph. It is an opening—one that exposes both the depth of her interior life and the profound inadequacy of the structures meant to contain it.

This chapter has not sought to prove what *The Awakening* is "about," but to demonstrate how it can be read when we attend carefully to what is felt, what is displaced, and what is never allowed to fully arrive. In doing so, it invites the reader not to accept a new conclusion, but to return to the text with sharpened perception—to read it again, and to notice what was there all along.

Chapter Twenty

Mammon: The Displacement of the Goddess and the Policing of the Sacred

Section I - When the Goddess Was Central

"Ye Cannot Serve God and Mammon." Matthew 6:24

Before the warning was given and before it was shaped into doctrine, the sacred world had a center that was neither abstract nor distant. That center was female, and her authority was neither symbolic nor secondary. Ishtar occupied a position of power that permeated every aspect of life, shaping how people understood survival, continuity, and legitimacy itself. She was not confined to a single domain or reduced to a specialized function. She governed fertility and sexuality, but also war, sovereignty, and the fate of cities. These were not separate realms in her world, but interwoven expressions of the same divine force moving through the material and social order.

Her presence was not experienced as metaphor. It was structural. Cities rose and fell under her protection, and kings derived authority through her favor. Political legitimacy, military success, and communal stability were understood to be inseparable from her approval. Ishtar's divinity was not invoked after the fact to justify power; it was the source through which power was recognized and sustained. Her worship was therefore not peripheral to civic life but embedded within it, shaping institutions rather than merely ornamenting them.

Nowhere was this integration more evident than in her temples, which functioned as living centers of communal organization rather than secluded religious spaces. These were places where goods were stored, redistributed, and produced, where labor was organized and survival coordinated. Offerings moved through these spaces not as acts of appeasement directed toward a distant deity, but as acknowledgments of participation in a sacred order that bound people, land, and life together. To give was not to diminish oneself, but to affirm belonging within a system understood as reciprocal and sustaining.

In this world, the material was not opposed to the sacred. Nourishment, sexuality, labor, and continuity were not suspect categories requiring moral defense. They were the means through which the divine was encountered and expressed. The body was not a problem to be solved, nor the land a resource to be mastered. Both were sites of presence, animated by a divinity that did not require distance to assert authority. Ishtar ruled through immanence, through visibility and participation, rather than through abstraction or command.

This understanding shaped how life itself was interpreted. Survival was not individual but communal, dependent on cycles of giving and receiving that extended across generations. Abundance was not an end in itself, but a sign that the relationships sustaining life were intact. Loss and destruction were not failures of divinity, but part of the same sacred rhythm that governed renewal and continuity. Ishtar's power held these contradictions together without requiring resolution, allowing life to be understood as both generative and destructive without moral fracture.

This was the sacred order that preceded the warning, and it was coherent in a way that later systems would find intolerable. Divinity did not stand apart from the world; it moved through it. Authority did not descend from above alone; it emerged from participation in life itself. The Goddess did not require belief to exist, because she was encountered through living. It was this integration, rather than any single attribute, that made her indispensable to those who lived within her domain and dangerous to any system that required separation as the foundation of control.

Section II - The Threat of an Embodied Sacred

A sacred order centered on Ishtar could not be absorbed into a system that required authority to function through separation. Her power was too immediate and too deeply woven into lived reality to be subordinated without consequence. She was not a figure who could be repositioned quietly within a new hierarchy, nor a symbolic presence whose meaning could be safely redirected. Ishtar represented a way of understanding the divine that was incompatible with a theology built on transcendence, distance, and exclusive control.

The threat she posed was not simply that she was female, but that her divinity was embodied. Ishtar did not exist apart from the world. Her authority flowed through bodies, through land, through sexuality, nourishment, conflict, and continuity. She governed life as it was lived rather than life as it was regulated. This form of sacred presence could not coexist with a god whose legitimacy depended on separation from the material world, because it denied the premise that holiness required distance from flesh and soil.

As patriarchal religious systems consolidated power, divinity had to be redefined in ways that removed it from immediate experience. The sacred was lifted out of the world and placed beyond it, and in that movement the body became suspect. Sexuality, once recognized as a divine force, was reframed as excess. The land, once understood as alive with presence, became something to be managed rather than honored. Holiness shifted from participation in life to obedience within structure, and authority moved upward, away from the rhythms of daily existence.

Ishtar's continued presence made this transformation unstable. Her worship affirmed that power did not flow only from above, but emerged from relationship, reciprocity, and continuity. Her temples were not marginal religious sites but visible centers of communal life, shaping how labor, nourishment, and legitimacy were organized. As long as those structures remained intact, the claim that divinity now existed solely beyond the world could not be fully secured.

Because of this, the Goddess could not merely be diminished; she had to be displaced. Her authority needed to be severed not only from theology, but from legitimacy itself. This was not accomplished through sudden destruction, but through gradual reinterpretation. Myths were altered, symbols reassigned, and meanings reframed so that what had once been central could be made peripheral without appearing to vanish entirely. The process was careful, because the systems shaped by her presence were too foundational to dismantle all at once.

Yet even as Ishtar's divinity was denied, the structures associated with her did not disappear. The rhythms of life she governed continued, and the material world she animated remained unavoidable. This created a tension that could not be resolved through erasure alone. What had once been sacred could no longer be acknowledged as such, but it also could not be eliminated. The Goddess was gone in name and authority, yet her presence continued to surface in altered forms, pressing against the boundaries of a theology that could not fully contain what it had displaced.

That unresolved tension sets the stage for what follows, where what cannot be named directly must survive indirectly, and where metaphor becomes the means by which suppression is enforced without ever fully succeeding.

Section III - The Goddess Survives Only as Metaphor

The removal of the Goddess did not occur as a clean rupture. Sacred systems that have endured for centuries rarely collapse in a single moment, and Ishtar's authority was too deeply embedded in human understanding to be eliminated without residue. What followed was not disappearance but displacement, a gradual stripping away of name, legitimacy, and presence while traces of her influence were allowed to linger in altered form. She could no longer be acknowledged as divine, yet she could not be erased from memory altogether, and it was in this tension that metaphor became the means of survival.

Once Ishtar was denied as a living sacred authority, she could no longer be permitted to remain recognizable. Her power had never been abstract or distant; it had been experienced through the body, through nourishment, sexuality, continuity, and the rhythms of survival. Those associations did not vanish simply because doctrine changed. People still sensed that life emerged from relationship rather than command, from participation rather than obedience, and that intuition had to be redirected rather than destroyed. What could no longer be honored directly was allowed to persist only in symbolic form, stripped of reverence and rendered suspect.

In this transformation, the Goddess was reduced to metaphor. She was no longer named as source, but recast as an object lesson. The qualities that had once defined her—generativity, abundance, continuity—were detached from her personhood and reframed as dangerous attachments rather than sacred realities. The feminine source of life was not argued against openly; instead, it was displaced into a warning, a prohibition, a line drawn between what was acceptable and what was not. The sacred order she represented was not defeated through debate but dissolved through reinterpretation.

The figure of mammon emerges within this process not as a subject in its own right, but as a vessel for what could not be acknowledged. It functions as a stand-in, carrying the displaced presence of the Goddess in a form that could be named and rejected without ever speaking her name. What is being warned against is not material excess, but the persistence of a feminine sacred memory that refuses to disappear. The metaphor allows rejection to masquerade as morality, transforming theological suppression into ethical instruction.

This is why the warning is framed as incompatibility rather than moderation. The issue is not behavior but allegiance, not conduct but recognition. To acknowledge even a symbolic survival of the Goddess would be to admit that divinity once dwelled within the world rather than above it, that life itself had been understood as sacred without mediation. That possibility could not be allowed to remain intact. Metaphor became the final acceptable container, preserving just enough of her presence to justify its condemnation.

Yet the very need for such displacement reveals the limits of erasure. If the Goddess had truly been eliminated, there would be no need to warn against her shadow. The persistence of the metaphor signals that something remains unresolved, that memory continues to press against prohibition. Ishtar survives here not as deity, not as worship, but as a resonance that cannot be silenced, a presence reduced and distorted yet still powerful enough to require resistance. What remains is not devotion but hostility, not reverence but prohibition, and even that hostility bears witness to the endurance of what it seeks to suppress.

Section IV - Language as the Last Refuge

When a goddess is stripped of divinity, language often becomes the last place she is allowed to exist. Not as doctrine, not as sanctioned belief, but as residue embedded in sound and association, carried forward long after names are erased and temples dismantled. Theology can forbid worship and institutions can dismantle ritual, but language forms earlier and deeper than belief. It is learned through the body before abstraction, shaped by need, nourishment, and survival long before meaning is regulated. Because of this, it resists complete control, preserving traces of what once structured human understanding even after those structures are declared illegitimate.

Across cultures and across time, certain sounds recur with remarkable consistency, always circling the same experiential ground. The *mamm-* root appears repeatedly in connection with the maternal and with nourishment, naming the breast, the act of feeding, and the capacity to sustain life. These words do not emerge from theology or philosophical reasoning; they arise from embodied recognition. They form in infancy, before hierarchy, before moral instruction, before any concept of divinity is imposed. Language here is not symbolic in the abstract sense but mnemonic, carrying forward knowledge that predates conscious belief.

When Ishtar is removed as divine authority, the understanding of where life comes from does not disappear with her. Bodies still know what sustains them. Children still recognize nourishment as relational rather than imposed. The land still teaches dependence, reciprocity, and continuity. What changes is not this recognition, but whether it is permitted to be named as sacred. Once the Goddess is erased, the feminine source of life can no longer be honored directly. It must be disguised, fragmented, and reinterpreted in ways that strip it of authority while allowing it to persist just enough to be managed.

The term *mammon* belongs to this linguistic afterlife. It carries an echo of nourishment and provision without being allowed to acknowledge its origin. The sound itself gestures toward maternal continuity, but the meaning attached to it is carefully inverted. What once would have signaled life-giving presence is reframed as danger. The association is not eliminated; it is condemned. In this way, language becomes a site of containment, preserving memory while enforcing its distortion.

This process reveals the limits of theological erasure. Doctrine may insist that the sacred exists only beyond the world, but language continues to anchor meaning in the body. Even as transcendence is elevated, words return again and again to immanence, to feeding, birthing, sustaining, and continuing. These associations persist because they are not taught as belief; they are carried as memory. The Goddess no longer survives in sanctioned worship or public ritual, but she endures in the structures of language that still recognize life as something received and sustained rather than commanded. In this way, Ishtar remains present not as name or figure, but as resonance, embedded in the sounds through which humans first learn what it means to live.

Section V - The Necessity of the Warning

Once the Goddess had been displaced into metaphor, the work of suppression was not complete. What survived in symbolic form still posed a problem, because metaphor is not neutral. It carries memory forward even when it disguises it. The displaced presence of Ishtar, stripped of divinity but not of resonance, continued to press against the boundaries of a sacred order that insisted divinity now existed only beyond the world. As long as that resonance persisted, it threatened to undermine the claim that the material, embodied, and relational aspects of life were no longer legitimate sites of the sacred.

This is why the warning became necessary.

The statement that one cannot serve both God and mammon is not a general ethical observation about divided attention or misplaced priorities. It is a line drawn with precision, marking the boundary between two incompatible ways of understanding the sacred. On one side stands a transcendent male god whose authority depends on exclusivity and distance from the world. On the other stands the lingering memory of a feminine sacred order in which divinity was encountered through life itself. The warning does not address behavior so much as recognition. It demands not moderation, but severance.

What cannot be named directly must be rejected indirectly. By framing the surviving trace of the Goddess as something dangerous rather than sacred, the warning recasts theological suppression as moral necessity. The feminine source of life, already reduced to metaphor, is further diminished by being associated with corruption and disobedience. The problem is no longer that the Goddess once ruled, but that people might still feel drawn to what she represented. The warning teaches that such attraction is not memory, but failure.

In this way, hostility replaces worship. The sacred feminine is no longer encountered as presence, but as threat. Any association with embodiment, nourishment, continuity, or generativity that once pointed toward Ishtar must now be disciplined, restrained, and denied sacred meaning. The world itself becomes suspect, not because it is flawed, but because it still carries traces of a divinity that has been declared illegitimate.

Yet the persistence of the warning reveals what it seeks to control. If the Goddess had been fully erased, there would be no need to insist on incompatibility. The very act of naming what must be rejected confirms that something remains unresolved. The displaced presence of Ishtar continues to surface, not as devotion, but as anxiety, requiring repeated condemnation to keep it contained.

The warning therefore functions less as guidance than as enforcement. It polices memory rather than behavior, ensuring that what survives of the Goddess does so only in forms that can be repudiated. The sacred order that once integrated body, land, and life must be replaced by one that separates them, and the warning serves as a guardrail against return.

What is ultimately being protected is not holiness, but authority. The insistence on exclusive service secures a theology that cannot tolerate competition from an older truth, one that understood the sacred as immanent rather than distant and life-giving rather than commanding. The Goddess must not only be gone; she must be resisted wherever her memory threatens to reappear.

In this way, the warning stands as both evidence of suppression and proof of endurance. It marks the point at which erasure fails and must be reinforced through prohibition. Ishtar no longer stands at the center of the sacred world, but her absence must be actively maintained, because even reduced to metaphor, her presence remains powerful enough to challenge the order that replaced her.

Section VI - What Remains After Erasure

What follows the warning is not resolution, but inheritance. Once the Goddess has been reduced to metaphor and then disciplined through prohibition, what remains is a sacred landscape reorganized around absence. Ishtar is no longer named, no longer invoked, no longer permitted authority, yet the world she once animated has not been replaced so much as constrained. Life continues to unfold through bodies, land, desire, birth, and loss, but these are now treated as domains to be managed rather than sites of meaning. The sacred has been relocated, not discovered, and the cost of that relocation is carried quietly by everything that still insists on being lived.

This inheritance reshapes how people understand their relationship to the world. Where the Goddess once affirmed continuity through participation, the new order demands separation as proof of fidelity. The material world is no longer a partner in sacred exchange but a test of obedience. The body is no longer a site of encounter but a liability to be governed. What was once integrated must now be divided, and what was once sustained through reciprocity must be justified through restraint. In this shift, the sacred does not disappear from life; it is withdrawn from recognition, leaving behind a sense of tension that never fully resolves.

Yet erasure is never complete. What has been suppressed does not simply vanish; it persists in altered forms, shaping anxiety, doctrine, and vigilance. The need to warn, to prohibit, and to insist on incompatibility reveals an ongoing struggle to contain something that refuses to disappear. The Goddess remains present not as reverence, but as pressure, not as worship, but as memory that surfaces where control is weakest. The warning itself becomes a kind of ritual repetition, reaffirming boundaries that would otherwise blur.

Over time, this tension produces a strange inversion. What once gave life coherence is now framed as threat, while what demands distance is framed as purity. The sacred order that replaced Ishtar must constantly reinforce itself, because it is built not on integration but on exclusion. Authority depends on maintaining the absence of the Goddess, even as the world continues to echo with the logic she once embodied. Life still arrives through relationship and nourishment, still unfolds through cycles rather than commands, and still resists full abstraction, no matter how insistently doctrine attempts to impose it.

What remains, then, is not simply loss, but endurance under constraint. Ishtar survives not as deity or myth, but as a pattern of understanding that cannot be fully extinguished because it is grounded in how life is actually lived. The body remembers what theology denies. The land continues to give without permission. Continuity persists without sanction. These are not acts of rebellion; they are facts of existence that refuse to conform entirely to imposed categories.

In the end, the warning stands as a marker of unresolved conflict rather than final triumph. It testifies to the success of erasure, but also to its limits. The Goddess no longer rules, yet she has not been silenced. She remains present in the tension between world and doctrine, in the discomfort that surrounds embodiment, and in the persistent need to name and reject what continues to surface. What was once sacred has been driven underground, but it has not been destroyed, and its survival continues to shape the very system that sought to erase it.

Chapter Twenty-One

The Serpent and The Labrys: Symbolic Language, Power, and the Erasure of Coherent Meaning

Section I — The Boundary of Symbolic Language

There are symbols that function as decoration, and there are symbols that function as language, and the difference between them is not aesthetic but structural. Decorative symbols can be admired, borrowed, emptied, or repurposed without consequence because they are not bound to rules. They float free of obligation. A symbolic grammar, by contrast, carries constraints. It orders meaning, establishes relationships, and encodes assumptions about power, body, time, and authority. When such a grammar threatens an emerging order, it is not merely forgotten or allowed to fade. It is dismantled through distortion, inversion, and selective survival.

The serpent and the labrys belong to this second category. They are frequently discussed today as interchangeable tokens in a loose symbolic grab bag: fertility here, danger there, goddess imagery, ritual violence, mystery cults, or vague invocations of the feminine. Treated this way, they lose their coherence. They become curiosities rather than carriers of knowledge. What disappears in that flattening is the fact that these two symbols once functioned together, not as ornament, but as a coherent grammatical system that articulated authority, legitimacy, and continuity in cultures that predate patriarchal hierarchy.

Grammar governs how meaning moves. It determines what can act, what can receive action, what can transform, and what must remain fixed. In this sense, the serpent and the labrys did not operate as metaphor in the modern sense. They functioned as operators, describing how power circulated rather than where it was owned. They encoded a worldview in which continuity mattered more than conquest, and regeneration mattered more than dominance, and in which authority was exercised through competence rather than accumulated through force.

Across Anatolia, the Aegean, the Black Sea region, and into the Scythian steppes, the serpent was never simply an animal symbol. It marked continuity through transformation. A creature that shed its skin without dying, that moved between surface and underworld, that lived at the threshold of human settlements rather than beyond them, it carried associations not of chaos but of regulation. Seasonal cycles, boundary maintenance, ancestral return, and the persistence of life through change all gathered around the serpent as a way of understanding time as recursive rather than linear.

The labrys has been persistently misunderstood by being read backward through later assumptions about weapons and violence. While it could be used as a tool of force, its primary symbolic function was not martial. It was administrative and judicial. The double blade does not simply cut; it distinguishes. It separates without hierarchy and balances without annihilation. In Minoan and pre–Indo-European Anatolian contexts, the labrys appears not on battlefields but in spaces of ritual authority, associated with oath-making, adjudication, and the maintenance of communal order.

Together, these symbols articulated a grammar of power that was neither centralized nor hereditary in the later patriarchal sense. Authority was not possessed as property; it was enacted. It moved through individuals temporarily and conditionally, often through ritualized roles rather than permanent status. The serpent encoded continuity across generations and lifetimes, while the labrys encoded responsibility within the present moment, one governing time and the other governing action without collapsing the two into a single locus of control.

As Indo-European, patrilineal systems consolidated power through conquest, lineage, and singular divine authority, older symbolic systems of this kind could not be absorbed intact. They contradicted the emerging logic at a foundational level. A grammar that understands time as cyclical undermines a theology of final judgment. A grammar that distributes authority destabilizes kingship. A grammar that embeds legitimacy in ritual competence rather than bloodline erodes inheritance as destiny. The incompatibility was structural rather than ideological.

What followed was not erasure but inversion. The serpent was recast as treacherous and deceptive, its association with renewal displaced by narratives of temptation and fall. The labrys, stripped of its judicial and ritual context, was reduced either to a crude weapon or to an exotic curiosity, severed from governance and deprived of legitimacy. What survived were fragments that could be displayed without consequence because the relationships that once animated them had been removed.

This pattern repeats across cultures. Suppression rarely requires the destruction of images; it is accomplished through the destruction of their relationships. Once grammar is dismantled, symbols can be aestheticized, sexualized, demonized, or trivialized without recovering their original force. Endless arguments arise about what a serpent means or what a double axe represents, while the deeper structure that once linked them remains unnamed and inaccessible.

Yet grammar leaves traces. It persists in ritual patterns that no longer align neatly with later hierarchies, in gendered distributions of authority that appear anomalous under systems that insist on linear inheritance, and in myths that feel disjointed because their connective logic has been stripped away. These symbols continue to surface in art, religion, and cultural memory long after their original contexts have been dismantled, not as relics but as residues.

To recover the serpent and the labrys is not to reclaim a goddess figure or resurrect a lost religion. It is to recognize that an entire way of structuring meaning—of understanding power, time, and responsibility—was deliberately rendered incoherent because it could not coexist with domination-based systems. When these symbols are approached again as grammar rather than ornament, their persistence begins to make sense, not as nostalgia, but as continuity that was never fully extinguished.

Section II — Disarticulation and Survival

When symbolic grammars are dismantled, they rarely disappear all at once. What occurs instead is a process of disarticulation, in which elements that once functioned together are separated and reassigned new roles within an emerging order. The symbols remain visible, but the rules that governed their interaction are lost. Meaning becomes unstable, not because the symbols are unclear, but because the structure that once organized them has been deliberately disrupted.

This disarticulation allows suppression to proceed without appearing destructive. Images continue to circulate, rituals persist in modified form, and fragments of the older grammar are folded into new systems where they no longer threaten coherence. The appearance of continuity masks a deeper rupture. What is preserved is not the logic of the system, but its residue.

In the case of the serpent and the labrys, this separation was gradual and uneven. The symbols did not vanish from material culture, nor were they confined to a single region or tradition. Instead, they migrated. They appeared in altered contexts, stripped of their reciprocal function and reinterpreted through frameworks that emphasized dominance, hierarchy, and singular authority. The serpent, once associated with regulated cycles and boundary maintenance, was increasingly cast as an external threat, a figure of disorder that had to be mastered or expelled. The labrys, detached from its role in adjudication and ritual balance, was reduced to a signifier of force, its double blade read as excess rather than equilibrium.

This process did not require widespread literacy or formal doctrine. It operated through repetition, through the gradual accumulation of stories, images, and associations that reframed the symbols over time. As these new associations hardened, the older grammar became increasingly difficult to access. The symbols appeared familiar, even ubiquitous, yet their persistence no longer conveyed knowledge. Familiarity replaced understanding.

Disarticulation also altered how authority itself was imagined. In the older grammar, authority moved through roles that were enacted rather than possessed. It was contingent, situational, and often collective. Once the grammar was broken, authority could be redefined as a permanent attribute of individuals or lineages. The shift was not merely political; it was symbolic. Without a language capable of articulating distributed power, centralization appeared natural rather than constructed.

Despite this, fragments of the older system continued to surface in ways that resisted full assimilation. Ritual practices retained gestures whose original significance was no longer fully articulated but remained stubbornly present. Myths preserved sequences that felt unresolved or contradictory, their internal logic obscured but not erased. In some cases, the persistence of these fragments produced discomfort, prompting reinterpretation rather than abandonment. In others, they were dismissed as superstition, folklore, or aesthetic flourish, categories that neutralized their disruptive potential.

What survived most consistently were not complete symbols, but relational echoes. The association between renewal and danger, for example, lingered in the serpent's transformed role, even as its original regulatory function was obscured. Similarly, the labrys retained an aura of authority even when its judicial context was forgotten, its presence suggesting power without explaining its source. These echoes functioned as reminders of a grammar that could no longer be spoken fluently but had not entirely vanished.

The survival of such fragments complicates any attempt to draw a clean line between suppression and continuity. The older grammar was neither preserved intact nor fully destroyed. It persisted unevenly, embedded in practices and images that no longer aligned with their original logic. This uneven survival allowed later systems to claim antiquity and legitimacy while quietly severing themselves from the structures that once gave those claims meaning.

Over time, the disarticulated symbols became available for appropriation in ways that would have been impossible within the original grammar. They could be detached from responsibility and redeployed as markers of identity, transgression, or exoticism. The serpent could signify temptation without regeneration, knowledge without accountability. The labrys could signify violence without judgment, power without obligation. In each case, the symbol's surface appeal increased as its grammatical depth diminished.

This availability made the symbols safe. They could circulate widely without destabilizing the systems that had displaced them. Their presence no longer implied an alternative order; it suggested only difference, spectacle, or nostalgia. The older grammar was rendered unintelligible not through prohibition, but through excess, overwhelmed by interpretations that obscured rather than clarified its function.

Yet the persistence of these symbols, even in altered form, indicates that suppression was never complete. The fragments remained because they continued to answer questions that the new systems could not fully resolve. Cyclical time, distributed authority, and ritual responsibility did not disappear as needs simply because they were incompatible with domination-based structures. They reemerged in disguised forms, sometimes misrecognized, sometimes misused, but rarely absent altogether.

This tension between disarticulation and survival sets the stage for the later recovery of symbolic grammar, not as restoration but as recognition. The fragments alone are insufficient. Without the relationships that once bound them, they cannot function as language. What is required is not the retrieval of images, but the reconstruction of structure, an act that demands attention to how symbols once interacted rather than what they individually represented.

In this sense, the survival of the serpent and the labrys is less about endurance than about latency. Their continued appearance signals not a completed past, but an unresolved one. They remain present because the conditions that required their suppression have not entirely eliminated the questions they once addressed. Meaning persists, even when its grammar has been deliberately obscured.

Section III — Misrecognition and Recovery

Once symbolic grammar has been disarticulated, encounters with its remnants rarely register as encounters with a coherent system. What remains is approached piecemeal, filtered through assumptions inherited from the structures that displaced it. Recognition, when it occurs at all, is partial and often misdirected. Symbols are seen, named, even revered, but they are not understood as elements of a language. They are treated instead as isolated signs whose meanings can be freely assigned.

This misrecognition shapes how later cultures attempt to recover what has been lost. The search is frequently directed toward origins rather than relationships, toward identifying first appearances rather than reconstructing function. Symbols are cataloged, compared, and classified, but their grammatical roles remain obscured. The serpent becomes an object of fascination across traditions, its recurrence noted but its structural role flattened into archetype. The labrys is traced through iconography and material culture, its presence acknowledged while its administrative and judicial functions are left largely uninterrogated.

Such approaches create the illusion of recovery while leaving the underlying logic untouched. By isolating symbols from the systems that once governed their interaction, recovery efforts reproduce the very fragmentation that suppression relied upon. Meaning is sought in accumulation rather than structure, in breadth rather than depth. The result is a proliferation of interpretations that gesture toward significance without restoring coherence.

This process is reinforced by disciplinary boundaries that privilege categorization over integration. When symbols are studied within narrowly defined frameworks, their relational capacities are further constrained. The serpent is assigned to myth, the labrys to archaeology, ritual to religion, authority to politics. Each domain extracts what it can use and discards the rest. What is lost is the recognition that these domains were not separate within the original grammar. They were interdependent, mutually informing, and inseparable from one another.

Recovery, under these conditions, becomes speculative rather than reconstructive. The absence of a living grammatical tradition means that later interpreters must work indirectly, assembling fragments and testing relationships that are no longer self-evident. This work is necessarily tentative. It relies on pattern recognition, on attention to repetition and anomaly, and on a willingness to consider that meaning once operated differently than it does within contemporary frameworks.

Misrecognition persists not because evidence is lacking, but because the implications of recognition are unsettling. To acknowledge that the serpent and the labrys once articulated a coherent grammar of power is to confront the contingency of current systems. It suggests that alternative structures were not only imaginable, but operational, and that their suppression was neither accidental nor benign. Recognition therefore carries consequences that many interpretive traditions are reluctant to face.

As a result, recovery often takes place obliquely. Elements of the older grammar reappear in movements that challenge centralized authority, in ritual practices that emphasize cyclical time, and in symbolic systems that resist linear hierarchy. These reappearances are frequently dismissed as revivals, appropriations, or romanticizations, categories that allow them to be acknowledged without being taken seriously. The persistence of the symbols is noted, but the persistence of the grammar is not.

Yet misrecognition is never complete. The symbols continue to exert pressure on the systems that attempt to contain them. Their recurrence produces questions that cannot be fully resolved within domination-based frameworks. Why does renewal so often appear alongside danger? Why does authority continue to be associated with balance rather than accumulation? Why do certain symbols refuse to stabilize into single meanings, instead generating discomfort and debate wherever they appear?

These questions point toward recovery not as restoration, but as reorientation. The goal is not to recreate an ancient system intact, but to recognize the structural assumptions it encoded. Recovery, in this sense, involves learning to see relationships where only fragments have been acknowledged. It requires attention to how symbols function together, how they distribute responsibility, and how they articulate continuity without reliance on conquest or lineage.

Such recognition does not arrive all at once. It emerges through comparison, through noticing repetition across contexts that should not align if existing frameworks were sufficient. It appears in the gaps between disciplines, in moments where explanations falter or feel incomplete. These moments signal not failure, but the limits of the grammars currently in use.

What is being recovered, then, is not a set of answers but a capacity for different kinds of questions. The serpent and the labrys cease to function as curiosities once their relational logic is glimpsed. They become intelligible not as symbols to be interpreted, but as components of a language that once structured social life in ways that no longer fit dominant narratives.

This recognition does not resolve tension. It introduces it. To see symbolic grammar where ornament was assumed is to unsettle the comfort of inherited categories. It challenges the idea that meaning naturally evolves toward hierarchy and centralization. It suggests instead that suppression operates not only through force, but through the quiet dismantling of alternatives that continue to trouble the present.

In this way, misrecognition and recovery remain entangled. Each encounter with these symbols carries the possibility of both. They can be absorbed into existing frameworks and neutralized, or they can reopen questions about how power, time, and responsibility might be structured otherwise. The difference lies not in the symbols themselves, but in the willingness to attend to the grammar they once expressed.

Section IV — Gendered Custody

When a symbolic grammar is dismantled, it does not disappear evenly across a culture. What survives does so unevenly, settling where enforcement is weakest and where continuity is most difficult to police. In the case of the serpent and the labrys, the remnants of their grammar persisted most visibly and most consistently in women's bodies, roles, and inherited practices, not because women were uniquely symbolic, but because they were increasingly excluded from formal authority as new systems consolidated power and redefined legitimacy.

As governance shifted toward centralized, male-dominated hierarchies, the public articulation of authority moved out of ritual space and into legal, military, and theological structures that no longer required cyclical legitimacy or distributed responsibility. What remained were domestic, medicinal, and liminal roles, areas essential to social continuity but devalued precisely because they did not align with conquest, inheritance, or expansion. These functions did not become marginal in practice, but they were rendered marginal in theory, reframed as auxiliary rather than constitutive of social order.

It is within these spaces that fragments of the older grammar continued to operate. Healing practices retained an understanding of the body as cyclical rather than defective, as something that moved through phases requiring guidance rather than correction. Midwifery, herbal knowledge, and seasonal observances carried forward an implicit logic of regeneration that echoed the serpent's earlier role, even when the symbolic language that once named that role had faded. Continuity remained present not as doctrine, but as practice.

Judicial authority followed a similar path of displacement. As formal law became codified and enforced through centralized power, communal and ritual mechanisms of discernment were reclassified as custom rather than governance. Yet the work of distinction did not disappear. It persisted in informal arbitration, in the regulation of social boundaries, and in rites of passage that marked transition without recourse to violence. These practices preserved aspects of the labrys's original function, not as an instrument of force, but as a means of separation governed by responsibility and balance.

What matters here is that these survivals were not symbolic performances enacted for preservation's sake. They were functional continuities. Women did not carry the grammar forward by consciously transmitting a forbidden system, but by continuing to perform forms of labor and judgment that societies still required even as they refused to formally recognize them. The grammar endured because it remained operational, not because it was protected.

This endurance, however, came at a cost. Once detached from acknowledged authority, these practices became increasingly vulnerable to suspicion and reinterpretation. Knowledge exercised without institutional sanction was reframed as dangerous. Authority enacted without official mandate became transgressive. The very invisibility that allowed the grammar to persist also made those who carried it exposed, their legitimacy fragile and easily withdrawn.

Over time, this shift intensified. As theological and legal systems hardened, the residual grammar embedded in women's practices was no longer merely ignored but actively pathologized. Healing was redescribed as superstition. Ritual competence was recast as witchcraft. Boundary maintenance became deviance. The serpent, already inverted in symbolic meaning, was increasingly associated with female bodies as an emblem of moral instability rather than continuity. The labrys, stripped of its judicial context, was recoded as evidence of violent or illegitimate authority when linked to women's power.

This process cannot be reduced to misogyny layered onto older symbols. It reflects a structural response to unresolved contradiction. Systems built on domination struggle to accommodate forms of authority that operate without ownership, finality, or accumulation. Women's continued engagement with cyclical knowledge, relational power, and embodied memory functioned as a living reminder of a grammar that had been officially dismantled but not functionally replaced.

What survived, then, was not a romantic remnant of a lost world, but a pressured inheritance. The grammar persisted in partial and constrained forms, carried through practices that were increasingly regulated, reinterpreted, or punished. Its custodians were rarely recognized as such. Instead, they were framed as anomalous, disruptive, or dangerous, not because they preserved the past, but because they enacted principles that remained incompatible with dominant structures.

This tension helps explain why the serpent and the labrys continue to generate unease when associated with women, even in contemporary contexts. Their persistence does not simply reference gender; it invokes alternative logics of authority and continuity that have never been fully resolved. The discomfort they provoke arises less from what they recall than from what they continue to expose about the limits of prevailing systems.

The suppression of the grammar did not eliminate its necessity. It displaced it into forms that were embodied rather than codified, relational rather than hierarchical. In doing so, it ensured that its survival would remain precarious, carried not through doctrine or institution, but through practice, memory, and the quiet labor of continuity that formal systems depended upon even as they refused to acknowledge it.

Section V — Literacy Without Revival

Recognizing a suppressed grammar does not require its resurrection, nor does it demand allegiance to the cultural systems in which it first operated. Grammar is not belief, but structure. To become literate in the relationship between the serpent and the labrys is not to return to an earlier religious world, but to understand how meaning was once organized in ways that remain legible even after formal authority has been dismantled.

This distinction matters because attempts at revival often reproduce the fragmentation they seek to correct. Symbols are lifted out of context and redeployed as identity markers, aesthetic statements, or personal talismans, and in doing so they remain isolated. The grammar is not restored; it is further obscured. What is required instead is fluency, an ability to see how these elements once functioned together to regulate power, continuity, and responsibility rather than to stand in for them individually.

Literacy begins with recognizing that the serpent and the labrys were not expressive devices in the modern sense, but operational ones. They did not signify abstract ideas so much as structure processes. The serpent encoded continuity through transformation, anchoring social and bodily systems to cyclical time. The labrys encoded the necessity of distinction, enabling action, judgment, and separation without collapsing into domination. Together, they formed a system oriented toward managing transition rather than securing conquest.

Understanding this grammar clarifies both the thoroughness of its suppression and the instability of its fragments when encountered in isolation. Contemporary systems have inherited many of the problems this grammar once addressed, but they have replaced its mechanisms with substitutes that often falter under strain. Authority is centralized yet contested. Justice is procedural yet frequently experienced as arbitrary. Healing is technical yet disconnected from lived continuity.

The earlier grammar did not resolve these tensions completely, but it approached them relationally rather than hierarchically, distributing responsibility rather than concentrating it.

This perspective also reframes the gendered survival of the grammar. What persisted through women's roles was not symbolic resistance, but practical competence. The work of maintaining continuity, regulating transition, and navigating thresholds continued because it was necessary. Formal recognition was withdrawn, but function remained. Seeing this clearly avoids both romanticization and dismissal, situating survival not in ideology but in ongoing use.

Approached in this way, the discomfort that continues to surround these symbols becomes easier to locate. Anxiety does not arise from their antiquity or their association with marginalized histories, but from the way they expose unresolved contradictions within contemporary systems. The serpent unsettles linear narratives of progress and finality. The labrys unsettles authority exercised without accountability. When their grammatical roles are acknowledged, it becomes clear why they resist assimilation into modern symbolic frameworks without distortion.

To become literate in this grammar is therefore not to adopt its symbols, but to recognize the kinds of structural questions they articulate. How power is regulated without ownership, how continuity is maintained without erasing change, and how separation is enacted without annihilation are not historical curiosities. They remain active problems, regardless of the symbolic vocabulary used to address them.

The value of literacy lies in restraint rather than revival. It does not require reenactment or allegiance, only sustained attention to relationship, function, and structure. Through that attention, the serpent and the labrys can be understood not as objects of fascination or identity, but as traces of a coherent system whose absence continues to shape how authority, memory, and responsibility are negotiated in the present.

What becomes possible through this kind of recognition is not the recovery of a lost past, but a clearer understanding of why certain tensions recur, why certain forms of authority feel incomplete, and why some symbols continue to resist settling into harmless meaning. Grammar, once apprehended, does not impose belief, but it alters how meaning is encountered, shifting attention away from isolated signs and toward the structures that once allowed them to function together.

Epilogue

What Persists: Memory, Constraint, and Responsibility

Across cultures, memory is often treated as something that fades—something fragile, dependent on care or attention. Yet the evidence examined throughout this book suggests the opposite. Memory is remarkably durable. What changes is not whether it survives, but **how it is shaped, constrained, redirected, or disguised**.

Before memory was widely textual, it was symbolic, material, and spatial. Meaning was carried not primarily through words, but through images, objects, gestures, and repetition—through symbols that could be recognized before they could be read, and through materials chosen for their durability, visibility, and authority. Tombstones and inscriptions emerged within this older grammar, functioning not simply as records of death but as interfaces between private loss and public recognition. Stone, placement, iconography, and wording worked together to determine whose lives were legible, whose deaths were authorized, and whose absence could be rendered permanent. What later appears as administrative memory did not replace this system so much as inherit it. Categories, documents, monuments, photographs, and procedures continue to rely on the same logic: that memory must be fixed in material form, repeated in space, and sanctioned by authority in order to endure. The technologies have changed, but the structure remains. What this book traces, across cemeteries, confinement, spectacle, and symbol, is not the disappearance of pre-literate memory, but its persistence—reconfigured, disciplined, and often obscured—within the very systems that claim to have surpassed it.

Burial grounds reveal this first. Cemeteries are not simply places of rest; they are spatial arguments about belonging, value, and legitimacy. Through layout, segregation, and ritual, they teach the living how to rank the dead. What is presented as reverence often doubles as regulation. Even grief, when permitted, is managed—contained within acceptable forms and spaces.

The same logic governs knowledge and identity. Women's intellectual labor persists even when authorship is stripped away. Networks form where formal recognition is denied. Scholarship survives by becoming invisible, embedded within disciplines that later claim neutrality. Memory does not disappear; it changes location.

Confinement and displacement follow similar patterns. Internment camps, removals, and enforced migrations rely on the language of necessity and temporariness, yet their effects endure long after the structures themselves are dismantled. What remains is not always the site, but the rationale—the ready-made logic that can be reactivated when fear or profit demands it. Memory, in these cases, is not erased so much as rendered abstract.

Spectacle offers a different solution to the same problem. Where silence might provoke discomfort, performance overwhelms it. Entertainment, exposition, and monument transform violence into inevitability and domination into heritage. Memory becomes loud, permanent, and difficult to question—not because it is accurate, but because it occupies space so completely.

And yet, alongside these systems of management, other forms of memory persist.

Folk practices, unauthorized rituals, and acts of private remembrance continue at the margins. Grave witching, pet cemeteries, and informal memorials do not challenge institutional power directly, but they refuse total compliance. They represent memory that has not been fully disciplined—remembrance that survives without permission.

Beneath all of this lies an even older layer. Symbols such as the bull, the serpent, and the labrys carry knowledge forward in forms that resist easy removal. Long before memory was archived or monumentalized, it was embodied, encoded, and repeated. These symbols endure not because they are decorative, but because they preserve meaning outside official record. When institutions fail or collapse, symbolic memory remains legible.

Taken together, these examples reveal a consistent pattern. Cultures do not forget indiscriminately. They **manage**. They decide which memories will be elevated, which will be softened, which will be hidden, and which will be allowed to persist only in altered form. What survives does so not by accident, but by adaptation.

This book has not attempted to recover a single lost history or to correct a definitive record. Instead, it has traced a system—one that operates across space, time, and institution. By attending to repetition, absence, and structure, the management of memory becomes visible, not as an abstraction, but as a lived and ongoing process.

What remains, then, is not a conclusion about the past, but an orientation toward it. Memory is not something we inherit intact. It is something we encounter already shaped. Learning to recognize that shaping—where it is enforced, where it fractures, and where it fails—is the first step toward understanding what has endured, and why.

Some memories are buried.
Some are performed.
Some are carved into stone.
And some persist quietly, waiting to be recognized.

Appendix – Photographs

The photographs discussed in Chapter Three were documented in publicly accessible cemeteries, primarily in Missouri and Kansas and are indicative of many Midwestern Cemeteries. They are presented in the chapter as material evidence of commemorative practice rather than as aesthetic objects or family records. In keeping with ethical standards for research in funerary spaces, individual names, plot numbers, and identifying family information are omitted unless already visible on public monuments or widely documented historical markers.

All photographs were taken by the author between 2005 – 2014. The site visits were conducted for the purposes of cultural and material analysis.

All images are reproduced or described with respect for the dead and for the communities in which these cemeteries remain active sites of remembrance.

Information on photographs in Chapter 5

The historical photographs referenced in Chapter Twelve are drawn from major public domain sources that preserve and provide access to documentary materials related to World War II civilian confinement, incarceration, and deportation. These institutions maintain collections that are widely used in historical scholarship, museum exhibitions, and educational contexts. Photographs are generally cited at the institutional level rather than at the level of individual photographers reflecting their use as documentary evidence within broader archival holdings.

The following are specific details for each photograph. Please pay attention to the wording used to describe different aspects of the camps:

Page 154	Japanese American family awaiting relocation – Library of Congress, Russell Lee
Page 155	European Jewish family awaiting relocation - United States Holocaust Memorial Museum, courtesy of Archiwum Dokumentacji Mchanicznej #XI-307/03
Page 156	Japanese Americans 9066 Notification of required relocation - Library of Congress
Page 157	Requiring Jews to be located to specific holding areas – United States Holocaust Memorial Museum, courtesy of Archiwum Panstwowe w Krakowie
Page 158	Japanese Americans businesses closed – Library of Congress, Dorothea Lang
Page 159	European Jewish businesses closed - Norwegian Museum of Cultural History
Page 160	Ouster of Japs in California - NARA
Page 161	Jewish Removal to Ghettos - NARA
Page 162	Japanese Americans walking to relocation – NARA #539961, Dorothea Lang
Page 163	European Jews walking to relocation in Poland - Bundesarchiv Bild 101III-Schilf-002-04, Polen, Ghetto Litzmannstadt, Straßenszene
Page 164	Japanese Americans registering for relocation - NARA
Page 165	European Jews registering for relocation in Krakow, Poland - United States Holocaust Memorial Museum, courtesy of the Instytut Pamięci Narodowej
Page 166	Japanese Americans with relocation tags awaiting removal – NARA
Page 167	European Jews with star of David awaiting removal - United States Holocaust Memorial Museum, courtesy of Yad Vashem

Page 168	Japanese American mother waiting with baby - NARA - #210-G-B23
Page 169	European Jewish mother waiting with baby - Hessisches Hauptstaatsarchiv, courtesy of USHMM Photo Archives – Yad Vashem
Page 170	Japanese American moving to relocation camp – Library of Congress
Page 171	European Jews moving to concentration camp – NARA #089827 Nach dem Umschlagplatz
Page 172	Japanese Americans waiting to board train – NARA
Page 173	European Jews on train headed to Auschwitz – Google Arts & Culture
Page 174	Japanese American relocation camp – Library of Congress
Page 175	European Jewish concentration camp – Westerbork, NARA
Page 176	Japanese Americans behind fence – Library of Congress
Page 177	European Jews behind fence - The Lvov ghetto, shown here in the spring of 1942 - Meczenstwo Walka, Zaglada Zydów Polsce 1939-1945. Poland. No. 107
Page 178	Japanese American camp observation tower - Library of Congress
Page 179	European Jewish Concentration Camp Guard Tower - Bundesarchiv, BildY 12-441-5372, Walter Sohst, Heiner Kurzbein

INDEX

www.ingramcontent.com/pod-product-compliance
Lightning Source LLC
LaVergne TN
LVHW041114080826
845145LV00007B/1806

* 9 7 8 0 9 8 2 3 4 2 3 4 3 *